Place Names
of the
Highlands and Islands
of Scotland

Place Names
of the
Highlands and Islands
of Scotland

Alexander MacBain,
M.A., LL.D.

with an Introduction by
William J. Watson, M.A.,LL.D.

Glasgow
The Grimsay Press
2003

The Grimsay Press
an imprint of
Zeticula
57 St Vincent Crescent
Glasgow
G3 8NQ

http://www.thegrimsaypress.co.uk
admin@thegrimsaypress.co.uk

Transferred to digital printing in 2003

First published in Great Britain by
Eneas MacKay in 1922

ISBN 0 902664 09 3

Contents

INTRODUCTION.

DR ALEXANDER MACBAIN'S work on Names of Places deals with the Celtic names of pre-Gaelic origin which he calls "Pictish"; with Gaelic names, and with names of Norse origin which have been transmitted through Gaelic. The area from which he took his materials was chiefly Inverness-shire, Sutherland, and Lewis. His views on the language spoken by the Picts are given in his paper on "Ptolemy's Geography of Scotland" (published separately), in his edition of Skene's "Highlanders of Scotland," and in several papers contained in this volume, particularly that on the "Place-Names of Inverness-shire." His position is that the Picts spoke Early British or a dialect of it, and that the Celtic language of early Britain was practically homogeneous from the English Channel to the very North. He agrees with Kuno Meyer in holding that "no Gael ever set his foot on British soil save from a vessel that had put out from Ireland." Further, assuming that the terms *Cruthen* (which is the Gaelic form of Briton) and *Pict* are co-extensive and mutually convertible, he includes under " Picts " the whole of the Celtic settlers in Britain prior to the Belgæ, thus ignoring the facts that the Picts are not heard of till about 300 ~~B.C.~~ A.D., and that all old authorities (Gildas, Nennius, Bede, &c.) state that their original seat in Scotland was in the far North.   To him too, as well as to other modern writers, the Cruithne of Ireland are " Picts."   These assumptions do not, however, affect the linguistic part of Macbain's argument, and his views on the language of the Picts have been generally accepted.   No one nowadays would suggest, as Sir John Rhys did once, that the Picts spoke a language that was non-Aryan, and very few would hold that Pictish was other than Early British.   It must be admitted at the same time that some of Macbain's " Pictish " examples are really Gaelic (*e.g.* Dores, Loch Oich), or at least capable of being explained from Gaelic (*e.g.* Feshie, Mashie, Geldie).

By his treatment of Norse names, Macbain laid a firm foundation for further investigators to build on.   He was the first to recognize in practice that the changes undergone by these names in the mouths of Gaelic speakers are not arbitrary, but are capable of classification, and that no derivation which ignores the current Gaelic pronunciation, or which goes against it, can be accepted as certain.

In dealing with place-names in general, Dr Macbain's method was first to make sure of the actual pronunciation in Gaelic, and then to compare the old written forms of the names when such are available. He also paid attention to the physical characteristics in cases where there might be more than one possible explanation. In the case of Idrigill, for instance, I remember how he learned first that there is no " gill " there, and then that there is a knob-like hill at the extremity next the sea. This is, of course, the only scientific way of treating the subject. He was not always right, and in the papers that follow it will be seen that he changed his views in particular instances; but he was on the right lines. Sometimes he was misled by wrong information : this is most notable in his paper on Sutherland. The only work on Scottish place-names comparable to Macbain's, done by a man of his generation, is the late Professor Donald Mackinnon's series of eighteen articles in the *Scotsman* on the Place-Names and Personal Names of Argyll, which has not been reprinted.

The present volume contains practically all that Macbain printed on the subject of Place-Names. It may be proper to state that before the work came into my hands, the selection and sequence of the papers had been already decided, and pp. 1-64 printed off.

In the notes that follow, I have indicated the chief points on which, as it seems to me, one might venture to differ from Dr Macbain's explanations.

PAGE

1. Cataobh, Gallaobh, being certainly datives, are correctly spelled Cataibh, Gallaibh.

6. Ptolemy's tribes : In his paper on Ptolemy's Geography of Scotland, Macbain places the Caereni '' in Western Sutherland up to near the Naver '' ; '' the Cornavii occupied Caithness, the horn or corn of Scotland '' ; '' neighbours to the Cornavii southwards were the Lugi, occupying Easter Sutherland. Around Loch Shin were the Smertae, and Easter Ross was occupied, up to the Varar estuary, by the Decantae.'' The name of the Smertae was discovered (by myself) to survive in Carn Smeart (also, sometimes, Carn Smeartach), the name of a hill in the ridge between Strathcarron and Kyleside. Smertae is a participial form, from the root *smer*, smear; compare M. Ir. *smertha.*

Travedum, Travedrum : read Tarvedum, Tarvedunum.

8. Creed river—A' Ghriota : correctly Abhainn Ghrìde.

Pittentrail : in Gaelic Baile an Tràill, Thrall's Stead, which makes it post-Norse, for *tràill* is a loan from Norse *thraell*.

Aberscross : in Gaelic àbarscaig; Norse; no connection with *aber*, a confluence.

10. Rogart : in Gaelic *Raghart*, i.e. Ro-ghort, Ra-ghart, Big-field.

Assynt : assendi will not do, for initial *a* of Norse *áss*, ridge, is long. There is another Assynt in Ross-shire.

11. Skinaskink : a ghost-name found on maps for the real Slonasgaig.

Clyne : as Mr C. M. Robertson has pointed out, Clìn, which is the Gaelic form, is an oblique case of *claon*, sloping, a slope.

Dornoch : place of fist-stones, i.e., rounded pebbles or *dornagan;* the locative case is found in Dornaigh, Dornie, in Lochalsh, and elsewhere—*v.* Place-Names of Ross and Cromarty.

Kildonan : Kelduninach c. 1230; in view of other early spellings and of the modern Gaelic, *Cill Donnain*, there is no doubt that " St Donnan's Kirk " is the original, and that Kelduninach (presumably inter-preted by Macbain as Kil-domnach) is either an error or refers to another place.

Lairg : in Gaelic *Luirg*, dative-locative of *lorg*, shank; compare Lurgyndaspok,

1390, " the Bishop's Leg ". (Ant. of
Aberdeen and Banff); Magh-luirg, Moy-
lurg, in Connacht.

Reay: in Rob Donn Mioghradh, genitive
Mioghraidh (rhyming with *inntinn, cinnt-
each, gnìomh sin*); in Strathy now Meagh-
rath; cannot therefore be from *magh*; the
second part is *ràth;* compare Dù(n)rath,
Dounreay.

Embo: may be Eyvind's Stead; Elvind is
probably a misprint.

Creich: in Gaelic *Craoich*, possibly locative
of *craobhach*, tree-place; not from *crìoch*.

13. Ashore: in Rob Donn, and now, Aisir (*a*
long); anglicised on maps Old-shore.

Hysbackie, in Gaelic Hei(ll)sbacaidh; the
phonetics clearly indicate an original *ll*
(or possibly *nn*); compare Heisker.

Coldbackie, in Gaelic Callbacaidh.

14. Migdale: in Gaelic Migein; not Norse,
wholly at least, and to be compared with
Migvie, Miggovie, Miggernie, etc.

Keoldale: in Gaelic *Cealldail;* the palatal *c*
is decisive against *kaldr*, cold.

Duible, in Gaelic Daigheabul; the first
syllable is sounded like *aoi* short.

Leirable, in Gaelic Lìreabol; not from leir,
loam; it may be from Norse *líri*, a tern,
also a man's nickname.

Eldrable, in Gaelic Eilldreabol, which cannot be from the source suggested in the
text.

Mudale, in Gaelic Modhadul.

Halladale, in Gaelic Healadul.

15. Navidale : in Gaelic Nei(mh)eadail, which
may be a hybrid from *neimhidh*, a sanc-
tuary, holy place, and Norse *dalr*, a dale.

Conamheall : properly Conmheall, either
High Lump or Hound Lump; *con* may be
the compositional form of *cu*, hound, or
it may represent Early Celtic *cunos*, high.
As Conmheall is the highest part of Ben
More in Assynt, it probably represents
Early Celtic *Cunomello-*.

Rimisdale, in Gaelic Rumasdal; the *u* is
almost *ao* short.

16. Meall Rinidh, in Gaelic Meall Roidhinigh
or Reidhinigh (possibly Roithinidh,
Reithinidh); Loch More is in Gaelic Loch
an Rei'inidh; there is also Allt an Rei'-
inidh; the *ei* is close. My informant
connected these names with reidhneach,
reithneach (in the glossary to Rob Donn,
1829, reidhne), "bó sheasg," a yeld cow.

Reisgill : there is another Reisgill in Sutherland, which is in Gaelic Ridhisgil; I am
not sure of its position.

Smigel, in Gaelic Smidhigil; not from
smuga; it appears to represent Norse
" smidhju-gil," Smithy-gill.

Fresgill, in Gaelic Freisgil, perhaps from
Norse fress, a tom-cat.

Suisgil, in Gaelic Sithisgil or Sidhisgil;
Norse "seydhir," from which Macbain
takes the name, means a fire-pit, cook-
ing-fire, roasting fire. The derivation is
somewhat doubtful.

Ben Loyal: in Gaelic *Beinn Laghail*, Norse
laga-fjall or *laga-völlr*, Law-fell or Law-
field.

Tralagill: Thrall's Gill, not Troll's Gill.

Baligil: the *a* is long, therefore Norse
Bale-gulley, Flame-gulley.

Melness, in Gaelic Mealanais; cf. Meala-
bhaig, Bent-grass Bay.

Shinness: more likely Gaelic *sean-innis*,
old-haugh.

17. Conesaid, in Gaelic Caonasaid; the phon
etics point to a Norse "kein-"; compare
"Thórgeir Keingr" (genitive Keings)
of Landnámabók, where "Keingr" is
explained as "uncus," hooked.

Falside, in Gaelic Feallasaid, correctly explained in text.

Melvich, in Gaelic Mealbhaich, Place of
Seabent; not from Norse vik.

Golval, in Gaelic Golbhal, where *o*, being
short, cannot represent *au* of Norse,
which would give *o* long in Gaelic.

Musal, in Gaelic Musal; the explanation is
probably correct.

Marrel, in Gaelic Maraill, Seafield.

Rossal : the grass here causes congestion
and inflammation in cattle, but not in the
case of horses.

18. Hielam, in Rob Donn *Huilleum;* may be
Hound-holm.

Scourie; in Gaelic *Sgobhairidh*, probably
from Norse *skógr*, a wood, ''Shaw-
shieling.''

Bighouse : in Gaelic *Biogas*, genitive *Biog-
ais;* an alternative explanation is Norse
bygg, barley : Barley-house.

Olave : in Altas, a fancy name given to a
cottage.

32. "A well called Dobur Artbranani": read "a
stream,'' etc.

" Losing himself in a dense wood " : read
'' entering a dense wood.''

Clar Sgithe : in poetry *clàr* is common in
the sense of '' surface, district,'' e.g.
Clár Chormaic, Clár Conghail, Clár Cobh-
thaigh, etc. (bardic names for Ireland),
Clár Monaidh (North Britain); Clár
Mumhan (Munster); Clár Rois (Ross);
Clár Fionnghall (the Western Isles,

Hebrides), etc., etc. "Clar Sgìth," therefore, is in no way influenced by Norse *skídh*. The term occurs often in unpublished bardic poetry, regularly in the form of *Clár Sgíth* or *Sgí*.

33. Dun Sgathaich : read *Dùn Sgàthaich;* so in Skye now ; the Dean of Lismore has genitive *Scáthcha*, rhyming with *clárdha.* The poem in the Dean's Book has also the dative *Scáthaigh* rhyming with *d' fhágais;* both forms occur in Early Irish.

35. Swordale : in Gaelic *Suardail;* Norse *Saurdalr* would become *Sòrdail* in Gaelic. It is " Sward-dale."

Sleat : the derivation from *sléttr* is supported by the spelling *Sléite* in an unpublished poem by Cathal MacMhuirich.

Bracadale : in Gaelic Bràcadail (Bràchdadail); therefore not from *brekka*, a slope.

36. Raasay : in Gaelic *Ratharsa;* MacVurich *Raarsaigh* (genitive); *v.* p. 169.

Trodday : in Gaelic *Tròndaidh*, evidently connected with *Tròndairnis*, but " Thrond's Isle " ought to be *Tròndaraidh*.

Ascrib Isles : initial *a* is long, which negatives the explanation.

Wiay : in Gaelic *Fui'aidh*, which does not consist with the explanation.

37. Broadford: a translation of *an t-Ath Leathan*, the Broad Ford; not Norse.

Oskaig: *óss-skiki*, Stream-mouth Strip.

Loch Eishort: Gaelic, as got by me, Loch Ai(ll)seort, does not consist with the explanation.

Scavaig: in Gaelic *Sgathabhaig;* hardly from Norse *skógr*, wood, shaw

Osdail: initial *o* short negatives the derivation.

39. Garry: in Gaelic *geàrraidh*, Norse *gerdhi*, a fenced field, garth.

46. Kilmallie: the suggested derivation from Amhalghaidh is impossible; *Màilidh* is most probably connected with *mál*, a prince; found also in Coire Mhàileagain (Place-Names of Ross and Cromarty) and in Dail Mhàilidh, Dalmally.

An Linne Sheilich: read "An Linne Sheileach," which is from *seile*, locally said to mean here "brackish water"; compare *seile*, saliva.

47. Loch Leven: I have heard it called "Loch Lìobhunn," but the true form appears to be "Loch Leamhain" or "Leamhna," from *leamhan*, elm. The river Leven in Lennox is certainly *Leamhan;* so in the poem by Muireach Ua Dálaigh, "Saer do lennan, a Leamhain." Glen Lyon is *Gleann Lìo(bh)unn.*

48. Glen Loy : in Gaelic *Gleann Laoigh;* Laogh, calf, is the name of the river. A well at Tara was called Lóig-les, " vitulus civitatum," Calf of the Courts.

Callart : in Gaelic *Callaird*, Hazel Point.

49. Dun Dearduil : only two *forts* of this name are known to me, one at Inverfarigaig on Loch Ness, the other this one, in Glen Nevis.

Bothuntin : the local pronunciation in Gaelic is *Both-thionntainn.*

53. Loch-aìs' : the lingering, dragging sound that indicates the loss of *ll* is attached to the *i*, not to the *a*.

56. Ulhava : if Ulfr were a person's name, it ought to be rather Ulfs-ey; in Gaelic, Ulbhsa; but the *s* of the Norse genitive seems to be dropped sometimes in the Gaelicized forms.

57. Avernish : *afar*, bulky, seems to be used only of qualities and actions, not of things like nesses.

Loch Calavie : in Gaelic *Loch Cailbhidh*, from *calbh*, a plant-stalk, etc.

Strathasgaig : in Gaelic *Srath-àsgaig;* Norse *á-skiki*, water-strip.

60. Conchra : more probably " Dog-fold "; compare Ir. *con-chró*, a wolf-trap; K. Meyer's Contribb.

AGE

61. Strathie : as it has the singular form of the article, " abhainn an t-Srathaidh," the form must be diminutive.

Palascaig : in Gaelic *Feallasgaig*, Norse *Fjalla-skiki*, Hill-strip. Palasgaig was formed on the assumption that *f* was aspirated *p*.

Monar : the phonetics are decisive against the reference to *monmhur*; the Gaelic is Monar, from root of *mon-adh*, hill, mountain.

63. Loch Hourn : the couplet quoted from the Dean's Book is in Deibhidhe metre, and should be read—

Léigid deïreadh do mhuirne
eadar Seile is Subhairne.

They make an end of jollity between Sheil and Subhairne.

John MacÇodrum has—

O cheann Loch-Uthairn nam fuar bheann
Gu bun na stuaighe a Morrair,

which I have printed in *Bardachd Ghàidhlig* " Loch Shubhairn," following the Dean. At the head of the loch there are *Coire Shubh* and *Loch Coire Shubh*, from *subh*, small fruit, berry, raspberry, etc.; and Subhairn is therefore *Subh-bhearn*, Berry Gap. Similarly *A' Mhor-*

bhairn, Morvern, is from *mor*, the compositional form of *muir*, sea, and *bearn*, "the Sea Gap," with reference probably to the deep indentation by Loch Sunart.

68. Sainea: the equation with Shuna is impossible phonetically, for Sainea would become Saoine in modern Gaelic, while Shuna is now Siùna.

Maleos: read Malaios.

69. Colonsay: in Gaelic *Colbhasa;* in the Dean's Book, "cholfissay"; in the so-called "Red Book of Clanranald," "Colbhannsaigh"; with Dean Monro, "Colvansay"; on record "Coluynsay," etc.—plainly Norse, "Kolbein's Isle." Adamnan's Colosus is now Coll.

Terra Ethica: there is no reason to doubt the equation with Tiree, but the reference to Old Irish *ith*, genitive *etho*, corn, is doubtful, in view of the fact that Tiree appears in very old Irish poetry as Tír Iath, which indicates that *e* of "Ethica" is long.

73. Harris: another suggestion is Norse *héradh*, a district, but the fact that *e* of *héradh* is long while that of Na h-Earradh is short is fatal to this idea.

Hirt: *v.* p. 177; perhaps the more probable, if more prosaic, connection with Old Irish *irt*, death, is the extremely dangerous

character of the rock-bound coast of
Hirt. The term recurs in *an Duibhirt-
each*, "the Black Deadly One," the
name of the sea-rock west of Colonsay on
which a lighthouse now stands.

74. Coilsay : read " Gilsay."

75. Fuidhaidh : *v.* note on p. 36 above.

Benbecula : the Gaelic form is properly
Beinn na bhFaoghla.

Heisker : in Gaelic *Hei(ll)sgeir;* old spellings have *l* regularly ; the name is Norse
hellu-sker, flat skerry, contracted into
hellsker.

Hasker : in Gaelic *Haisgeir, haf-sker*, deep-
sea skerry.

76. Trodday : the derivation from *trodh*, pasture, is impossible, for Norse *dh* would be
in Gaelic here *dh*. See note on p. 36
above. The correct explanation of
Trotternish appears on p. 166.

Raasay : *v.* p. 169 ; Hraunsey is not possible.

77. Kerrera : in Gaelic pronunciation there is
still distinct trace of *bh*—Cear(bh)ara;
kjarr, copse, is therefore insufficient to
explain the phonetic facts.

78. Colonsay : see note on p. 68 above.

Hersey : it is difficult to see how this could
have been a Norse attempt at pronouncing
Arran.

Bute : in modern Gaelic rather Bód; Baile
Bhóid is Rothesay; there is Old Irish *bót*,
fire, but the connection is not obvious.

79. Snizort : *v.* p. 34.

81. Creed : this is all wrong; see p. 8 and note
thereon above.

82. Diebek : this is the same as Dìobaig,
" Deep Bay," in Ross-shire.

83. Leurbost : cannot come from *leir*, which
would yield *laor* in Gaelic.

Garbost : cannot come from *geir*, which
would yield *gaor* in Gaelic.

84. Habost : the derivation proposed by Captain
Thomas is impossible, for *ll* would not
disappear here.

85. Haugr : becomes Hógh and Tógh in Gaelic.

88. Bragar : in Gaelic Bràgar.

89. Orfris-ey : read Orfiris-ey.

90. Rodel : in an Adv. Lib. MS. *Roghadal*
(poem of 1705).

92. Taransay :Taran was a Pictish personal
name; see Index to Skene's Chronicles of
the Picts and Scots.

93. Resort : in Gaelic *Reusort;* Capt. Thomas's
explanation is impossible phonetically.

95. Coinn-mheall : see note on p. 15 above.

96. Gardhr : throughout this article, read
gerdhi, a fenced field, garth. The Gaelic
is *geàrraidh*.

PAGE

Rusigarry : in Gaelic *Ruisigearraidh*, which makes a derivation from *hrís* improbable.

97. Tralagill : in Gaelic *Tràlaigil*, Thrall's Gulley.

Crisigill : the explanation " Cross-gill " is phonetically unlikely. I do not know the Gaelic pronunciation.

100. " Joyce is wrong " : Norse *múli* would not become *maol, maoil* in Gaelic; Joyce is right so far as the Mull of Kintyre is concerned, and probably also as to the Mull of Galloway. The Mulls of Orkney, etc., represent *múli* doubtless.

103. Callernish : in Gaelic *Calanis*; " Cala " is found at the beginning of several Lewis names, and probably is the personal name Kali. Mr Kenneth Mackenzie of Shader, Barvas, believed the form Callernish to be wrong; it is indicated, however, by Martin's " Classerniss." In any case, *kjalar-nes* does not suit the fact that *c* of *Calanis* is not palatal, as it would be if it were Norse *kj*.

104. Barvas : the derivation is certainly wrong as to the first part, and very doubtful as to the second part.

107. Linshader : in Gaelic *Lìseadair*, with nasal *i*; Flax-stead.

109. Vatisker : the first part has no connection with *vádha*; probably for *vatns-sker*,

water-skerry, i.e., skerry covered at high
water.

Hasker : Deep-sea Skerry, *haf-sker.*

112. Clach an Truiseil : derivation unsatisfactory
phonetically ; a more likely one will ap
pear in Mr Kenneth Mackenzie's forth-
coming book on the Place-Names of
Lewis.

113. Teangue : rather from Gaelic *teanga.*

121. Inverness : in the Dean's Book, Inverness
is " y'nvir nissa," i.e. Inbhir Nise (the
metre requires a dissyllable) ; in 17th
century bardic poetry (poetry by profes-
sional trained bards) it is Inbhir Nis,
without the genitive inflection, as now.

Clachnaharry : Clach na h-Aithrigh(e),
Stone of Repentance, suits the phonetics
exactly ; cf. Clach a' Pheanais, in Colonsay.

Tomnahurich : in literature *iubhrach* is used
in the sense of a " barge, goodly vessel " ;
also " a pretty girl."

126. Bona : well known in Gaelic as *am Bànath,*
the White ford, and named so, according
to the local *seanchaidhean,* from white
stones in it.   Similar formations are common, e.g., *an Damhath,* Dava, the Ox
Ford ; *an Garbhath,* Garva, the Rough
Ford ; *am Bannath,* Bonar, the Bottom
Ford, etc.   Macbain's suspicion was

perhaps due to the fact that there is no ford at Bona now, but that is due to the raising of the level of Loch Ness when the Caledonian Canal was made.

Dores : see note to p. 157.

127. Moy : The Mackintosh is " Tighearna na Moighe."

Nairn : in Gaelic *Narunn* (?Narrunn); Srath Narunn and Srath Naruinn, Strathnairn; Inbhir Narunn and Inbhir Naruinn, Nairn town. The name belongs to the small but important class of river names that end in -ann, -unn, e.g., Comhann, Coe; Lìobhunn, Lyon; Carrann, Carron. Macbain regarded these as representing the Early Celtic ending *-ona;* they may, however, be names of river divinities in the genitive case, from an old nominative ending in -u; compare Domnu, gen. Domnann; Manau, gen. Manann.

128. Croy is in Gaelic Crothaigh.

Partick is in Gaelic Pearraig (for Pearthaig?).

Blairour : the fact that the confluence of the Blair-our burn with Spean is Inverour indicates that Blair-our represents Blar-dhobhair, Moor of the Water, i.e. Stream.

129. Peffer : there are other streams of this name in addition to those mentioned. In

"Inbhir-feo'arain," *f* is of course really
ph. The final -an (open *a*) is not in-
flected; i.e., it is not -ain. This lack of
inflection in the case of the final -án (from
-agnos) is common in the early language,
and in some parts of Scotland is still
regular in saints' names, e.g. Ciaran, etc.

147. Don : I have not heard Dian.

151. "A mediæval MS." : the Book of Leinster
(*circa* 1150 A.D.), 371, b. 37 : "Donnan
Ega—Ega nomen fontis i n-Aldasain i
Cataib i tuasciurt Alban"; Ega is the
name of a well in Aldasain among the
Cats (i.e. in Sutherland or Caithness) in
the north of Alba. An interlinear gloss
on Aldasain says correctly, ".i. carrac
etir Gall-Gedelu 7 Cend-tiri i n-a camair
immuich"; "(Aldasain is) a rock between Galloway and Kintyre facing them
out (in the sea)"; it is Ailsa Craig in fact.
With "Ega nomen fontis" compare
"enga, aqua super petram, .i. fons,"
"enga, water over a rock, that is, a fountain" (Book of Armagh), where "enga"
might be written, in Greek style,
"egga."

Morvern, which has *o* short, cannot contain *mór;* the first syllable is the compositional form of *muir*, sea; Morvern means

"Sea-gap," just as Subhairne means "Berry-gap." See note on p. 63 above.

— Portree : there is another Fort-righ in Kin-tyre, a very old name. The Skye name may be much older than James V.

152. Morbhearnaibh : see note to p. 63.

157. Duthil : anglicized from Gaelic Daoghal or Daodhal; similarly Culduthel, near Inverness, is Cuil-daoghail, -daodhail; this puts " tuathail " out of the question.

Dores, in Gaelic Duras : there is no phonetic difficulty in equating this with *dubhros*, *dubhras*, which in fact occurs as Durrus in Cork (Joyce). Terminal -as here is dull, whereas the so-called " Pictish " ending -*ais* has open *a*. Dorus, locally darus, a door, is the Gaelic name which is anglicized Dares, in the parish of Dores. The local rhyme beginning "Mile o Dhuras gu Darus," " a mile from Dores to Dares," is very well known.

Loch Hourn : see note to p. 63 above.

158. Dalarossie, Dulergusy : the ending -ie or -y represents the old genitive ending of Fergus, an u-stem with genitive Ferguso, Fergusa.

164. Loch Hourn : see note to p. 63.

169. Ben Loyal : see note to p. 16 above. Macbain's *leidh-fjall* would yield *laodhal* in Gaelic.

Coylum : from *cuing-leum*, "gorge-leap";
cong, a deep narrow gorge in a stream
(or even between rocks in the sea), is with
us *cuing*.

Rothiemoon : "Rat a' Mòine"; we should
have expected "na mòna."

Geldie, etc. : it is to be feared that here we
have Old Irish *gelda, geldai*, bright; e.g.,
"Aedan in grian geldai," in Féilhre
Oengusa; "Aedan the brilliant sun"; and
elsewhere *passim*.

183. Scaniport : the stress being on the first part,
the meaning is rather "Cleft-ferry," i.e.
ferry near the cleft.

319. Ach-gourish represents "gobhair-innis,"
Goat-haugh, Goat-mead. Compare Coin-
innis, Hound-mead; Daimh-innis, Ox-
mead.

327. This is a review of the first edition of the
work; the second edition (1903) benefited
by the criticism.

331. abh, O.Ir. ab, means stream, river; it is
feminine; genitive "na habae, na haba,"
in Early Middle Irish.
"an, water" : so Kuno Meyer in Contribb.,
with reference to Stokes' "Metrical
Glossaries."

334. "Dal-uar, with the accent on the Dal" :
the stress would be on "uar," the qualifying term, not on "Dal," the generic

term. The fatal objection to connecting
names like Bal-four, Pit-four, with Gaelic
"fuar," cold, is that when these names
are preserved in Gaelic pronunciation, the
sound of "four" is not in the least like
that of "fuar."

343. "The Gael did not visit the Epidii for at
least forty years later." Macbain means
that Cairbre Riada's settlement took
place about forty years after the time
when Ptolemy wrote.
But Gael from Ireland may have
"visited" Kintyre much earlier; the
"regulus" who visited Agricola in
Scotland about 84 A.D. is not likely to
have been the first to come across.

346. Maol-rubha : the declension of the name
(e.g., mac Máile-Rubha in Cáin Adam-
náin) negatives *mál*, prince. Mael-rubha
is exactly equivalent to Mael-ruis or
Mael-rois, from *ros*, cape or wood; in
such names *mael* has lost its primitive
meaning of "cropped man, shaveling,"
whence "slave, devotee"; and is practically equivalent to *gille*.
Glen Finnan, see note, p. xxvi.

348. Ardnamurchan : the fact that the name is
stressed on the penultimate syllable puts
"Heights of the sea of Coll" out of the

question; the grammar, too, is impossible.

350. Colonsay : see note, p. xviii.

352. Nant is simply neannta, nettle; Abhainn Neannta, Nettle river; Coille Neannta, Nettle wood, etc.

354. Glen Brander (Branter) : I have not heard the name pronounced, but the Pass of Brander is Cumhang a' Bhrannraidh, from *brannradh*, an obstruction; Irish *brannradh*, a trap or snare; stocks, pillory.

Seil, in Book of Leinster 24b, Soíl; more likely pre-Norse; O.N. *seil* means a string, which is not satisfactory as an island name.

SUTHERLAND:

ITS EARLY HISTORY

AND NAMES.

SUTHERLAND.—ITS EARLY HISTORY AND NAMES.

THE name Sutherland was applied by the Norse to the portion of their Caithness south of the Ord, stretching to the Oikel river, now the southern boundary of the modern county. The water-shed in the middle of the county divided this Sudhr-land from Assynt, Durness, and Strathnaver; and the northern district of Strathnaver and its neighbouring valleys were known to the Norsemen as the Dales of Caithness. This restricted meaning of the name remained in historic force till 1601, when the Earl of Sutherland got the modern county, all save Assynt, raised into a separate Sheriffship, apart from Inverness, in the Sheriffship of which it had been till then included. The Earl of Sutherland's lands also were till then mostly confined to the district here indicated as early Sutherland. Through the fall of the Roman Church, which practically possessed north-west Sutherland, and through the turbulence of the native clans —the Mackays especially—the Earl of Sutherland in 1601 was either actual holder or legal superior of the present county, with the exception of Assynt.   In 1631 Assynt was also joined to the rest of Sutherland, and the present county was constituted, thanks to the efforts of the indefatigable Sir Robert Gordon.

The Gaelic name for Sutherland is Cataobh, and Brae-Chat is Sir Robert Gordon's designation for the upper regions of Lairg—the Barony of Gruids and the other inland and upland districts on the eastern water-shed, with Dirie-Chat, or the Desert of Cat, further north.   The Norse called both Sutherland and Caithness by the name of Caithness or Katanes ; but when greater accuracy was desired, modern Caithness was called Ness, that is, the Nose of the province of Cat, while the district south of the Ord was called Sudhr-land.   This distinction remained after the Norse power was overthrown, and we hear of " Catanesia cis et ultra Montem "—Caithness on this and beyond the Mound—the MONTEM being the Ord of Caithness.   In an important epitome of the geography of Scotland, written in 1165, and inspired by Andrew, the first Bishop of Caithness, we read :—" Septima enim pars est Cathanesia citra montem et ultra montem, quod mons Mound dividit Cathanesia per medium."   The division made by the Ord of Caithness suggested the usual derivation given for the Gaelic names of Sutherland and Caithness—the names Cataobh and Gallaobh.   They were explained by Shaw, the historian of Moray, as being for Cat-taobh and Gall-thaobh, the CAT-side and the GALL-side of the Ord ; Gall he explained as stranger or foreigner, and this is correct, and Cat he derived from Gaelic CAD, high, which is a non-existent word, or from St Cattan's name.   As a matter of fact the two names are the dative or accusative plural of the Gaelic nouns Cat and Gall.   The name of a people was in old Gaelic times used for the name of their country, in the plural number, and generally in the dative or accusative plural. The same thing occurred in Latin and in Anglo-Saxon.   The name Wales means

"Welshmen;" it is a plural of like force with Gall or Gallaobh, foreigners, or "Lowlanders" now. Caithness in Gaelic is Gallaobh, and means "strangers," "among strangers," "in the land of strangers," that is, AN GALLAOBH.

But what is Cataobh? Gaelic "cat" means a cat, as in English. Various interpretations have been offered. Careless investigators have correlated the name with the Chatti of Germany, mentioned in the first century of our era, and they have even asserted that Ptolemy places a Catti tribe in Sutherland. The tribe meant is the Decantae, which has been misread into Cantae, which even then is unlike Catti, and still more unlike the Chatti, or rather Hatti, now developed into the province of Hesse. The name Cat, Cait, or Cataobh is old; it is manifestly antecedent to the Norse, who made use of the tribal names they found on the mainland of Scotland—the Picts for Pettland, as in Pentland Firth; and so Cat and Cata was the name adopted for the province, which was divided into the Ness of Cat and the Souther-land. Katanes or Caithness latterly usurped the older name of Kata or Katar, which, as a matter of fact, does not exist in historical Norse literature; it is only inferred. The Gaelic records of mediæval times make Cat a son of Cruithne, the eponymus of the Cruithnig or Picts; he was one of the seven sons of Cruithne, who divided Scotland between them, and a verse is recorded which is attributed to St Columba, which says:

> Seven children of Cruithne
> Divided Alba into seven divisions—
> Cait, Ce, Cirig, a warlike clan,
> Fib, Fidach, Fotla, Fortrenn.

The four provinces of Cataobh, Fife, Athole (or old Ath-Fhodhla), and Fortrenn are clearly indicated; the other three names are difficult to fix. Mediæval Irish works refer to the northern province of Scotland as Crich Chat and I CATAIB, " in (the land of) Cats," or in the Province of Cats. There is every indication that the name anteceded the Norse ; and, further, the word CAT, cat, possessed by most modern languages, is probably Celtic, meaning the " wild cat." The name appears in Gaulish as a personal name—Cattos and Catta ; and there can be little doubt that the Gaelic name of Sutherland comes from an old Celtic tribe—the Catti—named so after the " wild cat." Such animal names were quite common as tribal names, and it is supposed that the Caereni (Assynt, probably) mentioned by Ptolemy as possessing western Sutherland were so named from CAORA, sheep.

Ptolemy, the geographer, who flourished about 120 of our era, has left half-a-dozen interesting names attachable to Sutherland and Caithness. The tribal names are the Caereni, already mentioned ; north of them, in the northwest corner of the county, occupying Durness, were the Cornavi, a name which might mean the people of the CORN or horn, as we have in Cornwall. The Lugi (or Lougi) inhabited eastern Catanesia ; and south of them were the Decantae, with the Smertae to the west, possibly of both. The latter name is from the root SMER, MER, mind, memory, which also appears elsewhere, especially in Ro-smerta, the Gaulish Minerva. These five tribes, with the Carnonacae, in the Loch-carron and adjacent districts, filled the whole of Scotland north of the Beauly Firth. Ptolemy mentions the capes, rivers, and estuaries. Curiously, Cape Wrath is missed ; but the river Naver is given plainly enough in his " Nabarus flumen," the root of the name being supposed to be NAV, flow, swim, as in our borrowed English words, NAVAL, NAVY. The Cape of Travedum or Travedrum may be regarded as one of the horns of Thurso Bay ; the word means " bull head," from TARVOS, now TARBH, bull. That this is the locality meant seems to be proved by the name Thurso, older Thórsa, for

Thjórsa, bull water, a name which appears also in Iceland. The name Orkas is also given to this cape, and Orkney is the Norse garb of the Celtic name Orcades or Whale-isles. Ptolemy gives also two other cape names further east: Duncansbay Head is Cape Virvedrum, and Noss Head is Verubium, which last possibly means " Spit-head." The Helmsdale river, Gaelic Ilidh, is rendered with fair exactness by Ptolemy's Ila flumen. With this name may be compared the other Isla of Perthshire, and Dr Stokes has proposed the root IL, EIL, move rapidly, as the root of the name. Further south Ptolemy places his Alta Ripa or High Bank, which is supposed to be the Ord of Caithness misplaced.

One or two misreadings of Ptolemy, besides supposititious names which the perfervid imaginations of antiquarians have conjured up, are responsible for some bad history and bad etymologising. The case of the name Chatti or Hatti has already been mentioned; but a bad reading of the name Lugi has been adopted, namely, Logi, which is made to explain the parish name of Loth. The Lougi may have been so named from the Celtic or Gadelic sun-god, whose name was Luga, possibly meaning the " bright and charming one," perhaps allied to the Norse Loki, the god of tricks and evil deeds. A name Abona has somehow " growed " in this connection, and it is made to explain Bonar.

The first Celtic inhabitants of Sutherland were the Picts; it was from them that the names recorded by Ptolemy came. They spoke a language like the Welsh, where P often answers to Gaelic C. The great test-word in place-names is PET, whose Gaelic equivalent is CUID. It signifies a farm or " town," the same as Gaelic BAILE, which, in fact, replaces it. Half-a-dozen names with the prefix PIT or PET meet us in Sutherland proper, for there are none now in the north and west of the county. There is, first, Pitfour; this is a common name in Pictland (occurring twice in Sutherland—in Rogart and near Lairg), and means, in all probability, "Pasture-town," allied to Welsh PAWR, pasture. Pitmean, in the old Barony of Skelbo, is also common, and possibly means "Mid-town," allied to Gaelic MEADHON, middle. It appears as Pait-mayne in 1525 and Petmayne in 1562. Pettakarsie and Pitfour are mentioned together in 1566. Pitgrudie shows a terminal part which seems to appear in Gruids and the Grudie river in Durness. It has been explained as from the Norse GRJOT, gravel; and as a river name it is classical in the Cumberland form of Greta. In Lewis we have it in the Creed river—A' Ghriota. But it can scarcely be the same word in Pitgrudy; such a hybrid is almost impossible in the circumstances. The Pictish language by the time of the Norse conquest of Sutherland was practically dead; a new combination with PET under Norse auspices is scarcely to be imagined. The old form of the name, in 1222-45, was Pethgrudi, which is unlike what we should expect from Norse GRJOT at that time, or indeed later. A form like GREED or GREOD is demanded by Norse-Gaelic phonetics. Compare the river name Fleet from Norse FLJOTR, fleet, flood, and the clan name Macleod, which comes from Norse LJOTR, ugly. The Welsh GRUT, of similar meaning, has been suggested, but the history of the Welsh word itself requires clearing up. Pittentrail (in 1566 Pittentrail) has been explained as Pet-an-tràigh— the town by the shore; but this does not account for the ending of the word.

The only other assured Pictish names are Abirscor and Oykel. In regard to Abirscor, there being Easter and Wester Abirscor, the word is generally plural—Aberscors, now Aberscross. The natives pronounce it Aberscaig. The etymology of the name still awaits elucidating. In 1518 it is spelt Abbirsco, in 1544 Abirscor. That it is Pictish is proved by the prefix ABER, instead of the Gaelic equivalent INVER, meaning "confluence." The Oykel river is probably so named from its banks: the name in Pictish means "high," and is the same as appears in the Ochil Hills and in Ochiltree ("High-town" or Uxello-trebos). The Norse sagas speak of Ekkjalbakki or the Oykel bank, and this fact also lends strength to the view that the river got its name from the high banks somewhere.

The Norsemen commenced their raids shortly before 800. At first they did not think of settling in the land. About 830 they began to establish a kingdom in Ireland, and they had evidently meanwhile subdued the Orkneys and Hebrides and colonised them, intending them as so many stepping-stones in their raids in Ireland and the west of England. The conquest of Sutherland and Caithness is recorded as having taken place about 880 under Thorstein the Red and Sigurd of Orkney. The Norse had possession of the province of Cat for over three hundred years. It was not till 1196 that King William finally established the authority of the Scottish Crown north of the Oikel; for it was only a nominal suzeranity that existed previous to that, and Earls like Thorfin (1014-1064) were quite independent of the King of Scotland; indeed, the latter ruled as a rival—a friendly rival—to Macbeth, possessing all Scotland north of the Beauly Firth, if, indeed, his power did not extend to Inverness. The name Dingwall ("Parliament-place") shows that they had established a centre of political authority there. The completeness of the conquest of Sutherland is shown by the great number of Norse place-names that still exist therein. In Cosmo Innes' map of Sutherland, attached to his "Origines Parochiales," where all the "public" names of the county appear as they were in the 16th and 17th centuries, the proportion of Norse names in Sutherland proper—Dornoch, etc.—is one in every three as against Gaelic, while in the "Dales" district—Tongue, etc.—the proportion is reversed, and Gaelic forms only a third of the names as against Norse. The conquest and occupation of Sutherland proper were slower and less complete than what took place on the northern coast. As we come through Easter Ross the Norse names fall away rapidly, and end altogether in the Beauly valley with Tarradale and Eskadale.

In northern Sutherland we meet with as many Norse place-names nearly as in Lewis. The general Gaelic names STAC, CLEIT, GEODHA and SGEIR, meaning respectively a precipitous hill, sea cliff, bay, and "skerry," are from the Norse; and these are common names along the coast of Sutherland from Assynt to Reay. Beinn Stack in Eddrachilles is one of the highest mountains in the county. Of the thirteen or fourteen parish names in Sutherland three are certainly Norse—Durness, which means "Deer's Ness or point," spelt about 1230 as Dyrnes; Golspie, spelt in 1330 Goldespy, which is a compound of the Norse BAER or BYR, a village, English BYE, as in Whitby, and whose first part is possibly GULL, gold, though usually explained as Gils-by or "Ravine-village;" and Tongue, which is from Norse TUNGA, a tongue (of land). Rogart is possibly Norse; its earliest spelling (1230) is Rothe-gorthe, then Rogert in 1542, and Roart in 1562, which is practically its local name still. It seems to be for Raudhar-garth or Rauth's garth or farm, the RAUDH signifying a person as well as "red." It is explained usually as ROTH-GART, "circle garth" in Welsh, as being of Pictish origin. If GARTH forms the final part of the name, it is infallibly Norse; for DAL and GARTH or GARRY (from GERDI) final are of Norse origin and use. Assynt has also been claimed as Norse, explained as A SYNT, "seen from afar," with reference to its conspicuous mountains. The earliest spelling is Assend, and for this we might suggest the derivation ASSENDI, the Norse for "Ridge-end." Its termination may be compared to that of the Caithness parish name of Skinnet, the older Scynend, the

Skinid of Tongue, which may be compared with the Icelandic Skinnastadr or "Skinstead;" and to these we may add the name of Loch Skinashink in Assynt.

The other parish names are Celtic or Gaelic. Clyne is the Clun of 1230 from G. CLUAIN, a meadow. Creich is Crech in 1230, and doubtless means the "boundary" parish—G. CRIOCH; Dornoch, which in 1230 is Durnach, seems of Pictish origin, pointing to a Celtic Durnâcon, the stem DURNO appearing both in England and on the Continent in Celtic place-names and meaning "stronghold" doubtless allied to Gaelic DORN, fist; Eddrachilles means the place "between the two kyles;" Farr, a name also appearing in Strathnairn, is possibly a compound from G. FOR, over, above, and means "upper land;" Kildonan was originally Kil-domnach or "Lord's Kirk," corrupted into "St Donnan's Kirk;" Lairg, in 1230 Larg, means a "hillside or moor," G. LEARG; Loth is from G. LOTH, mud, now obsolete; Reay, which is partly of Caithness and partly of Sutherland, is in G. RATH or MAGH RATH, "Plain of the Fort" (there is also Ben Rath), reminding us of the Ulster Maghrath or Moyra, famous in story. The earliest form of the Gaelic name appears in M'Vurich, who calls the first Lord Reay "Morbhair Meghrath," Mormaer of Moyra.

In rapidly reviewing the Norse names of Sutherland, I will first commence with personal names which enter into place-names. Persons' names often give names to farms, especially with the word BOL, farm. Thus Arnaboll of Durness, which appears in the sixteenth century as Ardeboll, Arnboll, Ardnaboll, and Arnobill, means Arni's stead, rather than "eagle or erne stead;" Embo, which in the early 17th century is Enbo, and in 1610 Eyndboll, means Elvind's stead, even though the modern pronunciation is Ereboll, a manifest and easily explained corruption; Skibo is the Scitheboll of 1230,

which suggests the name Skithi, the word SKIDH meaning
otherwise a log, tablet; Torboll of Dornoch, which appears
as Torroboll in Lairg, appears as Thoreboll or Thureboll
in the 13th century, and is so named from Thori, a favourite Norse name, derived from the god named Thor.
Another form of this name is Thorir, genitive Thoris,
which appears in Torrisdale of Tongue. Names in prefixed Thor or Tor are very common all over the Norse-
occupied portion of the Highlands and Isles. Unapool of
Assynt receives its name from Uni; it means Uni's BOL.
Allied to BOL is the word BOLSTADR, farm-stead; it
becomes BISTER or BUSTER in Caithness and Orkney, and
BOST in the Isles. Ulbster of Kildonan no doubt was
Ulli's stead, a favourite name, which also appears in Ullapool and Ulladale elsewhere; while Scrabster (in Tongue),
which in the Orkney Saga appears as Ská-ra-bólstadr,
means Skari's stead rather than "sea-mew stead," which
it may also mean. With DALR, a dale, personal names are
rare; yet we have Helmsdale in the Sagas as Hjalmundal,
which means Hjalmund's dale. Ospisdale, in Creich, is
from Ospis, which must be the genitive, degraded considerably, of Ospak or Uspak, another favourite Scoto-
Norse name. Ullipsdale, in Kildonan, is doubtless
"Wolf's dale," after Gaelic phonetics had hardened the F
of Ulfs (genitive of Ulfr) into a P before the S. Trantle,
in Farr, which appears in 1527 as Trountal and in 1626 as
Trontaill, stands no doubt for a Norse Throndar-dalr, or
"Thrond's dale;" and doubtless the same name accounts
for the Dronside or Thrond's SETR (seat) of Tongue.
Dal-Harald, in Farr, is a Gaelic compound, and, as conjec-
tured, commemorates the defeat in 1196 of Earl Harold,
son of Maddad (Gaelic MADADH—Hound) of Athole, by
King William, when the King was helped by the famous
Manx King Reginald, son of Godred, who undertook the
government of Cataobh for a season. Lochan Hacoin, in
Tongue, is named after some unknown or unrecognised

Haco or other, just as Kyleakin of Skye celebrates Haco
of Largs (1263). The name Grimr has left many place-
names in the Isles; two places in Sutherland get named
after some hero of this designation—Ben Griam, Sir R.
Gordon's Bingrime, and, below the ben, Griamacharry,
or "Grim's Garth"—that is, Griama-ghardhaidh in
the best old Gaelic phonetics. Not far away is Ben
Armin, the ben of the ARMANN, which in Norse means
steward or controller, and in Gaelic, which has borrowed
it, "a hero." Cyderhall is a fancy form for Sidera, which
in 1230 appears as Sywardhoch, in 1275 as Sytheraw; it is
no doubt justly regarded as standing for Sigurd's HAUGR
or "howe," where the first Sigurd of Orkney may have
been buried after his fight with and death by Malbrigd
Bucktooth, whose venomous tooth had killed him. Ashore
or Oldshores in Assynt was formerly Astlair (1559) and
Aslar (1551), and the late Captain Thomas regarded this
as a corruption of Asleifar-vik, Asleif's Bay, which is
mentioned in 1263 as one of Hacon's ports of call.

The most of the Norse names will now be classified
under their commonest, significant parts, such as bakki,
ból, dalr, and vik.

BAKKI, a bank. We have Backies above Golspie, "the
Banks;" Coldbackie in Tongue, which is either Cold Bank
or Charcoal Bank, probably the former; Hysbackie, also
in Tongue, for Hùs-bakki, "House-bank;" and the Saga
Ekkjals-bakki or Oikel Bank, where Oikel itself seems to
be the Pictish UCHEL, high, possibly applied to the river
banks.

BOL, a farm. Arnaboll, Embo, Skibo, Torboll, Torro-
bol, and Unabol have been explained above. In Dornoch
parish we have Skelbo, the older Skelbol and Skelbotil,
which means "shell town (ból or botl);" in Durness, Erri-
bol, "Beach-town," from EYRR, beach, and Loch Crossphuil
from Krossa-ból ,"cross-town," a name well known in the

Isles; in Kildonan, Duible, "Mud town," from DY, mud, and
Leirable from LEIR, loam, meaning much the same as
Duible—old forms of both are Doypull (1527), Duiboll
(1610), Lyriboll, Lereboll (1563-1566), to which compare
Lerwick, "mud bay;" Borrobale is Borg or Burgh-bol,
"fort-town," Borryboll (1563); Eldrable, older Eltriboll
(1610) and Altreboll (1566), which cannot be from ELDR,
gen. ELDS, beacon, as usually explained, must be equated
with the Caithness Alterwall, the Alterwell of 1455, which
points to a Norse Altara-völlr or "Altar-field;" hence we
may infer Eldrable to be for "Altar-ton."   Gailval in
1566 Galezboll, is possibly Galli's town: in Lairg we have
Colaboll, which may mean "Coal (charcoal) town," or
"Cold town," or even "Kol's town," the person Kol: in
Tongue we have Kirkiboll, Icelandic Kirkjubói, "Church-
town," and Ribigill, which in 1530 appears as Regeboll,
and may thus mean "Lady's town" (RYGR, lady).

DALR, a dale. In Creich there is Swordale, the
Swerdel and Swerisdale of 1275, meaning "Swarddale;"
Spinningdale, in 1464 Spanigidill, and in 1553 Spanzedell,
possibly "spangle-dale," from Norse SPONG, G. SPANGAR;
Migdale, the Miggeweth of 1275, seems from MYKI, dung.
In Dornoch there is Astle, which has undergone many
transformations. Askesdale and Haskesdale (1222-75),
Assastel (1360), Askadaile (1472), Assiedale (1610), which
is the Icelandic Eskidalr or "Ash-dale."   In Durness
there is Keoldale, in 1559 Kauldale, the Icelandic Kaldi-
dalr, "Cold-dale;" Strath-uridale, Strathwradell of 1530,
the dale of the URUS or auroch. In Farr are many dales
—Armadale, Armidill (1499), "Arm or bay dale;" Mudale,
Mowdaill (1570), Mowadale (1601), possibly from MODA
MODR, muddy river or snow-banks, which seemingly is
the root idea of Moydart also—"Mudfjord;" Halladale,
Helgadall in 1222, means "Hallow or Holy dale," though
the name may be a personal one, Helgi; Langdale is
exactly "Longdale." In Kildonan we found Helmsdale

SUTHERLAND—ITS EARLY HISTORY AND NAMES.

and Ullipsdale, already discussed; there are also Navidale (Navadaill, 1566) and Rimisdale (Rimbisdell, 1630), the former being explained as from NAEFR, birch (compare Icelandic Naefrholt, "Birch-holt," and the latter from RYMR, roaring, "Dale of the roaring stream." In Lairg we have Sletdale, "Evendale," and Osdale (Feith Osdale), "East-dale."

EY, island. Oldney off Assynt is possibly from ALDIN, fruit; the Channel Island Alderney has been compared in name. Soyea is Saudhar-ey or "Sheep-isle," a common name in the Hebrides; Chrona is possibly T-hraun-ey, the same as Rona, "Rocky-isle." Off Eddrachilles are Calva or "Calf-isle," a common name also, and Handa, "Sand-isle." Boursa, near Strathy Point, is apparently BURS-EY, "Bower-isle." In 1386 Ferchard Leche, or the Physician, gets from Robert III. the islands from "Rowestorenastynghe to Rowearmedale" (Rudha-Stór-an-Assaint to Rudha-Armadail), which are named Jura ("Deer isle,' possibly Oldaney), Calva ("Calf-isle,") Sanda (Handa, "Sand-isle,") Elangawne, Elanwillighe, Elanerone, Elanehoga, Elanequothra, Elangelye, and Elaneneyfe. In 1570 some of these are Handa, Choarie (Quothra in 1551), Gyld (Rabbit Isles?), Rone ("Seal Isles") and Colme, while Howga, now Hoan, also appears (Haga and Houga in 1601, 1613). The latter means the "howe" or "burial" isle; and itself and Isle-Colm or Neave, "Holy-isle," were ancient burial-places "to keep the bodies safe from the mainland wolves!"

FJORDR FJARDAR, a ford or sea-loch. Laxford (G. LUISEARD) and INCHARD are both on the coast of Eddrachilles; the former means "'Salmon-loch" and the latter probably "Meadowfjord," from ENGI, a mead.

FJALL, hill, fell. This suffix seems to have been replaced in Sutherland by BEINN and MEALL of the Gaelic. Suilven, from SULA, pillar; Conamheall, from Konna-

fjall "Lady's fell;" and Far-mheall, from FAER, sheep.
Ben Arkle must be from Arkfell, from its summit being
"ark-like;" Meall Horn is simply the Norse HORN, which
is common for hills and capes; Mcall Rinidh may be for
Hreinn-fjall, "Reindeer fell," for the Norse found reindeer, it is said, in Sutherland.   Beinn Loyal has the terminal FJALL, but the prefix is obscure; compare the
Icelandic Laufafell or "Leafy-hill."   In South Uist is the
similarly named Ben Layaval.

GIL, a ravine.   In Assynt we have Tralagill, usually
explained as Troll's gill, but Thrall's gill is also an Icelandic word, and suits here as well; Urigill, ravine of the
URUS or auroch; Gisgill, the "gushing gill," allied to
GEYSIR, hot spring.   The Reisgill of Eddrachilles is possibly from HRIS, brushwood.   Farr has Apigill, "Ape-gill,"
which recalls the Icelandic Apavatn, where API may have
been a person's nick-name; Baligill, gill of the grassy-
slope (BALI); Smigel, gill of the narrow cleft (SMUGA); and
Redigill, possibly Rétta-gil, the "gill of the sheep pen or
adjusting pen."   Fresgill, in Durness, is explained as the
"noisy gill" (FRAES, noise).   Suisgil, in Kildonan, is in
1527 Seyisgill and Suisgill in 1545, which may be compared to the Icelandic Seythisfjordr, "Seethe-fjord."   Mr
Mackay refers it to SUS, roaring.

GJA, a rift, geo, G. GEODHA, borrowed.   The Gaelic
form of this word is very common on the northern shores
of Sutherland; its Norse use is found in Sango-more and
Sango-beg, "Sand-bay," in Durness, and Lamigo or
"Lamb's bay," in Tongue.

NES, a ness, cape.   Melness, in Tongue, means
"Bent-grass-ness" (MELR); Unes, in Golspie, "Yew-ness,"
from YR, yew, the Owenes of 1275; and Shinness, which
in 1630 is Chinenes, "Ness of Shin or Loch Shin," called
in Gaelic Ard-na-sinnis.

SETR, a seat, farm, sheiling. It often appears as SIDE in Sutherland: in Tongue, Conesaid, Konnasetr, "Lady's-ton," the older Kinsett (1570) and Kennyside (1601); Falside, "Hill or FJALL seat;" in Creich, Linside, Linsett in 1541 and Leynside in 1552, possibly "flax-seat" (lin); in Golspie, Clayside, possibly "Cliff-seat" (KLEIF); Bosset and Bowsett (Creich and Farr), "Dwell-ing-seat" (BUSETR), while in Reay Sandside, the older Sandset, means "Sand-seat."

VIK, bay. In Assynt are Melvich ("Bent-grass") and Kirkaig (Kirkjavik, "Kirk-bay"); in Farr, Melvich; in Durness, Cearbhaig, or Kerwick, Karfavi, "Galley bay." Port Chaligaig, in Eddrachilles, is Cellach or Kjallak's wick.

VOLLR, g. VALLR, a field. Carrol, in Clyne, Carrell in 1610, is Kjarr-vollr or Copse-field. Rossal, in Rosehall, is Hross-vollr, "Horse-field," Rosswell in 1553; Langwell and Dal-Langal are both from Langi-vollr or "Long-field;" Sletell, in Tongue, is "Even-field;" Golvall, in Farr, the older Gauldwell (1559), may be Galli's field or Gaular-vollr, "field of the sounding stream," Norse Gaular-dale. Musal, in Durness, is Moswell in 1560, that is "Mossfield;" while Marrel, in Kildonan, is explained as "Sea-field."

Other names that do not often recur and do not come under "heads" are these:—Stoer in Assynt, which is the very common Norse prefix STOR, big, Stór-áss, "Big-ridge," Stór-isandr, "Stour-sand," etc.; Brora (Bruray 1601, Brora sixteenth century), which is the Icelandic Brúará, "Bridgewater" exactly; Uppat, Uphald in 1528, is from UPP, up; Kyle-strome and Ben-Strome, admissable hybrids of Gaelic and Norse, come from STRAUMR, stream, ocean current; Smoo, Cave of Smoo, in Durness, from SMUGA, a rift or narrow cleft to creep through, SMJUGA, to creep; Rispond, from HRIS,

copse; Cape Wrath or Am Parph is from the Norse name
HVARF, turning point; Hope, ben and loch, from HOP, a
bay, as in Oban, Ob, etc.; Hielam is a compound of
HOLMR, a holm or island, but the old forms are puzzling—
Unlem (1542), Handlemet (1551), Hunleam (1601);
Sandwood in Eddrachilles is for Sandvatn, " Sand-water "
—it is Sandwat in 1559; Scourie, place of sheds or
shiels (?), from SKURR, a shed; Borgie in Farr is from
BURG, a fort, the Borve or Borr of the Isles; Port Skerra
and Skerray are from SKER, a sharp rock, whence "skerry"
and Gaelic SGEIR; Forsinard, etc., the " twa Fursyis "
(1527), Forseyis (1626), are from FORS, a waterfall;
Swordly is probably " Sward-lea;" Skullomie may be
Skolla hvamur, " fox's slope;" and the following may be
Norse:—Gearnsary, Grodsary, Modsory, Pronsy, Maikle,
Sciberscross, Olave, Shigra, Skericha, Syre, Kirtomy, Bighouse and Garty. Grumbeg and Grumbmore (also Grubeg
and Grubmor) have been etymologised by Rev. A. Gunn
as from Druim-beg and Druim-mor, a phonetic impossi-
bility. The old forms explain their origin: in 1570 we
have Grubmor and Grubeg, but in 1551 it is Gnowb
" Mekle and litil," which is the common Icelandic place-
name word GNUPR, a peak, " a knob." Bighouse is probably BYGD HUS, " Dwelling-house."

EARLY CLAN AND FAMILY NAMES.

Before passing on to the Clan and Family Names of
Sutherland, I have, firstly, to acknowledge my deep
indebtedness, in my study of the Norse names of Sutherland, to Mr John Mackay of Hereford, whose excellent

series of papers in the Inverness Gaelic Society's Transactions on "Sutherland Place-Names" made my task comparatively easy—in fact, made it a matter of judicial, if not judicious, selection.

MURRAYS, SUTHERLANDS, AND GORDONS.

The oldest family name in Sutherland is that of Moray or Murray. The noble family of Sutherland hailed originally from Moray; Freskin, the ancestor of the Earls of Sutherland and the great families of Morays of Bothwell and Tullibardine, whence the Duke of Athole and the Earl of Dunmore, held the lands of Duffus, in Moray, about 1150. His son, called Hugh Freskin, got Sutherland—that is, Sutherland proper—from King William, no doubt at the time of his conquest of Catanesia in 1196; and William, his son, was created Earl of Sutherland about 1235, much about the same time as Magnus, son of Gillebride, Earl of Angus, was made Earl of Caithness proper. Freskin's son William was ancestor of the De Moravia family—the Morays—famed in the 13th and 14th centuries, the best known of them being Sir Andrew Moray of Bothwell, the Scottish patriot.

It cannot be proved that Hugo Freskin was called "of Moray," nor was his son so called, for he calls himself "Dominus de Suthyrlandia, filius Hugonis Freskyn;" but his friends were Moravians. Gilbert, Bishop of Caithness, 1222-1245, was "de Moravia," acquiring the lands of Skelbo from Hugh Freskin, and latterly granting them to his brother, Richard de Moravia of Culbyn, in whose family they remained for two centuries. Next to Sutherland the name Moray is the commonest met with in old documents dealing with Dornoch and the adjacent parishes. The Province of Moray is called in early Gaelic

Mureb, and in Norse Morhaefi, which points to a Pictish Morapia, roots MOR (sea) and AP (water), meaning "coastland."

As a name Sutherland is naturally very common in Sutherland proper. Its origin is simple: it arises from the title "de Sutherland," or "of Sutherland." In its older form it appears as "Nicholas of Sutherland of Duffus," for example. Scions of the noble house only had the name, just as "de Isles" or "Isles" did duty for the surname of the early Macdonald Chiefs—Alexander Isles of Glengarry and Marion de Ilys, sister of Alexander, Earl of Ross (1439). The name Sutherland is, therefore, on a different footing from any other county-named surnames, such as Nairne and Fyfe. The tenants of Cupar-Abbey lands were sometimes from the neighbouring "kingdom," and such are called, for lack of other surnames, Henry of Fife and James of Fife, as the case may be, that is, James, from Fife, "James the Fifer," which latterly settles into James Fife.

The Gordons became Earls of Sutherland in the 16th century on the failure of the Moray family in the male line, Adam Gordon, second son of the Earl of Huntly, marrying the heiress Elizabeth, and their son Alexander being infeft in the Earldom in 1527. The Gordons thereafter became fairly numerous in the county. The name is derived from the lands of Gordon, in Berwick, "de Gordon" being its original form as a designation. One of the most noted Sutherland men of this name was Sir Robert Gordon of Gordonston, tutor of Sutherland from 1615 to 1630, being uncle to the young Earl. He wrote that valuable work, "The Genealogy of the Earls of Sutherland," which is our most important guide for the early history of the northern Highlands.

GUNNS, MACPHAILS, POLSONS.

Sir Robert Gordon gives as the principal surnames in Sutherland proper (leaving out Strathnaver, Durness, Eddrachilles, and Assynt, which last was joined to the county by Sir Robert's efforts in 1631) in his day the following:—Gordon, Sutherland, Moray, Gray, Clan-Guin (the Gunns), Seil-Thomas, Seil-Wohan, and Seil-Phaill. I have already discussed the first three clan names. The Grays had their chief holding at Skibo, which was possessed by them in the 16th and 17th centuries. The first of them came North from Forfarshire about 1456, being the son of Lord Gray of Fowlis, who had to fly for killing the constable of Dundee.

The Clan Gunn were of Caithness origin. The name is Norse, the common one of Gunni, from GUNNR, war (allied to Eng. GUN). Their ancestor was Gun, crowner of Caithness, about the middle of the 15th century (1450). He was a man of great power in his day, and a descent from the King of Denmark was claimed for him—a son of that King called Gunni having settled, ages before Sir Robert Gordon wrote the story, in Caithness. The Crowner's daughter was mother of Donald Gallach of Sleat, slain in 1506, ancestor of Lord Macdonald. The Crowner was treacherously slain by the Keiths, along with many of his clan. His son James escaped to Sutherland, and the chief centre of the clan in Sutherland came to be Killernan in Strath-ully. William Mac James Mac Crowner Gunn distinguished himself against the Mackays in 1517, at the battle of Torran-dow. During the 16th century the history of Clan Gunn was a very chequered one; the clan had branches in Caithness, Strathnaver and Sutherland proper, and they could not please the rival heads of the houses of Sutherland, Sinclair and Mackay.

They generally sided with the Earl of Sutherland.   In 1585 the earls agreed to destroy the Gunns, and for three years the plucky clan was harassed by the earls, until another disagreement intervened to save the Gunns.   John Gunn Robson was leader of the Caithness Gunns in 1616, and no doubt the northern Robsons may be traced to this branch of the clan.   Colonel Sir William Gunn, his son, rendered himself famous in the Continental wars, becoming by 1648 a Baron of the Roman Empire.

The Seil-Thomas and Seil-Phaill, mentioned by Sir Robert Gordon, were cadets of the Mackay clan.   There is some doubt as to the Seil-Thomas, for Sir Robert, in his attempt to wean them from the Mackay alliance, declared them to be from Ardmeanagh, in Ross.   But the Seil-Phaill or McPhails were really Mackays, descendants of Paul, son of Neil Mac Neil Mackay, the latter Neil being a brother of Angus Dubh, the great Mackay Chief of 1411.   This Neil Mac Neil was the first Mackay to get land from the Crown under charter; King James, in 1430, gave him lands in Creich and Gairloch.   The Polsons, or Paulsons, are supposed to be the same as the McPhails, sons of Paul Mackay, but this is not the case. The real Polsons go back as such to the 15th century, and were settled before 1430 in Creichmore in Creich, where John Poilsone is mentioned in 1545, and Thomas Poilsone in 1567.   They are regarded by Cosmo Innes as descended from Paul MacTire, who got these lands in 1365. Paul MacTire, or " Paul the Wolf," was a famous man in his day.   One or two ecclesiastics appear with the name of Polson in the 16th century.   The name Paul was a favourite one among the Norse, and hence its popularity in Cathanesia.

MATHESONS: DORNOCH NAMES.

Seil-Wohan, or Seil-Wogan, as Sir Robert Gordon has the name, were Sìol-Mhathain, or the Sept of Mathesons. The name Mathan simply means "bear," and was extremely common in Ireland, especially in Norse times, when Thor's Wolf and Thor's Bear formed the model for warlike names. The Mathesons or Mac Mahons were located on the north side of Loch Shin, their Chief being tacksman of Shiness. They are traditionally regarded as descended from the Lochalsh Mathesons, one of whom, Donald, son of Alexander, fled for his country's good to Caithness or Cataobh. It was his grandson, "John Mac-ean-Mac-Konald-wain" whom Sir Robert Gordon in 1616 induced to assume the chiefship of the sept and to separate his name and kin from the Seil-Thomas, who were on the side of their kinsmen, the Mackays, and who were bringing the Mathesons over to the Mackay side. In this way Sir Robert, as he says, weakened the power of Seil-Thomas. The first mentioned in the county is William Matheson in 1512, who acted among other prominent citizens and tacksmen at Dornoch as juryman in a succession case. Sir John Matheson was Chancellor of the Bishopric from 1544 to 1554, and Robert Matheson, saddler and burgess of Dornoch (1566 to 1603), was a man of property, a fact to which we owe a list of the chief burgesses of Dornoch Burgh in 1603, who held an "inquest" over his estate. Colonel George Matheson of Shiness made his name on the Continent with Lord Reay; and from him are descended the Mathesons of the Lewis —the late Sir James Matheson and Donald Matheson, the present proprietor of that island.

The list of Burgesses of Dornoch referred to above must be given to show the character of the better class of the population, at least from the standpoint of names. They are these in 1603:—

> Richard Murray,
> Alexander Murray,
> William Murray M'Kane M'Kwatt,
> John Murray M'Kane M'Kwatt,
> Thomas Murray Angus-sone,
> Donald Mackphaill,
> Alexander M'Kraith,
> William Clunes,
> Alexander Clark,
> Thomas Veir,
> Thomas Ratter,
> George Dicksone,
> Thomas Fiddes,

to whom add Robert Mathiescne, saddler, deceased. Earlier Dornoch names are:—Morays in plenty; in 1512 David Mudy (Moody), a family name introduced by Bishop William Mudy about 1450; in 1529, Ysaac Leslie and John Talyour; 1542, Walter Leslie, Ferquhard M'Gillespy, Alexander Rater and Alexander M'Culloch; 1544, David Dyksoun; in 1551 and 1552, in addition to these Leslies, Morays, M'Cullochs, and Dicksons, are Thomas Chesholme and John Gillepatrick Tailyeour; in 1583 Angus Polson is a citizen, and the name Sutherland also appears, though rarely. The McRaes are also common as burgesses and once as bailie; Robert McRaithe, bailie, 1570, with Angus McCraithe, holding Achloch in 1584, and Alexander McKraith, burgess in 1603. Sir Robert McCraith was vicar of Kilmalie or Golspie in 1545. Other names connected with Dornoch City are Donald McGillemor (1512), Alexander Gar (G. GEARR, short) in 1545, John Awloche (Atholeman?) in 1524 and 1545, Thomas Mowate, Robert Duf or

McDonald McDavid, 1562, John McDonald McMurquhe, 1568, etc. The name Mowatt, so common in Caithness early and late, is in the oldest documents given in its original form of " de Monte Alto "—High Mount, whence the modern name is contracted and degraded.

THE MACKAYS.

The clans outside Sutherland proper—those of Strathnaver, Durness, Eddrachilles and Assynt—did not in olden times comprise any great variety of names. This region is the cradle of one great clan—the Mackays of Strathnaver and Reay. The Mackenzies, with their dependants the McIvers, and the Macleods, with the Morrisons and other Lewis septs, are outsiders, comparatively speaking. Like all the other northern clans—the Macleods, Mackenzies, Mackintoshes, Camerons, etc.—the Mackay Clan begins its history really at the end of the fourteenth century—at 1400. True, historians do tell us that Alexander Mackay, hailing from Galloway, the seat of the similarly named septs of Mackie and McGhie, or from Aberdeenshire and the lands of the Forbeses there, settled in Strathnaver in 1196, he having, of course, helped King William to expel the Norsemen. Of course his son (or himself) married the Bishop of Cathanesia's daughter (as did the ancestor of the Morrisons of Durness, etc.), and got from him Church lands in Strathnaver. Equally, of course, Magnus, the 4th from Alexander, fought for Bruce at Bannockburn, as did 18 other Highland chiefs, inclusive of The Macpherson. The first assured chief is Angus Dubh Mackay, who in 1411 barred Donald of Harlaw's path at Dingwall, and got well " thrashed " for the same. From him the descent can be followed easily to the present Lord Reay. The Mackay chiefs got their first charters only in 1499.

Sir Robert Gordon calls them Clan Worgan—that is, Clan of Morgan—and though this title has been refused by the clan historian, under the impression that it was an invention of the enemy, it is the usual Gaelic name in literature for the Mackays of Sutherland, distinguishing them from the Mackays of Kintyre and "Mac Aoidh na Ranna," in Islay. In the famous "arming" piece in the Red Book of Clanranald they are called Clanna meram-oenmnacha, masgalacha, morbhrontach Morguinn agus Catuigh"—the merry-hearted, courteous, great-bestowing Clans Morgan and Cattach. This was written before Sir Robert's time, possibly. Niall McVurich says that Donald Duval Mackay O'Manus was "Morbhair Meghrath na chenn ar Mhorgannachuibh"—the Mormaor of Moyra (Lord Reay) was the chief of the Morgans.

The name Morgan has puzzled and annoyed the historians; it is Welsh, they thought. Now, the name is a good Pictish one, common in Aberdeenshire now, and especially in olden times, appearing in the roll of Earls of Mar and other dignities. It is also in the Book of Deer (circ. 1100). It is the old Celtic name Moricantos, "Sea-bright." Its preservation in Aberdeenshire and Strath-naver is interesting; and the fact shows that there is more in the Forbes myth than some wise historians think. The name Mackay is, in Gaelic, Mac Aoidh, son of Aodh, and this in old Gaelic was Aed, the Celtic Aidus, which was the word, declension and all, for "fire." That it was once a longer name—such as Aed-gal, Aed-gin, Aed-lug, etc.—is possible; but in historic times it has been Aed, and means "fire," neither more nor less. Cæsar's Aedui, whose name is directly from Celtic AEDUS or AIDUS, were the first Mackays!

ANTIQUITIES.

I have no intention of dealing with the purely physical antiquities of Sutherland, such as the cairns and stone circles of the Stone Age, or the brochs (of which there are 60) and earth-houses of the Bronze and Iron Ages. I will deal only with the literary monument left by early Christianity at Golspie in the shape of an Ogam-inscribed monolith usually known as the " Golspie Stone," now in the Dunrobin Museum. The inscription on this stone has received much attention in late years from Mr Nicholson, of the Bodleian Library, and from Professor Rhys. Both have written largely on the so-called " Pictish Inscriptions " in the Ogam character. The Ogam letters are an Irish invention—a sort of proto-telegraphic system where the letters of the alphabet are denoted by so many strokes—from one to five—above, through, or under a stem line respectively. The letters are easy to inscribe, but often difficult properly to read.

Professor Rhys has spent many years in deciphering these Ogam monuments, but Mr Nicholson " came, saw and conquered " all at once. As he says himself, it was on a visit to Golspie in 1893 he came " by chance " to study the Pictish inscriptions of Scotland, and two years later he gave his " chance " lucubrations to an astonished Celtic world in the pages of the " Academy." Since then he has put the articles together in book form under the title of the " Vernacular Inscriptions of the Ancient Kingdom of Alban." Celtic scholars have not thought it worth while to confute Mr Nicholson's views; his philology belongs to the good old days of Charles Mackay and Lachlan Maclean (" Lachunn nam Mogan.") The Picts, according to Mr Nicholson, were Gaelic-speaking Celts. Now, no Celtic scholar holds such a view; even Professor Rhys maintains that they were not Gaelic-speaking. In

his extraordinary paper in the Society of Antiquaries'
Transactions (1892), and lately in the report of the Welsh
Land Commission, the Professor strenuously holds that
the inscriptions are written in a lost language, which
was neither Gaelic nor Welsh, nor allied to them at all.
Dr Whitley Stokes and Professor Windish consider the
Picts to have been of Brittonic race and language, and
the place-names of Pictland alone ought to be enough to
bring any unprejudiced mind to this view.   It is, however,
probable that the inscriptions are in Gaelic, for they were
no doubt the work of the Gaelic-speaking missionaries
from Ireland who Christianised Pictland.   The Ogam
writing is, as already said, a purely Irish invention.   The
Ogams are, therefore, not " Pictish;" they are the " Ogams
of Pictland," and "Pictish inscriptions" is a misleading
term.   Mr Nicholson's greatest sin is his disregard of
what Professor Rhys calls "perspective in language."   He
explains 7th century Gaelic as if it were 19th century
Gaelic.   He forgets or overlooks the fact that " b " and
"m," for instance, were not aspirated for hundreds of years
after the Ogams were inscribed on the Golspie stone.
The readings of these Ogams are unsatisfactory in the
highest degree.   Professor Rhys pins his faith to an atrocity like this at Lunasting—xttocuhetts: ahehhtmnnn:
hccvvevv: nehhtonn.   He challenges the believers in the
Brittonic origin of Pictish to explain it, and says—" Let
them explain it as Welsh and I shall have to confess that
I have never understood a single word of my mother
tongue." ! ! !   As it stands printed above, it belongs to
a language that "was never heard on land or sea."   It
looks like the language of Luna, the moon—"Lunacy," it
may be named.

Mr Nicholson's reading of the Golspie stone is equally
as satisfactory as Professor Rhys's champion inscription
given above.   It runs thus—Allhhallorr edd m'qq Nu
uvvarrecch.   This he puts in Gaelic thus—Alhallr, ait Mic

Nu Uabhraich, " Alhallr, the place of McNu the Bold."
He takes Alhallr to be Norse, meaning " All-sloping."
The stone—indeed, all the inscribed stones—he regards
as boundary stones, not gravestones. McNu is compared
to the name of Columba's maternal grandfather Mac Naue,
a perfectly legitimate comparison, and to the Pictish
McNu Sir Herbert Maxwell correlates the Galwegian and
Dumfries names of McNoe or McNoah. Professor Rhys
reads the stone thus—Allhhallorr edd Maqq Nuuvva
rreirng. It is at present useless to speculate on the meaning of such a conglomeration of letters; the stone is evidently mis-read, and so are most of them.

A name about which much nonsense has been written
is Dunrobin; and the latest nonsense is in Mr Nicholson's
book on " Golspie." If the name had been Dun-Robert,
he says, it would be easily seen that it was named after
some Robert or other; but Robin he regards as a name
unlikely among a Gaelic population. This is a fallacy.
Diminutives like Robin in -in and -on were common in
early times with English names borrowed by the Gaels,
and in the Highlands we meet with many—Gibbon
(whence McGibbon), Robin (whence the present-day
McRobin), Paton (whence McFadyen), Wilkin (whence
McCuilcein), Rankin (whence McRankin, now obsolete),
Cubbin (from Cuthbert, whence McCubin, a Kirkcudbright
name), Michin (from Michael), whence McMichin or
McMeeking). In Ireland such forms were also common
—Tomin, Wattin, Philbin, Rickin, Robin. Dunrobin,
then, means the DUN or " fort " of Robin. The form
Drum-robin also occurs: " Robin's-ridge." Dunrobin
appears first in 1401 in Earl Robert's charters; it is no
doubt named after him.

PLACE NAMES

OF

SKYE.

PLACE NAMES OF SKYE.

THE Island of Skye is first mentioned by Ptolemy, the classical geographer of the second century. He calls it Skitis or Sketis, and misplaces it, putting it where the Orkneys should be. The island is next mentioned by Adamnan (700 A.D.), who calls it Scia Insula, the Island Scia, no doubt from Scith. St Columba, he tells us, was there once baptising a pagan chief called Artbrananus at a well called after him, Dobur Artbranani, at another time losing himself in a dense wood, for the island, we know, was once well wooded, as, indeed, were all the Hebrides till the advent of the Norse. The Irish annals tell us that in 668 the sons of Gartnait, with the people of Scith (or Sceth, gen. case), migrated to Ireland, but returned two years later. In 700 A.D. a battle of some consequence took place in Scii (dat. case), followed by the destruction of Dunolly Castle by King Selbach. Skye is mentioned several times in the Norse sagas, especially as being devastated in 1098 by Magnus of Norway: the Norse called it Skith, which in their language meant " tablet, log;" and, evidently from a remembrance of the Norse possession of the island and its Norse name, our poets have called the isle by the name of Clàr Sgithe. The Dean of Lismore (1512) speaks of

" McWllam oo Clar Skeith,"

the Dunvegan chief of the time. Rory M'Vurich's elegy on M'Leod (published 1776) has it—

> " Dh' fhalbh mo lathaichean éibhinn
> O 'n thréig sibh Clar Sgithe."

The early charter forms of the name are Skey (1292), Sky (1336, the 14th century form), Skye (1498); in the Chronicle of Man the name is Ski. The present Gaelic name is adjectival: An t-Eilean Sgiathanach, and Sgith-eanach, explained as the " Winged Isle." The older forms of the name, Sci or Scith, point to a shorter form of the same sort, as in Gaelic SGIATH, Norse SKITH, namely SKI, divide. The name may really be Pictish and mean the " Indented Isle," still having the same general force as " Winged."

It is usual to connect with Skye the early history of Cuchulinn, who received his martial education in the isle and DUN of Scathach, the Amazon Championess. The oldest tales make her live in an isle eastward of Alba or Scotland; the Scottish tradition has it that Dun-Scathaich in Skye is meant (Dunskahay in 1505—Dún-Scathaigh', the Dean of Lismore's Zown Skayth, and Skay for dative of Scathach), and this, after all, is likely.

Skye was one of the immediate causes of Hacon's invasion in 1263: with the rest of the Isles it owned Norway as its suzerain, but it formed part of the Kingdom of Man and the Isles till 1266, when the cession of the Isles took place. The Earl of Ross attacked it fiercely in 1262, with the consequence that complaint was made to Norway. Hacon in 1263 passed between Skye and the mainland

with his fleet, and there is little doubt that Kyleakin—
" Hacon's Sound," as it undoubtedly means—got its name
from the passing through of Hacon and his fleet. Similarly King James IV.'s punitive visit to Skye and the Isles
in 1540 is no doubt remembered in Portree, the King's
Port. The Earl of Ross received Skye as his portion of
the spoils of Largs and the events of 1262, and in 1292
the Sheriffdom of Skey was constituted from the Earl of
Ross's lands on the West Coast and northern Hebrides
(Skye and Lewis especially), for which Hugh of Ross has
in 1309 a charter from Robert Bruce. In 1335 King
Edward Balliol forfeited the next Earl and gave the Isles
of Skye and Lewis to John of Isles, the head of the Clan
Donald; but David Bruce, on his return, restored Skye to
the Earldom of Ross. It passed, with the Earldom of
Ross, into the hands of the Wolf of Badenoch, the Leslies,
and finally Donald of the Isles took it with the rest of the
Earldom of Ross. The forfeiture of the Lord of the Isles
towards the end of the 15th century brought the local
clans into direct relations with the Crown, and henceforward we have Macleods, Macdonalds, and Mackinnons as
leading chiefs and landlords in Skye.

The completeness of the Norse conquest and possession of Skye is proved by the place-names. The seven
natural provinces of the island have all Norse names—
Trotternish, Waternish, Duirinish, Bracadale, Minginish,
Strathordil, and Sleat; and the important townships and
" setters " also were occupied and named by the Norsemen. The Valuation Roll is the best proof of this. Some
250 different names occur in Skye in the present Roll, but
nearly a score of these are purely English. The rest are
Gaelic and Norse, and the proportion is exactly 60 per
cent. Norse names and 40 per cent. Gaelic. Naturally the
percentage is heaviest on the west and north, while Sleat
and Portree have the fewest Norse names. Black's tourist
map of 4 miles to the inch has 58 per cent. Norse names

for Kilmuir and 33 for Sleat; the latest map—2 miles to
the inch—gives 55 per cent. Norse names for Kilmuir, and
Sleat 30 per cent. It practically contains all the names in
the ordnance one inch to the mile map. As Duirinish and
Snizort show a higher percentage on the Valuation Roll
respectively than Kilmuir (viz., 68, 70, 61 per cent.), we
may roughly state that about 50 per cent. of the names on
the 1 inch map are Norse as against the Gaelic names.
Of course, as the maps increase in minutiæ and detail, the
Gaelic names correspondingly increase: the smaller features—fields, hillocks, and burns—are apt to be Gaelic,
having possibly been re-named since the Norse occupation.

Of the present parish names three are Gaelic—
Strath, Portree, and Kilmuir (St Mary's kil or church),
but the first is properly half Norse, being for Strath-
Swordale or Strathordil, where Swordale or Suordale is a
common Norse name, appearing otherwise in Skye (at
Dunvegan), in Lewis, in Ross-shire, and in Sutherland,
explained by Captain Thomas as " Sward-dale," which it
likely is, though Saur-dalr, " Swampy or Mud dale," may
suit the phonetics in this case. The other four parishes
have Norse names: Duirinish, like Durness, in Sutherland,
means "Deer's ness," NESS being the Norse NES, a cape,
nose; Snizort, Snesfurd 1501, Sneisport 1526, Snisport
1561, seems to be for Snaes-fjord, " Snow-firth," the suggested " Sneis firth," from the name Sneis (skewer) being
unsatisfactory. Bracadale (Bracadoll 1498, Braikodell
1541) stands for Brekka-dalr, " Slope-dale;" and Sleat is
the Norse slétta, a level or plain, it being, in fact, the most
even or level portion of Skye. Here we may add the districts of Trotternish, Waternish, and Minginish. The first
is spelt by Dean Munro (1549) as Trouternesse or Tronternesse, and a writer at the end of the 17th century also
spells the name with N, not U, before the middle T.
M'Vurich gives the Gaelic for it in the Red Book of Clan-

ranald as Tròntarnis; the modern Gaelic is practically the
same—Trò(n)dar-nis, with nasalised ò. It stands for
Thróndar-nes, " Thrond's ness," Thrond being a favourite
personal name, giving rise also to many place-names, inclusive of the Icelandic Thróndarnes quoted above, and
the modern Drontheim or Trondhjem, in Norway.
Waternish finds its counterpart in two Icelandic nesses
called Vatnsnes, " Water-ness;" while Minginish
(Myngnes, 1498, Mygnes 1511, Myngynnes 1549, Men-
zenise 1549) may stand for Megin-nes' " Main ness."

We may next deal with the islands belonging to Skye.
Pabay is for Pap-ey, " Pope or Priest Isle," a common isle
name, showing the Norse found the Gaelic hermits or
Culdees there. Scalpa, which also appears in Harris, is
found also in Orkney, but there stands for Skálp-eith,
" Ship isthmus," whereas in the Hebrides it means " Ship
isle." Raasay (Rasay 1501, Rairsay 1526, Raarsay 1549)
seems to stand for Rár-áss-ey, " Isle of Roe-ridge." Its
neighbour, Rona, is easily derived, for we have the Norse
name for it—Rauney, that is Hraun-ey, " Isle of the rough,
rocky surface " (HRAUN, lava-field especially), a derivation supported by Martin's description of it—" This little
isle is the most unequal rocky piece of ground to be seen
anywhere." Staffin Isle is so named from its basaltic
rocks, Norse STAFR, staff, etc.; it gives its name to the
adjoining bay and mainland. Altavaig, on the contrary,
must take its name from Alpta-vik, " swan-bay." Trodday,
to the north of Trotternish, may be Thrond's Isle, though
" Pasture (Trodh) Isle " has also been suggested. Holm
Isle, off Duntulm, gives its name to the latter place, " Fort
of Holm;" the Norse is HOLMR, a holm or islet in a bay.
The Ascrib Isles, called by Monro Askerin, seem to contain a reference to ASKR, ash, spear, ship. Isay is " Ice-
isle;" Mingay, " Lesser-isle;" Wiay, a common isle name
in the Hebrides, seems for Vé-ey, " Temple-isle." Oronsa,

off Bracadale and off Sleat (the latter Eilean Dhiarmaid;
17th century Island Diermand), is for Orfiris-ey, "Ebb-
tide-isle," joined to the mainland at low water. There are
three or more other such. Soay, also a common island
name, "Sheep-isle," as Lampay, at Dunvegan, means
"Lamb-ey," and Eilean Heast, or "Horse-isle," no doubt
gives its name to the mainland township of Heast, though
in Iceland a place gets its name Hestr on account of a
horse-shaped crag.

The sea-lochs or fjords have mostly Norse names ending in ORD or ORT, derived from fjord. Broadford, like
the Arran Brodick, has replaced a Norse Breidha-fjord.
Lochs Ainort and Eynort may be for Einar's fjord; Loch
Snizort has been already explained; Loch Harport is possibly Hafra-fjord, "He-goat" fjord; and Loch Eishort
may be for Eiths-fjord, or Isthmus fjord. The termination AIG stands for VIK, bay, and there are many such. In
Sleat we have Ostaig, "Eastwick;" Saasaig, Cask
bay (sás-vik);" Morsaig, "Ant-bay (Maurs-vik"); Aula-
vaig, "Olave's bay;" Tarskavaig, "Cod-bay (thorskr,
Gaelic trosg "); in Strath, Malag "Measure or Speech bay
(Mála-vik "); Boreraig, "Burg bay" (Borgar-vik "); in
Bracadale, Scavaig river, 17th century Scah-vag, "Shaw-
bay;" Fiskavaig, "Fish-bay;" Totaig, "Toft or Clearing
Bay;" in Duirinish, Varkasaig, "Castle-bay" (VIRKI);
Branderscaig, Ramasaig, "Raven's bay;" Boreraig and
Totaig as before, Camalaig; in Snizort, Pen-soraig, from
Saur-vik, "Mud bay;" Liuravaig, like Lerwick, "Mud-
bay;" Bearraraig, Bjorn's bay; in Kilmuir, Bornaskitaig
(Martin's Bornswittag), from Skipta-vik, "Division-bay;"
Volovig, "Field bay;" Loch Langaig, "Long-bay;" Bro-
gaig, "Breeches' bay;" Torvaig, "Thori's bay;" Cracaig,
"Crook-bay;" Tianavaig (Martin's Camstinvag), Tindar-
vik or "Peak-bay;" Oskaig (long o), in 1630 Oistage,
"Osk's bay or the Desire bay." A river mouth is OSS
or AR-OSS, and hence come Ose, Glen-ose, Osdal, Oisgill

(Oyce-burn), Aros Bay, Inveraros or Inverarish in Raasay.

The capes or nesses are numerous: Ard Thurinish, "Thwart or cross (THVER) point;" Ardnish, a hybrid, as also Kraiknish, Ullinish, "Ulli's point;" Crossnish, "Cross point;" Uignish, "Wick ness;" Unish, "Yew (?) ness; Greshornish, "Grice or Pig's ness;" Skirinish (Martin's Skerines), "Skerry ness;" Meanish, Mjo-nes or "Narrow ness;" Hunish, "Bear's (hùnn) ness;" Arnish "Erne or Eagle ness;" Manish (Maenes, 1630), "Sea-mew ness." The two south capes of Suisnish—Raasay and Strath— come from SNOS, projecting rock, head, in fact for "Sow's head." Eyrr, a pebbly beach, appears in Eyre of Snizort, Ken-sal-eyre, and Ayre Point, south of Raasay.

Hill and rock names are mostly Norse, showing VALL for FJALL, fell; CLEIT or KLETTR, a rock; STACK or STAKKV, a stack of a hill; SGEIR, skerry; SCORE and SGUVR, edge or cliff; HAMARR, rock (as in Hamara, "Rock water"); SGATH or SKAGI, a jutting hill or promontory (Beinn a' Sgath); and SCO, a shaw or woody rising (Birkisco, "Birk-shaw.") The Hoe and Cop-na-Hoe mean HAUGR, tumulus or burial hillock. Ben Cleit, Loch Cleit and such names are common. Stockval is "Stock-fell;" Arnaval, "Erne-fell;" Roineval, "Hraun-fell," as in Rona; Scoval, "Shaw-fell;" Horneval, "Horn-hill;" Helavall, "Hella or Flagstone fell;" Maehall, "Narrow-hill;" Reiveal, "Smooth-hill." Ben Storr is from STOR, big. To these must be added one or two names in BRECK or BREKK, a slope; Cross-breck and Scorry-breck.

All names with -DAL as an ending are Norse, and they are very numerous (Armadale, Meadale, etc.) There are many GILS or burns (Vidi-gill, Vikisgill, etc.); but Idrigill, which occurs twice, is a promontory, and must stand for Ytri-kollr or "Further (Outer) hill." There are three names from FORS, a waterfall—Forse and Forsan.

The township names show many -SHADERS terminally; this is the Norse SETR, a station or sheiling (Marishader, "mare-seat," Shulishader, "Pillar-seat," etc.) The suffix BOST means township—Husabost, "House-stead;" Breabost, "Broad-town," etc. Terminal STA is for STADR, a stead, holding—Shulista, as in Shulisshader, Lusta, Conista (Lady's-town), etc. Suffix GARRY is for GARTH—Bigeary, "Bigging-garth," etc. BURG or Borve is very common—Skudiburg, Raisaburg, etc.; so is TOT or TOBHTA, a toft or clearing.

PLACE NAMES

OF

LOCHABER.

PLACE NAMES OF LOCHABER.

THE earliest mention of Lochaber occurs in the pages of Adamnan, who died in 704. St Columba, he tells us, gave a miraculous stake, which attracted and killed wild animals coming near it, to a poor man from "the district which borders on the shores of the Apcric Lake;" and the poor man further catches by means of the stake a monster salmon from the river there—a river "which may be called in Latin Nigra Dea," or Dark Goddess. Dr Skene has ingeniously connected this river with another name given by Adamnan for a lake in the Drumalban Range, viz., Loch-dae, which means in old Gaelic "Dark Goddess," from obsolete LOCH, dark. Hence the Nigra Dea is the Lochy, either in Perth or Lochaber; and it is an interesting reminder of the fact that the ancient Celts were great river worshippers, which they often called "Mothers" (Matrona or Marne), or "Goddesses" (Déva or Dee, Divona or Don). Adamnan's Aporic comes from the old Gaelic APOR, a marsh), and the meaning of Lochaber is the Lake of the

Marsh. Fortunately, tradition supports this view, for, according to it, the original Lochaber was a lakelet in the Mòine Mhór—the Large Moss—near the mouth of the river Lochy. Tradition and philology thus go hand in hand in the etymology of the name Lochaber: no scepticism need apply. The old Gaelic APOR and Irish ABAR (marsh) are not the same as the Pictish prefix ABER or OBAIR (confluence, river-mouth), so common in place-names in Pictland, such as Aberdeen, Aberchalder, and the like. Indeed, only one characteristically Pictish name can be found in Lochaber, and that is the old Pitmaglassy (1500), or Pittenglass (1669), which is mentioned along with Achadrom and Culross, on the borders of Lochaber and Glengarry, but such names as Spean or Pean may be inferred to be Pictish names belonging to the main features of the country. It is clear that in Columba's time the inhabitants of Lochaber spoke Gaelic, not Pictish: they, in fact, belonged to the old Scottic invaders of Pictland that settled in Oirir-Ghaidheal ("coastland of the Gael," Argyll from Kintyre to Lochbroom) long ere the Sons of Erc founded the Kingdom of Dalriada. Hence the people of Lochaber speak the Northern Dialect of Gaelic, and good Gaelic it once was, and still is.

Romance makes Banquo of the Macbeth drama Thane of Lochaber, and respectable tradition connects the Cummings with Lochaber in the thirteenth century; and, of course, as elsewhere, there is a Cummings-tower at Inverlochy Castle. When we come to assured history, we find that the "lands of Louchabre" formed part of the Earldom of Moray, granted to Randolph between 1307 and 1314, though seemingly it soon left his hands, for in the "Index to Lost Charters" it is entered that Angus of the Isles got the lands of "Lochabre" from Bruce in 1309. Anyway, Lochaber was not long attached to the Province of Moray. The "good John of Isla" got the ward of it in 1335 in the minority of the Earl of Atholl, who pro-

bably got it through his grandmother, the heiress of the
Cummings. The Island Lord got it altogether in 1343.
Alaster Carrach, third son of the good John of Ile, is in
possession of the Lordship of Louchabre at the end of
the century, though the superiority still remained in the
hands of the eldest son, the Lord of the Isles.   Alaster
Carrach was the ancestor of the Keppoch Macdonalds, and
it was from him, as eldest direct descendants, that their
claims of Brae Lochaber arose. The last two Lords of the
Isles seem to have ignored Alaster Carrach's descendants;
at anyrate, in 1444, Mackintosh got from the Lord of the
Isles the lands of Glenluy and Locharkaig, west of Loch
Lochy, and the Brae Lochaber lands, at first as far down
as Loch Lochy, the chief demesne being Keppoch. Mackintosh's claims to these lands and his attempted possession of them as against the native Camerons of Glenluy
and Locharkaig and the Macdonalds of Keppoch, kept
the country in a state of turmoil for two hundred years.
Finally, in 1666, Lochiel unwillingly bought Glenluy and
Locharkaig, Argyle being guarantor; but the Keppochs
kept forcible possession longer, which practically ended in
the last clan fight in Scotland, on Mulroy, above Keppoch,
in 1688. Though then defeated, Mackintosh made good
his right, and still holds the property.

The Camerons also incurred the displeasure of the
Lords of the Isles for deserting them in 1429 in their
quarrel with the King. Their brave and energetic chief,
Donald Dubh, fought against Donald Balloch at Inverlochy in 1431, when the latter defeated the Royal forces.
Donald Dubh and his clan suffered severely over this, and
became somewhat Ishmaelite for a century or two thereafter. Maclean, first, of Coll, then, of Lochbuy, received
the barony of Lochiel, there being a charter to the latter
in 1461 of these lands. The Lord of the Isles' cousin,
Celestine of Lochalsh, who appears to have received the
lordship of Lochaber from the Earl, favoured Cameron as

against the Macleans, and granted him Lochiel in 1472—
a grant renewed in 1492 by Celestine's son. The final forfeiture of the Lord of the Isles in 1493 brought the lordship of Lochaber into the King's hands. In 1494 Maclean again got Lochiel, but next year Cameron received
it from the Crown. The Macleans kept up their claims
or sold them, and the frequent forfeitures of Cameron gave
his enemies plenty of opportunity to get charter rights to
his property. After passing through the hands of Macleans, Campbells of Cawdor and Argyll, and Huntly, it is
gratifying to record that the Chief of Clan Cameron still
holds the barony of Lochiel—the land north of the loch
and west of Loch Lochy.

The portion of Lochaber between Glen Nevis and Loch
Leven, east of Loch Linnhe, had the general title of Maw-
more, the "Great Màm," MAM meaning a "large round hill."
The name is still preserved in Mamore Forest. Maw-
more was still in the King's lands after the forfeiture of the
Lord of the Isles in 1502, but then it was granted to
Stewart of Appin, and in 1504 to Huntly, who as Lord of
the Lordship of Lochaber sold it in 1522 to Argyll.
Mamore came thereafter into the hands of the Gordons,
but on their decline the western half of it came into the
hands of Lochiel, and the eastern half, inclusive of Glen-
Nevis, belongs to Mrs Cameron-Campbell of Monzie representative of the Camerons of Fassifern. Glen Nevis of
old belonged to the Camerons. The district about Fort-
William and Inverlochy, now the Abinger estate, was
acquired by Maclean of Duart in 1496, who sold to Stewart
of Appin and to Huntly parts of the estate, and in 1531
Lochiel got Appin's lands, including Inverlochy. But the
Duart family again recovered the land (1540), and in the
17th century it finally came into Huntly's hands, who held
it in the 17th and 18th centuries. The Gordons parted
with the estate some fifty years ago, and it is now Lord
Abinger's. The leading proprietors of Lochaber are

therefore Cameron of Lochiel, Mackintosh of Mackintosh, and Mrs Campbell of Monzie—three good Gaelic family names as against one "Scarlett" Sassenach, who holds a big fourth of the country!

Lochaber now comprises the two parishes of Kilmallie and Kilmonivaig; but formerly Mamore formed part of the old parish of Elan-munne, the other part belonging to Argyll.   The name Elan-munne, or St Munn's Isle, is still known, corrupted in English to Mungo.   It is an islet in Loch Leven, where St Munn's Church once was, and the burial-ground still is.   Munn, or Munna, is a con- traction for Mo-Fhindu, "My Findan," and is a pet name for St Finnan.   Kilmonivaig, in 1449 Kilmanawik, in 1500 Kilmonyvaig, stands for Kill or Church of St Mo-Naomhóc, or St Naomhan.   Kilmallie appears in 1292 as Kilmalyn, in 1532 Kilmale, and 1552 Culmaly.   This was also, spell- ings and all, the old name of Golspie.   A Kilmayaille is mentioned in Tarbert of Kintyre.   The name is a difficult one at best.   There is no St Málli—the A is long—though there is a literary Charles O'Malley from an ancestral O'Máilli.   Possibly our saint here is Amhalghaidh or Aulay, confused with Norse Olave (whence M'Aulay), with the usual MO prefixed.   Kilmallie would then stand for Cille-mo-Amhalghaidh.

In examining the place-names we may begin with the great natural features, the lakes, rivers and mountains. Loch Linnhe is known in the locality as An Linne, "the Pool" or "Sea-loch;" the Lochiel part is called An Linne Dhubh, "the Black Pool," the part outside Corran An Linne Sheilich, "the Willow Pool." Lochiel, in 1461 Locheale, Lochheil in 1492, and Lochiel in 1520, still awaits explanation. Loch Lochy has already been explained as the lake of the river "Dark Goddess." It must be remembered that lakes and glens take their names from the rivers that flow from or through them, a fact noted by Adamnan in speaking of Loch Ness, which he calls the "Lake of the River Ness." Loch Arkaig is named from the River Airceag; its etymology is unknown. The root ARK means "defence" in Celtic; but possibly the root here is ERC, darkish, the "dun" river being perhaps the force of the word. Equally enigmatical is Loch Treig and its river Treig, where the E is long. In modern Gaelic TREIG means "forsake." Loch Eilde means the River and Loch of the Hind; Loch Gulbin, Torgulbin, etc., come from GULBAN, a beak. Loch Leven and the River Leven, Gaelic Li'un, point to a Celtic Li-vo-na, root LI, flow, Gaelic LIGHE, a flood. There is a Leven in Lennox and another in Glen-Lyon similarly pronounced. The name is Pictish originally, as, indeed, may be the other difficult names above passed in review: perhaps older still.

In regard to the bens and glens, the latter follow the river names, and the former are nearly all easily derived by anyone that knows Gaelic. Ben Nevis is the exception. There we have Glen-Nevis and the River Nevis. A sea loch in the south of Knoydart is called Loch Nevis, and hence we are sure that it is the river that has given its name to Glen and Ben Nevis. The local pronunciation is Nibheis (Eng. Nivesh), which would give a primitive form, Nibestis, but probably Nebestis is the right form, from NEB, burst, flow; the name may have been a goddess name allied to "Nymph" by root and idea. Glen-Spean, of course, takes its name from the River Spean, and the SP initial is hardly ever native Gaelic— certainly not old Gaelic. We may conclude that Spean is Pictish, originally Spesona, the root SPES, SPE or SQES, SQE, as in Spey, to cast forth, squirt, vomit, Gaelic SGEITH; and the old Italian river name, Vomanus (root VOM), may be instanced as analogous. The idea is that of a fast-flowing, "spatey" river, the word "spate" being also distinctly allied. Glenfintaig comes from the River Fintag, the "white river," a common river name. Mrs Mackellar explained Glendessary (Glendessorach, 1505) as the "Glen of the South Shealing," DEAS-AIRIGH: anyway the root is DEAS, right or south. Glen-pean (so in Blaeu, Glen-pona, 1505), Glen-kingie (Glen-Kinglen, 1505), and Glen-gloy must be left alone at present; Glenroy is the "Glen of the Red River;" Glen-sulag, from Suileag river, the river full of "eyes" or pools; and Glen-luy (Glenloy, 1505, Glenlie, 1516), "Glen of Calves."

Fort-William gets its name from the fort built for William of Orange near there in the end of the seventeenth century, but the village was originally named after his consort, Mary, hence Maryburgh. A hundred years earlier (1597) an Act of Parliament directed the creation of three burghs in the West Highlands to maintain the cause of "civility and policy;" these were to be in Kintyre, Lochaber, and Lewis. The final result came to be the erection of the towns of Campbeltown, Fort-William, and Stornoway, but only the former procured the benefits of the Act in becoming a Royal Burgh. The Gordons, who owned the Inverlochy estates till their demise with the last duke (1836), changed Maryburgh into Gordonsburgh when the fit of "Orangeism" was past, and the village was last century so known. Sir Duncan Cameron of Fassifern, in succeeding the Gordons, changed the name to Duncansburgh! This has also given way to the "garrison" name of Fort-William, it being An Gearasdan in Gaelic. Auchintore-beg (Auchintor-beg, 1496) was its pre-village name, the field of the TODHAR or manure.

Only a few of the leading farms and other such names can here be taken. Callart, so in 1522, is explained as Cala-ard, the "high bay" literally, but "upper ferry" really, as opposed to the Ballachulish one. Ballachulish (Ballecheles, 1522), "Straits town," Kinlochmore, Coruanan ("Lamb's Corry,") Blar-nan-cléireach, and such in "Mamore" are easy. Onich, Offanych in 1522, is, as its older form proves, from OMHANACH, "foam-frothed" place; Cuilchenna is shown by the old form, Culkenan (1522), to mean "Back of the Head-ie;" Corran means a small promontory between two bays, not a "sickle," as usually explained; Drumarbin, Blaeu's Druimerbin, Drumarbane of 1522, is no doubt "Ridge of Roes." Lundavra is in 1502 Dundabray, a fort or forts in a small isle in Mamore, explained by Mrs Mackellar as Dun-da-ràth, "Fort of two RATHS or enclosures," there being two islets. Mr Livingstone explains the name as wave (LUNN) of the double crest (brà); but Lundavra seems a phonetic assimilation arising from Loch Dun-da-bhrà. Dun-dearduil is etymologised in the Ordnance maps into "Fort of the Foreign Bard!" The Dearduil here is a common fort name, usually explained from the heroine Deirdre, Macpherson's Darthula.

In Kilmonivaig the most interesting farm name is Keppoch; it is from the old Gaelic CEAPACH, a tillage plot, a holding, in root the same as CEAP, block. Fersit, the "two Fersenas" of 1500, and Blaeu's Farset, comes from FEARSAD, an estuary, sand-bank, which suits the place. Names like Blarour, Tirandrish, Achluachrach, Achaderry, Tulloch, Innerroy, and Innis or Inch have only to be pronounced in Gaelic and their secret is out. Lianachan is from LEAN, a mead; Sliabh Lorgach, east of Loch Treig, gets its name from its moraine "tracks" or lines; Bothuntin, Gaelic Both-hundainn, Bothinton in 1444, is one of the many BOTHS or "steads" of Brae-Lochaber, and it is a puzzling name, for Hundaidh or Hundainn did duty in Gaelic for Huntly; only here the appearance of the name in 1444, 1466, and 1476 precludes connection. It is evidently the same name as we have in Contin, a "confluence" place.

In Kilmallie we may note Corpach, so named, as the
Old Statistical Account says, from the fact that here they
rested with the bodies before embarkation on their way to
Iona. Annat comes from the obsolete ANNAID a mother-
church, doubtless where the anchorite had his cell and little
chapel. Fassfern is the "abode" or FASADH of the alder;
Errocht means in old Gaelic a "meeting;" Moy, a "plain;"
and Glastor is etymologised correctly on the ordnance maps
Glas-doire. Other Lochaber names of interest—and there
are many more such—are worthy of record and study.

PLACE NAMES

OF

LOCHALSH.

PLACE NAMES OF
LOCHALSH.

LOCHALSH is undoubtedly the Volsas or Volas Bay
of Ptolemy, the geographer, of the early part of the
second century. It is therefore one of the oldest
names in Scotland. Its next appearance in written
form is more than thirteen centuries later: this is
in 1464, in a Crown charter to Celestine of the Isles, where
the name is spelt Lochalsche. A common form in early
writings was Lochalch or Lochelch, and then Lochalse
(1576), now Lochalsh (Gaelic Loch-aills' or even Loch-àis',
where the L, as usual, drops before the s. Probably the
form Volsas is the ancestor of our modern form; Volas
might be apt to land in Loch-aill, whereas Volsas would
give, according to well-known phonetic laws, latterly
Fallas or such. That root may be VOL, roll, as a wave;
Eng., WELL.

Lochalsh formed part of 'Argyle, which anciently
stretched as far as Lochbroom; it belonged to North
'Argyle, the present county being South Argyle. It also
belonged to the Earldom of Ross. It was the " patria,"

or habitat, of pre-Mathesons, and the TOISEACH, or thane, of Lochalsh—the Chief of the Mathesons—was one of the Earl of Ross's leading vassals. Similarly Kintail was no doubt held by a TOISEACH, who latterly was Mackenzie of Kintail. The Edinburgh MS. (1450) indicates four clans in early times (1200-1400) as inhabiting from Lochalsh to Lochbroom—Mathesons in Lochalsh; Mackenzies in Kintail; Gillanders or Rosses in Gairloch; and Nicolsons in Lochbroom. Applecross was holy ground, and belonged to the Church.

In 1427 Mackmaken or Matheson of Lochalsh is mentioned as leader of two thousand by Fordun; he was vassal to the Earl of Ross, and concerned in his rebellious conduct. In 1449 Lochalsh was in the hands of Celestine, brother to John, Earl of Ross, granted to him by the Earl or his father, and confirmed by the Crown in 1464. What became of the Chief of Mathesons or how he was treated we do not know: at anyrate he had a new overlord. Sir Alexander of Lochalsh succeeded Celestine (died 1476), and in 1492 granted with other lands elsewhere to Ewin, son of Alan, Chief of the Camerons, the half of Lochalsh, 14 merklands out of the 26, and the King confirmed it in 1495, and renewed it in 1539. Meanwhile Sir Donald Gallda succeeded Alexander, and died in 1518, leaving his two sisters co-heiresses. One was married to Glengarry, the other to Dingwall of Kildun. The other half of Lochalsh thus belonged to these two. They shared the farms between them. Thus the Davoch land of Balmacarra belonged half to Glengarry and half to Dingwall, and so with the other holdings. In 1539 Glengarry has a direct Crown charter for his share of Lochalsh. Owing to circumstances arising from Blar-na-Leine and the consequent raid on Glens Moriston and Urquhart by Glengarry and Lochiel, their shares of Lochalsh passed by forfeiture into the hands of the Grants—Freuchy and Glenmoriston. But they don't seem to have reaped any benefit from this

" sheepskin " allotment to them of these lands. Dingwall in 1554 sold his share of Lochalsh to Mackenzie of Kintail, who was fast acquiring territory and power ever since the fall of the Earldom of Ross. Freuchy in 1571 made peace with Glengarry, and over a marriage contract with Glengarry's son and Freuchy's daughter gave him back his lands and his (Freuchy's) share of Lochalsh. Lochalsh was thus in the hands of three men in 1571—Glengarry, Kintail, and Grant of Glenmoriston (5 merklands). The quarrels between Kintail and Glengarry began about 1580. Glengarry was not popular in Lochalsh—the old Mathesons had not yet, possibly, forgotten the Macdonald usurpation—and at anyrate Glengarry himself was unwise and harsh. The Mackenzie Chief fomented the quarrel, then openly intervened in it, hostilities breaking out about 1580, which went on intermittently till 1603, with much loss in blood and status to Glengarry. The final result was that in 1607 Glengarry was compelled to part with the lands of Lochalsh to his more astute rival of Kintail, who thus in that year acquired the whole of Lochalsh save Glenmoriston's five merks and the Church lands, the latter of which, however, became his in 1610, and in 1633 the Earl of Seaforth is retoured for all Lochalsh.

The Mackenzies held Lochalsh for two hundred years, the last Lord Seaforth parting with it in 1801. The purchaser of Lochalsh was Mr, afterwards Sir (1818), Hugh Innes, who had made his fortune in London by commerce. He was some time member for the Wick Burghs, and, dying without issue, his property came into the hands of his grand-niece (Katherine Lindsay), who married Mr Isaac Lillingston. The Lillingstons were much beloved by the Lochalsh people, and receive great praise from Duncan Matheson, one of the clan historians of the time. After the death of her husband Mrs Lillingston sold Lochalsh to Mr, afterwards Sir, Alexander Matheson in 1851, whose son, Sir Kenneth, is the present proprietor.

The place-names of Lochalsh are nearly all Gaelic. The Norse names are remarkably few—nine or ten in all. There is at least one Pictish name—Lundie and Loch Lundie (Lunde, 1495; Lundy, 1527). It is a common name in Pictland, from Fife to Sutherland inclusive. It is possibly the same name as we have in London, ancient Londinium. The root may be a nasalised form of LUD, marshy, boggy; Gaelic, LODAN.

The Norse names are as follows:—

STROMEFERRY. This is a hybrid; "ferry" is English and "strome" is the Norse "straumr," current, stream, applied to the Strome channel here. It is common in the Orkneys and in the Norse regions generally.

ULHAVA, an islet near Duncraig. This is the same as Ulva, near Mull; it means "Wolf's Isle"—ULF-EY. Ulf may have been a person's name.

DUIRINISH (Durris, 1548, Durness, 1554, Dowrnes, Durinische, 1607). This means Deer's Ness or headland —"dyra-nes." The name appears as Duirinish in Skye and Durness in Sutherland.

ERBUSAIG (Arbesak, 1554, Erbissok, 1633, pronounced now Earbasaig with two r's for euphony's sake). It appears to mean Erp's Wick or bay, Erp being a personal name borrowed by the Norse from the Picts. The Gaelic form of Erp is Erc, a common name in ancient times, as in the case of Fergus Mac Erc, first King of Dalriada.

PLADAIG. The Norse chief root here is FLAT, flat; compare Pladda and Fladda for Flat-ey, "Flat Island." Whether AIG is a Gaelic termination or the Norse VIK, a wick or bay, is hard to say.

SCALPAIDH, pronounced Scalpa, means Shallop or Ship River—" Skálp-á." Scalpa, in Skye, is Ship Isle, and in the Orkneys it is for Ship-isthmus (EIDH).

RERAIG (Rowrag, 1548, Rerek, 1554, Rerag, 1607, 1633), Gaelic Rèiraig, seems to be for REYRVIK, Reed Bay. There is another Reraig in Lochcarron.

AVERNISH (Awernis 1459, Awnarnys 1527, Avarrynis 1548, Evernische 1607, Averneis 1633); Gaelic A(bh)arnis. It is likely Norse "Afar-nes," Big or Bulkyness.

CEANN-AN-OBA; Gaelic, "Ceann an òib." Head of the ob or bay; the word OB is in Norse HOP. It appears as Obbe in Harris, as Oban, and Ben Hope in Sutherland. Ob-an-Duine is a little north of Plockton.

These are the undoubted Norse names. It is tempting to refer Loch Calavie, far eastward among the hills, to the Norse KALFR, calf, especialy as in the next Glen is Loch an Laoigh, beside which is Coire Seasgach (corry of the heifers). The difficulty in regarding it as Norse · is two-fold: it is far inland and the pronunciation is Cailbhidh, where the termination in "i" is unaccountable from Norse sources. There is a Glen Calvie in Strathcarron. Strathasgaig, Gaelic Srath-àsgag, may be hybrid, Asgaig coming from the Norse "Aska-vik," Ash or Ship Wick; but the Norse ASK has the vowel short, and this makes the etymology doubtful. No Gaelic root in ASG, FASG, or even TASG or SASG can be suggested.

We shall now deal with the Gaelic names mentioned in the old records, commencing at the north end of the parish and working around the coast.

ARDNARFF, G. Ard-arbha, Ard-an-arbha; "Height of the corn(land)." In 1554 Ardnanarf 1574 Ardenarra, 1607 Ardonarrow.

INCHNAIRN; G. Innis-an-fhearna; "Inches or the Links of the Alder." In 1548, 1554, and 1607 Inchenarne, 1574 Inchnairnie.

FERNAIG; G. Fearnaig, "Place of Alders." In 1495 Fairnmoir, Fayrineagveg (there were two Fernaigs), in 1527 Fayrnagmore, Fayrinaegveg, &c.

ACHMORE, "Big Field"; in 1495 and 1527 Achmoir, in 1548 Auchmoir. Along with it went Killochir (1548, 1607) or Cuyloir (1527), a name seemingly lost.

ACHACHONLEICH, "Field of the Straw or Stubble"; in 1495 Achechoynleith, 1527 Achchonelyth.

BRAEINTRA; G. Bràigh' an t-Srath, "Upper part of the Strath." In 1495 Brayeintraye, 1633 Breaintread, 1548 Brayeyntrahe.

CRAIG, Duncraig, from G. CREAG, hill. In 1548 Cragy et Harsa, 1554 LIE Craig; in 1607 Craig et Harsa. The latter name is unknown to the present writer.

ACHANDARRACH; G. Achadh-nan-darach, "Field of the Oaks." In 1495 Achenadariache, 1527 Achendariach, 1548 Auchnadarrach.

ACHNAHINICH; G. Achadh-na h-ìnich; 1548 Auchna-howgych, 1554 Auchnaheuych, 1574 Auchinnahynneych, 1607 Auchnahinginche, 1633 Auchnahenginche. Duncan Matheson spelt it Acha na Shinich, and he says that at Achadh-da-ternaidh (Field of two descents) there the Mathesons used to rally as to a rendezvous when they took the field. They drank of the sacred stream of Altan-rabhraidh (Burn of the Murmuring) and started. If AONACH, fair, gathering, were dialectically feminine in old Lochalsh, as well it might, for the word was originally neuter, then we might explain the name as Achadh na h-Aonaich, "Field of the Fair"—even "Field of the Rendezvous." A word INGNEACH suits the old forms and pronunciation best.

BALMACARRA, G. Bail' mac-ara. The old forms are —1548 Ballimaccroy; 1554, 1607, and 1633 Ballamaccarra; 1574 Ballemakcarra(ne). The name looks as if it meant "Township of the M'Ara family" (M'Ara being genitive plural). The surname M'Ara or M'Carra is and was common in Perthshire; but it is not found elsewhere. Balmacarra may be a corruption, like Ben Mac Dui; perhaps, Whale-ton (Muc-mhara)?

AUCHTERTYRE, G. Uachdarìridh, for Uachdar-thire, "Upper part of the Land." Old forms are—Wochterory (1495), Ochtertere (1527), Ochbertirie (1548).

ACHTAYTORALAN, G. Achadh-da-toralan. Old forms are—Auchtatorlyne (1548), Auchtatorlane (1554), Auchrid-tidorillane (1574), Auchtatorrelan (1607). The word TORALAN or TORRALAN is of doubtful force; it may be a derivative like TORRAN, knoll, from TORR, but the name Achadh-da-tearnaidh, already referred to, makes it possible that here we have a name of similar form and force, viz., TORLUINN, descent, better TUIRLING. With Achtay-toralan went Ardach (1548), Ardache (1607), Ardacht (1574); it means " Highfield."

NOSTIE. G. Nòsdaidh; in 1548 and 1574 Nosti, 1554 Noyste, 1607 and 1633 Nostie. It seems to be from OSD-THIGH, inn, with the article in the dative (or locative) before it, as 'N-Osd-thigh, just as we have it in Nonach further east.

ARDELVE, G. Aird-eilghidh, " Height of the Fallow Land." In 1548 Ardelly, 1554 Ardelf (which suggests a locative Ard-sheilbh, " High-property,") Ardillie in 1574, 1607 Ardelleive, 1633 Ardelve.

CONCHRA, G. Conachra, which appears to be a derivative of CRO or CRA, an enclosure, fold (compare the Cro of Kintail, Crà in the north of Arran, and elsewhere in both forms). The CON is the old preposition CO, CON, with; it means here a collection of CRO-s, the whole word Conchra meaning " Place of folds." In 1548 Connachry, 1554 Concry, Conchra in 1574 and 1633, in 1607 Conchara.

SALLACHY, G. Salachaidh, " Place of Willows;" old Gaelic SAILECH (gen.), willow, now SEILEACH, the Scotch SAUGH, for SALCH, old English SALH. Sallachy is common as a place-name. Compare Sauchie-burn for older Salchie (Stirling), where possibly the word is Scotch. Old forms are Sallach in 1548, Salche in 1554, Sallachie in 1574 and 1633.

Old names that seem to have dropped out of the running are these—With Fernaigbeg go Fadamine (1495), Fynimain (1527), Fineman (1548), and Acheache (1495), Acheachy (1527), Auchcroy (1548, 1607). The two merklands of Culthnok, Achnacloich, Blaregarwe and Acheae are mentioned in 1495 and 1527 (Achiae in 1527) and later. With Auchtertyre appears Achich in 1548, Achiche in 1607.

Names that do not appear in the old documents will now be taken.

PORT-A-CHULLIN, G. Port a' Chuilinn, " Holly Port."

PLOCKTON, G. Am Ploc, " The Lump," applied to the humpy promontory which ends in Ruemore (G. Rudhamór, " Big Cape "). Duaird is G. Dubh-àird," " Black Point. Lon-buidhe is " Yellow mead."

STRATHIE, G. Srathaidh, " Straths." A plural locative.

SEAN-CHREAG, "Old Rock."

PORT-EORNA, G. Port an Eórna, " Barley Port."

DRUMBUIE, " Yellow Ridge."

PORTNACLOICHE, " Port of the Stone."

PALASCAIG, Loch Palascaig; doubtful.

BADICAUL, G. Bada-call, " Hazel-Clump." There is a Badcall in Rosskeen and another in Eddrachilles.

KYLE OF LOCHALSH. Kyle in G. is Caol, a narrow.

COILLEMORE, " Great Wood."

GLEN UDALAN. In Gaelic, UDALAN signifies a swivel or swingle tree. It is difficult to explain the connection here. It is likely that the river was first named Udalan. There is a Ben Udlaman on the confines of Badenoch.

KIRKTON. The Gaelic is Clachan, "village," " church." The burying-ground is called Cnoc nan Aingeal, " Angels' Knoll."

KINNAMOINE, G. Ceann-na-mòine, "Moss-head."

EILEAN TIORAM, "Dry Island" (a common name), is at the entrance to Loch Long, "Ship Loch," a name found in South Argyll and elsewhere. Camas Longart, "Bay of the Encampment," from LONGPHORT. The River Ling is in Gaelic Abhainn Luinge, "Ship's River," connected with Loch Long.

AULTNASOU, G. Allt-nan-subh, "Berry Stream." It was called Aultnasou in 1721.

NONACH, G. Nònach. Loch na h-onaich, not far off, shows that we have here the article AN with ONACH. We may compare Onich, near Ballachulish, which is derived from Omhanach (locative Omhanaich), "Place of Foam."

POLL-AN-TARIE, G. Poll-an-tairbh, "Bull's Pool," where the legendary battle between the Mathesons and Sutherland men took place.

PATT, on Loch Monar, G. Pait, "Hump." The shootings of Riochan (Riabhachan, "Brindled Place,") and Sàil-riabhach (from a hill so called, "Brindled Heel,") are near here.

The names of the rivers, lochs and hills not already mentioned are easy, save in the case of Loch Monar. The word Monar seems to be merely a more phonetic form of G. MONMHUR, a murmuring noise; purling of a stream or of water would be its meaning in this case. Coire-na-sorna, near Loch Calavie, is interesting as giving a feminine genitive to G. SORN, furnace, gully; but the word was both mas. and fem. in early Irish. We have the correct genitive in Loch Hourn, which stands for Loch

Shuirn, the loch taking its name from SORN. This is proved by the Dean of Lismore's line—

" Leggit derri di wurn
.eddir selli is sowyrrni "

(" An end of merriment between Shiel and Hourn;" that is, in the Clan Ranald country).

PLACE-NAMES

OF

THE HEBRIDES

PLACE-NAMES OF
THE HEBRIDES

PART I.

THE name Hebrides is, like the name Iona, due
to a clerical blunder; and Hector Boece is the
author of it. He misread the Classical Hebudæ
with a middle vowel u, as Hebridæ, with a
medial ri. The oldest form of the name appears
in Mela (1st century A.D.) as Hæmodæ, of which
he says there were seven. Pliny accepts Mela's
Hæmodæ, and adds 30 Hæbudes, while
Ptolemy (2nd century) has only the Aiboudai,
that is, Aebudæ, 5 in number. These he
separately names Aebuda, one and two, Ricina,
Malaeos, and Epidium. An attempt has been
made to identify the two Uists with the two
Aebudæ. Uist appears as Ivist in the old Norse
poetry, and it has been possibly modified to

sound like the Norse *i vist*, a habitation.   In any case, we cannot be certain that either in Aebudæ or in Uist we have anything resembling a Celtic spelling of the original word meant.   Uist, as we now have it, has been handed down on Norse lips.   Of Ptolemy's other three islands, Malæos is clearly Mull; Adamnan mentions it also as Malea and the Norse as Myl.   Adamnan besides mentions Iona, that is, Hii or I, St Columba's Isle, and he further notices Coloso (Colonsay), Egea (Eigg), Ilea (Islay), Longa (Luing or Lunga?), Sainea (Shuna), Scia (Skye), Terra Ethica (Tiree), and the unidentified ones, Airthrago, Elena, Hinba, Oidecha (Texa?), and Ommon.   Many of these were re-named by the Norsemen, and their locality can only be guessed.   Ptolemy doubtless also means Skye by his Sketis, though it is placed eastward of Cape Wrath and his Orcades Isles.

That the names of the western islands before the advent of the Norsemen were Celtic is probable; that Celts inhabited them is equally so.   The names Orcades is distinctly Celtic; the root is *orc*, pig, allied to the Latin *porcus*, and the English *farrow*, for the Celtic languages have lost initial *p* in every native word.   The name Skye, Norse Skidh, Adamnan's Scia and Ptolemy's Sketis, has been properly identified with Gaelic *sgiath* or *sgiadh*, wing.   The name of Malaeos, now Muile, that is, Mull, may come from a root *mal*, which Dr. Whitley Stokes compares with Albanian *mal*, mountain range, border, Lettic *mala*, border; to which we may add Gaelic *mala*, eyebrow. The idea would therefore be "the mountainous island"— "Muile nam mórbheann." Ptolemy's Epidion has not been identified; but the root is clearly the British or Pictish *epo*, horse, and the Epidii of Kintyre must have been so named, as the Echaidhs and Eachanns of Gaelic old and new, from their horsemanship. The name Colosus in Adamnan, now Colonsay, Gaelic coll-asa, may have something to do with *coll*, hazel. The word Hii, or I, or Iona, is extremely puzzling— Dr Whitley Stokes suggests a connection with Latin *pius*, holy, or Celtic *i-ios*. Tiree is in Adamnan Insula or Terra Ethica, "land of corn," *eth* being his form of old Gaelic *ith*, corn.

We are, so far, justified in assuming that the Western Isles were under the sway of the Celts, and that their inhabitants spoke a Celtic language until the advent of the Norsemen. The latter people appear first about the year 794, and terrible was the confusion and havoc that they caused. They completely colonised the Orkneys and Shetland, which the Celtic population never recovered; and almost the only remembrance of them there is the name of the Orkneys. Nowadays, the old idea that the

Teutonic invaders of the Celts annihilated the previous population has been abandoned, both for Saxon and for Norse conquests. But if it was anything like the truth anywhere, we may claim it as such for the Long Island. The Gaelic names were clean swept out of the island; the present Gaelic names are post-Norse imports. But the further we go south among the isles, the less sweeping does the clearance seem to have been. Lews was evidently re-named by the Norsemen, but in the southern isles the preponderance of Gaelic names shows that the Gaels were absorbed gradually, not extirpated, as they were in Lews. At present, the proportion of Norse names to Gaelic ones in Lewis is as 4 to 1; in Islay it is as 1 to 2; in Arran as 1 to 8; and in Man it is about the same, or rather 1 to $7\frac{1}{2}$. It is not clear if Gaelic was ever completely exterminated in Arran and the more southerly isles. It is most likely that it was not; inter-communication between Ireland and Scotland would help its continuance. The battle of Clontarf (1014) undoubtedly wrought harm to the Norse and Danish power. The Islands asserted their independence of Norway, but were cruelly subjugated again by Magnus Barelegs in 1098. In 1156 those islands south of Ardnamurchan were ceded to Somerled, a Norse Celt, who started seemingly a Gaelic-Norse kingdom of the Isles. In 1266 the Hebrides were finally ceded to Scotland, after being 470 years under Norse sway. The Gaelic language seems to have rapidly spread itself through the Isles in the time of the Norse decadence, and at the cession of the Isles. At the present time, to parody the expression "Hiberniores Hibernis ipsis," we may say that the Norsemen of Lewis at present are Goideliores Goidelis ipsis—more Gaelic than the Gaels themselves.

We may quote a passage from the lays of Magnus Barefoot's time, recounting his doings in the Isles. It will also serve the purpose of showing the early twelfth century form of the island names :—"Fire played fiercely to the heavens over Liódhús (Lewis); he (Magnus) went over Ivist with flame; the yeomen lost life and goods. He harried Skídh (Skye) and Tyrvist (Tiree) .... the Mylsk (people of Mull) ran for fear. Far over the flats of Sandey he warred. There was a smoke over Il (Islay); the king's men fed the flame. Further south, men in Cantyre—Santíris—bowed beneath the sword-edge. He made the Manxmen—Manverja—to fall."

So much did the Gaelic population of the mainland feel that the Isles were Norse that the proper Gaelic name of the Hebrides has been Innse Gall, "The Islands of the Galls or Strangers." The word Gall now means a Low-lander or English-speaking person; originally

the word was used by the Gael, as by the
Romans, to designate the Gauls of France and
Britain, who came as strangers in contact with
the Gael of Ireland in the earlier centuries of our
era.   Similarly the name Welsh comes originally
from that of the Volcae, a people on the northern
border of Gaul, and marching with the Teutons,
who named all Celts after them.

Dean Munro in his survey of the Isles in
1549 mentions and describes 209 of them.   Of
these names many are repeated—there are about
eight Fladdas, and many more are easily understood on the score of derivation; so that at this
part of our subject we need only refer to the
more important islands.   The first name that
claims attention is that of Lewis.   This in Norse
times was Ljódh-hús, the contemporary Gaelic
of which was Leódhús.   The Norse word may
mean "loud house" and "lay house," the
latter meaning either song or people; but these
meanings are unsatisfactory, and resort has been
had to Gaelic, old and new.   Martin (1703)
derives the name from a Gaelic word *leog*,
"water lying on the surface of the ground," a
word for which he is the first and sole authority.
The fact is that we do not know the pronunciation of Martin's word.   The modern Gaelic
name is spelt Leódhas, and pronounced in Gaelic
phonetics as Leó's.   In the present state of our

knowledge, it is impossible to say what the name may mean.

The Harris portion of the Long Island is in Gaelic called Na h-Earradh. In old documents of three centuries ago the name appears variously as Har(r)ay, Her(r)e, Herrie, and, with a plural form, Harreis (1588). Captain Thomas adduces other places so called, such as Harris in Rum, Herries in Dumfries, Harray (Orkney), and Harrastadhir in Iceland; and he further derives the root word from Norse hár, high, with a plural havir, and a comparative hærri, higher, allied to a noun haedh, height, whose plural is haedhir, which, he thinks, might develop into har-ri by a shifting of the r. The name Harrastadhir is rather to be referred to Norse harri, master, king, and the Orkney Harray may be of the same origin or descended from the word hérad, district. The meaning which Captain Thomas attached to the name Harris was that of "The Heights." Unsatisfactory as the phonetics are, this is the best derivation as yet offered for Harris. The final s in the English name Harris is, of course, the sign of the plural.

St Kilda is known in Gaelic as Hirt, which is its old name, the term St Kilda being only two centuries old and of doubtful origin. In ancient Gaelic irt signifies "death," and possibly the island received its name from its remote western position, for the Celts connected the West with the abode of the dead.

The Uists we have already discussed; and before passing on we may notice the most important islets in the Sound of Harris and thereabout. Taransay is St Taran's *ey* or island; Scalpay (in Harris and Skye) is "Ship-isle," from Norse Skálpr, a ship, whence also the old Orkney Skálp-eidh or " ship isthmus "; Scarp is the Norse Skarpr, sharp, and is the same as the English scarp, escarpment; Pabbay is a common name, appearing in Iceland and the Orkney and Shetland Isles as Papey or Papa, and it signifies Pope's or Priest's Isle; Shillay, or Shelley signifies " seal-isle "; Ensay is for engis-ey, " meadow-isle "; Tahay is for Há-ey, high-isle, the same as the Hoy of the Orkneys; Coilsay is for " gill's isle," *gill* being a ravine; Boreray is for Borgar-ey, that is, " Burgh-isle " or " fortress-isle," not, as Captain Thomas suggested, Boru-ey, " bore-isle "—thus, Dunvorrerick is the Dun or Fort of Borgar vík, that is, Fort-bay. Personal names appear often in these island names—Bernera is for Björn's-isle (Bear-isle); Grimisay is for Grimm's-isle; Hermetray is for Hermund's isle, as Gometra, further south, is for Godmund's isle; Eriskay is doubtless, as Professor Munch said, Eric's isle, by metathesis of the *s*; and Barra is St Barr's isle. The Flannen Islands (na h-Eileanan

Flannach) are called after St Flannen. Taransay
we have already explained as St Taran's isle.

The name Benbecula is a curious perversion
of the Gaelic Beinn-a'-bh-faoghla," " Hill of
the Ford." Scaravay and Scarba are for skarf-
ey, " cormorant (skarfr) isle "; Haskir is the
Há-sker, high-skerry, and Heisker is probably
for heidh-skar, bright-rock; Vallay is for " field-
isle," from völlr, field; Lingay is for ling or
heath-isle, from Norse lyng, heath; Hellisay is
from hellir, cave, also appearing in Orkney.
The names Vatersay and Sandray easily explain
themselves, from water and sand (vatn and
sandr of Norse); Foula, or Fula, is for " fowl
(Norse fugl) isle." There are four islands called
Wiay, Dean Munro's (1549) Buya or Bywa, now
pronounced as Fuidhaidh, to which we may
compare the Icelandic Véey or " house-isle,"
Vé being very common in Norse place-names.
Names like Fuday, Fiaray, Killegray, and Mingulay, (pronounced *Meall'a*), we pass over as
inexplicable to us, and come to Skye and its
environs.

Raasay and Rona are slumped together in
the Norse name applied to them, viz.,
Rauneyjar, the raun-isles, a word which Professor Munch explains as meaning experiment.
Despite the absence of initial *h*, we should refer
it rather to hraun, lava, rough ground, which is
characteristic of the several Rona Islands that

exist. The Norse Raunen are bare rocks in the
sea. Captain Thomas explained Raasay as " roe
isle," from rá, roe; but this would give a genitive rár, not rás. It is difficult to say what the
root word in Raasay is. Hrauns-ey is possible.
There are some eight Fladda Isles on the West
Coast; these all mean Flat Isle, the Norse
Flat-ey. Another common name is Soa or
Sheep-Isle, from the Norse Saudhr, sheep;
again Haversay is for hafrs-ey, " he-goat isle."
Isay is ice-isle; and Troddday appears to mean
pasture isle, from trödh, pasture, a name which
appears in Trotternish, which Captain Thomas
strangely refers to trylldr, enchanted, or Troll-
ness, though how this result could phonetically
occur one cannot see.

We now come to the parish of Small Isles,
which comprises Canna, Rum, Eigg, and Muck.
The first name—Canna—has been explained
from the Norse Kanna to mean the " can shaped
isle "; it appears as Kannay in 1549.   Rum,
pronounced like the English " room," appears
in the Annals of Ulster under the year 676 with
the genitive Ruimm; and Dr Stokes refers this
" lozenge-shaped island " to a root identical
with Greek rhombus. As the root of this
appears to be *vreng*, wrench, the comparison is
doubtful. Nor is Captain Thomas's derivation
at all happy; first he refers Uist to I-fheirste, or
Isle of Fords or sandbanks (Gaelic fearsad), and

then Rum is taken from I-dhruim, ridge-isle. The
supposed Gaelic *i* for isle is, as Dr Stokes says,
clearly the Norse word *ey* borrowed; as a matter
of fact, it does not exist in Gaelic at all.   Eigg
is Adamnan's Egea, and may be referred to an
oblique form of Gaelic eag, a notch.   Muck is
good Gaelic; it is "pigs' isle"; Eilean nam muc.
There is also a Horse Isle near.

Further south we meet with Coll, Tiree, and
Mull, names already discussed.   The name
Gunna recalls the Norse gunnr, war, so common
in proper names among the Norse.   Lismore is
Gaelic—the great lios or enclosure.   The islands
variously called Luing and Lunga or Lungay,
seem all to be of Gaelic origin, and to contain
the Gaelic word for ship (long) as base.   Lunga
and Lungay have certainly submitted to Norse
influence.   The two isles called Shiuna, and the
isle of Shona, seem to be formed from Norse
sjón, sight, a root which appears in Norse place-
names in connection with "scouting" positions.
Kerrera is in the Sagas called Kjarbarey, and
possibly means "copse isle."   The Calf of Mull
is in Norse Mylarkalfr, Mull's Calf, and in Gaelic
it is Calbh.   These Calf islands are common.

Passing island names like Treshinish, Erraid,
and Seil, we meet with Ulva, that is úlf-ey, or
wolf's isle, Ulf, or Ulfr, being really a person's
name here; Staffa is staff-ey, from stafr, a staff,
referring to its basaltic pillars, as Professor

Munch pointed out; Jura is, as the same authority says, for Dyrey, that is, Deer's Isle, whence also Duirinish and Durness, Deer's Ness. Colonsay (Norse Koln) is in Adamnan, as we already saw. There are some half-dozen isles called Oronsay, Gaelic Or'asa, without *n*, and Captain Thomas happily explained the name as Orfris-ey, from the Norse örfiri, ebbing. As Vigfusson says, Norse "Orfiris-ey is the proper name for islands which at low-water are joined to the mainland." And this is true of the Scottish isles so called. Gigha, of which there are two at least, is pronounced Gidhaidh, and appears in the Sagas as Gudhey or Gudey, that is, God-isle, or good-isle. Arran is in the Norse called Hersey or Herey, doubtless an attempt at the Gaelic name Arann. This is an oblique use of Gaelic *ára*, a kidney, as Dr Cameron pointed out. The Arann isles off Galway are similarly named and explained. The island is kidney-shaped. Bute is in Norse Saga and modern Gaelic called Bót, but what the name means it is not easy to say. The Cumbraes were called by the Norse Kumreyjar, the isles of Kumr, which name is usually explained as referring to the Kymry or Welsh of Strathclyde.

PART II.

THE ubiquity of the Norsemen in the Western
Isles is indicated further by the fact that even
lonely St Kilda fell under their sway, and its
leading features show Norse names. The names
of the adjacent islets are Norse; Boreray and
Soa are the isles of the Borg (burgh), and the
Saudhr (sheep). A hill on the east of St Kilda
itself is variously given as Oiseval or Ostrivail,
which stands for Oserveaul—that is, Norse
Austr-fell, or "East-hill." The Norse *fell*,
hill, as a rule, appears in Gaelic as bhal or val.
Other Norse words undergo wonderful changes
in passing into Gaelic, so much so that at times
their own mother (language) would have difficulty in recognising them. Norse *setr*, a seat,
holding, appears in Gaelic as siadair or seadair,
and in the place-names as shader. Bólstadhr
and Bústadhr come to be bos, bost, or bus; and
fjördhr, genitive fjardhar, a firth, becomes
terminally *art*, *ard*, *ord*, *ort;* and it may even
disport itself as *port*. Snizort is Sneisfjördhr,
spit-frith; Cnóideart is for Cnut's or Canute's
Frith, etc. Violent initial changes also take
place in borrowing these Norse words. Many
Norse names begin with *h*, and it is a peculiarity
of Gaelic that *h*, as Macalpin humorously remarked in regard to the singularity of Highland

character and institutions, though not recog
nised as a letter in Gaelic, " is used not only in
every word, but almost in every syllable
expressed or understood." It is a parasitic
letter, and leans upon some other consonant.
Hence Norse words beginning with *h* may be
supported by a *t*. Norse holmr appears as tolm,
genitive tuilm, an island or inch. According to
Captain Thomas, this word appears terminally
as *am, um,* while in the Northern Hebrides it
becomes by metathesis " mol," as in Kisa-mol,
for Kastel-mol. Compare Cobhsamul or Cos-
mul, Linmul, etc. Habost, that is, há-bólstadhr
or high-town, appears as Tabost; Loch Thamna-
bhaidh stands for t-hamna-vagr, that is, haven-
voe, haven-bay; Loch Thealasbhaidh is for
Hellis-vagr, cave-voe, etc.

In considering the place-names of the
Western Isles, we intend to utilise more or less
in full the work of the late Captain Thomas,
R.N., who wrote one or two papers on this subject for the Society of Antiquaries, in whose
Transactions they lie buried unknown to the
general public. The first paper on the " Extir-
pation of the Celts in the Hebrides " appeared
in 1876, and the other on " Islay Place Names "
in 1882, wherein Captain Thomas was helped
by the well-known Gaelic scholar, Mr Hector
Maclean, Islay. We shall take in alphabetical

order the leading Norse words that enter into the composition of these Island place-names.

A, that is, *á*, a river.   This word, which forms the stem of so many place-names in Iceland, is rare in Lewis and the Isles.   Laxá in Iceland, and Laxa of Shetland, are synonymous with Laxay of Lochs in Lewis.   It stands for lax-á, that is, salmon-river, lax being the Norse for salmon.   Other salmon rivers will be mentioned when we come to dalr, a dale.   Few of the small rivers in Lewis have distinctive names, but the Creed seems to be an exception, and tells of odoriferous plants and flowers; for krydd means spice, and krydd-jurt signifies spice-herbs.

Ass, that is, *áss*, a rocky ridge.   A strange corruption has befallen this word in Shetland, where Vind-áss has become Wind-house.   So Burn-house gives us the well-known name of Burns.   There are two places called Valtos in Lewis, and a third in Skye, and there is no óss, that is, oyce or river-mouth, there.   Further, we have Garry Valtos in South Uist.   In the Orkneys, Waldbrek, Waldgarth, and South Wald seem to be cognate words.   Assuming this, we may put Vold-áss, that is, field-ridge, down as the original form where Völd is an olden form of Völlr, a field.   For the phonetics we may appeal to Norse threskjoldr, a thrashing floor,

6

where we have vollr as oldr; and further, that
the Lawman in Shetland in 1307 dates from
Tingvold, that is, thing-völlr, the field of
assembly, which appears in Dingwall also.
Perhaps Valdarás in Iceland may be exactly our
Valtos.

Bekkr, a rivulet, brook.   This rare word in
Norse topography appears to occur only in Diebek in Harris, the Gaelic of which is Ceann-
Dhibig.   Dubec in Skye is no doubt the same
name.   As Captain Thomas remarks, we do not
know the meaning of the prefix, except that it is
not *Dubh*, Gaelic *black*.

Bakki, bank.   It was hardly to have been
expected that this word should have been retained
so near its original form as in *Back*, Stornoway;
Hábac — Highbank (Gaelic form Tabàc), in
Bernera of Lewis; Bakka in Taransay (Taransay-
banks), Harris; and Bachd in Barra.   Bacca-
skill occurs in the Orkneys; Backa and Bacca in
Shetland; while Bakki is the name of thirty
farms in Iceland.

Ból-stadhr, a homestead.   This word is
widely diffused over the northern and western
islands.   In "Landnámabók" it only occurs
twice, and it forms no compound except with
Breidh—broad, which is repeated eight times
(Breidhabólstadhr).   In the Shetland directory
there are (2) *Busta*, (4) *Bousta*, but in combina-

tion it is written (27) -*bister*, and but once
-*buster* only. In the Scottish dialect *i* has frequently the sound of *u*. The Orkney rental of
1595 contains (44) -bustar and (3) -buster; only
a few of which are named after men. In the
Lewis rental Bólstadhr occurs as Bosta in
Bernera, Uig; and when used as a generic term
it is shortened to -bost. Many of these names
are easily interpreted; thus, Melbost—there are
two of them—is for Mel-bólstadr, Links-Farm;
Leurbost, Leir-bolstadr, mud or clay farm;
Crossbost, Kross-bolstadr, Cross-Farm; Calbost
is shortened in the same way as in the Orkneys
and Shetland (Caldale, Calback) from Caldbost,
Kald - bólstadhr, Cold - Farm. Garbost, as
written by Martin, would be pronounced Garrabost by the Gael, and was originally Geira-
bólstadhr, Geirr's-Farm; Geirr is a proper
name. The Orkneys give Garraquoy; Shetland,
Garragarth or Gerragarth; and Iceland, Geira-
bólstadhr. It is but right to say that Geira may
mean a " gore " or slice of land.

At Shawbost, on the west of Lewis—variously written Sheabost, Shabost—is a lake, into
which the sea sometimes flows; this is the *Sjár*.
Loch Seaforth gets its name from the pent up
salt lake, *Saer*, which forms its head; hence
Sæfjördh, Sæfirth, Seaforth; and the oyce at
Kirkwall is called the " Little Sea "; Shawbost,
then, is Sjá-bólstadhr, that is, sea-lake-farm.

There are two Habosts in Lewis; neither of
them are upon high ground; the adjective, therefore, is the same as in so many places called
Holland, Hallandi, Hall-lendi, in the Orkneys,
and the still more common Houlland in Shetland. *Habost* has been *Hall-bolstadr;* from
Hallr, a slope, declivity. So Captain Thomas
thought.

Swanibost is the same as Swanbustar, in the
Orkneys; and is cognate with Swynasetter in
Shetland, and Sveinseyri, and Sveinavatn in
Iceland. Swanibost stands for Sveina-bólstadr,
Svein's-Farm; from Sveinn, a proper name.
Shelibost (the Gaelic form of which is Seilabost),
in Harris, is identical with *Skelbustar* in the
Orkneys, and cognate with Skeljavik in Iceland;
and in its Icelandic form is Skeljar-bólstadhr,
Shelly-Farm; from skel, a shell. Besides Nisa-
bost, in Harris, there is another in Skye, and
Nesbustar, in the Orkneys; all of which represent Nes-bólstadhr, Ness-Farm, from Nes, ness.
Horgibost, Harris, must be written in Gaelic
Torgabost; the Norse hörgr signifies a heathen
place of worship. Captain Thomas thought
that in the Orkneys it appears as Howbister; and
cognate names in Shetland are Houby, Huxter,
Hogsetter. "In this case," he adds, "as in
several others, the name has suffered less
change among the Gael than in the northern
islands. On this farm is a fine Cromlech, figured

in the Crania Britannica, hence its name, Hauga-
bolstadr, How-Farm; from Haugr, How, cairn,
sepulchral mound." As a matter of fact, hörgr
and haugr are different words of like meaning.

Borg—1, a small dome-shaped hill; 2, a wall,
fortification, castle. In Iceland ten different
places are called Borg, but " it may be ques-
tioned whether those names are derived simply
from the hill on which they stand (berg, bjarg),
or whether such hills took their name from old
fortifications built upon them; the latter is more
likely, but no information is on record, and at
present ' Borg ' only conveys the notion of a
hill." In Shetland Borg is still represented by
" Burgh " in two places, but the influence of
Scottish speech has changed it to " Brough " in
eleven others; in the Orkneys also " Brough "
prevails. In the Hebrides, when written in
English, it is "Borve"; in Harris (twice); in
Barra, and in Skye. Borve, in Barvas, Lewis,
appears as Borg, Bora (error for Borva),
Barove; and the Gaelic form is Borgh (in pronunciation the *r* is duplicated, Bor-rgh); hence
arises the English form Borve. The name is,
archæologically, of great importance, for in
Shetland, the Orkneys, and the Hebrides it
almost always indicates the location of a pre-
Norse Pictish tower; but there are a few exceptions, at anyrate in the Orkneys, viz., Burrow

Head, Stronza; Burwick, Sandwick; and the Brough of Birsa.

So completely is the original meaning of the word forgotten in the Hebrides, that it is usual to put Dun (that is, castle) before it; thus, Dun Borgh (grammatically Dun Bhuirgh) means Castle-castle. Captain Thomas thinks Professor Munch wrong in saying "that it (Shetland) has had no fixed settlers upon it before the arrival of the Norsemen."—(P. 90, Mem. Soc. Nor. Antqs., 1850-1860). He has here for a moment forgotten the Borgir or Pictish towers, which have never been claimed as Scandinavian, and are consequently pre-Norse. Says Captain Thomas :—" But my more immediate business is with a long paragraph on pp. 103-104 of the same volume, to this effect—Burra, in Shetland, following the analogy of the Orkneys, should be Borgarey, but it is almost certain that in ancient times it was called Barrey; this theory depending on the statement that a part of King Hacon's fleet, coming from Norway, passed south of Shetland, sailed ' vest fyrir Barreyjarfjordr,' and saw no land till they made Sule Skerry, west of the Orkneys. Barreyjarfjordr was, therefore, the Bay of Scalloway, and the present Burra was Barrey. To all this it is answered, that a ship leaving Norway and seeing no land until she arrived at Sule Skerry must have passed between Shetland and Fair Isle, which part of the sea

may very well have been called Frithareyjar-
fjördr or Fridhareyjarfjördr, *i.e.*, Fair Island
firth, and that Barreyjarfjördr is certainly a mis-
copy of either of these names, so that the ship
would not enter or be near the Bay of Scalloway.
Besides, I myself have been on the site of the
Picts' Castle, of which the stones were carried
away to build the pier of Scalloway. Burra in
Shetland, like Burra in the Orkneys, is Borgarey,
Castle-isle.

"It follows that Alfdis, Konálsdottir, of
Barrey (Barreysku), did not come from Shetland, and we are at liberty to suppose that she
was a native of Barra, Hebrides. We are told
in Gretti's Saga (Danish translation) that the
father of Alfdis, the Barra girl, was Konáll; her
grandfather, Steinmoor; her great-grandfather,
Olver Barnakarl (*i.e.*, Olver the child's-man);
he obtained this honourable title because he
objected to join in the Viking sport of throwing
the children of their victims up into the air and
catching them on the points of their spears.

"There is no further mention of Konáll; it
may be hoped he met an early death; Alfdis
would then come into the family of Ofeigr
Gretter, her uncle, who had fled, with all his
family and servants, from Harold Fairhair to
the Barra Isles. It may be gathered that these
islands formed the stronghold of a clan of
Vikings; and a cousin of Alfdis, Aldis by name,

was there married to a wooden-legged Viking.
Ultimately, we are told, they all went to Iceland;
but the topographical names prove that either
some remained behind or that other Vikings
supplied their places—probably both.   Alfdis,
the Barra girl, was married in Iceland to a
grandson of Olaf the White, King of Dublin."

Bragor, in Barvas of Lewis.   This word does
not occur in Cleasby's "Dictionary," perhaps
from the misfortune of neither author nor editor
being nautical men.   Braga is applied to reefs
on which the sea breaks with extra violence, and
Bragor is named from the shoal water lying sea-
ward of it.   Mackenzie's chart has "Bragd"
for a reef off Skegersta, Lewis; and if this is not
—but probably it is—a clerical error for Braga,
it would show how well the old Norse forms have
been retained in Lewis, for the word is probably
Bragd-arr, and formed from "Bragd," the
"fundamental notion of which is that of a
sudden motion."   In the Orkneys are two reefs
called Braga, and Break-ness is Bragir-ness.
(Captain Thomas).

Brú, a bridge.   This word is represented by
Brú in Iceland; Brow, Brugarth, in Shetland;
and Brogar in the Orkneys.   Brue, in Lewis, is
at the outlet of Loch Barvas.

Bœr, bœr, byr—(1) a town, village; (2) a
farm, landed estate.   The only certain "by"
in Lewis island is Eoropie, which has caused the

ridiculous appearance of "Europa Point" on some maps, and explained as meaning the extremity of Europe. Eoropie is simply Eyrar-baer, *i.e.*, Beach-village; from Eyrr, a beach. In Shetland they would say, "The boat is at the ayre"; that is, on the beach as distinguished from rocks. There are at least four islands in the Outer Hebrides and two in Skye bearing the name Oransay, Ornsay. "In every case that I know of they are connected at low water by a reef to another island." (Captain Thomas). The real name is Orfiris-ey, or Ebb-isle, from orfiri, ebbing, not from eyrr, beach.

Dalr, a dale. *Dœl*, a little dale. There are over 130 names compounded with dalr in the Landnámabók, and the "dales" are proportionally numerous in the Orkneys and Shetlands. They are scarcely so frequent as farm names in Lewis. Swordale occurs twice in Lewis, and the map of Skye has three dales of that name. The Ny Jardharbók has Swardbœli. Swordale is for Swardhardalr—Sward-dale; from Norse Svördhr, sward, green-turf. Swordale in Lochs contains a coppice of willows and birches which are the last living trees of the native forest, of which the name is commemorated in the adjacent "Birken Isles." Laxdale indicates the presence of a salmon river. There are no salmon caught in the Orkneys, nor is Lax contained in their name system. Neither are there

salmon in Shetland, yet there are Laxfirths and
Laxa, so that either the salmon have deserted
the country or the Northmen have given the
name of Lax to the fine sea trout.   Laxdale, in
Lewis, and Lacasdle, in Harris, are synonymous
with Laxár-dalr in Iceland.   Salmon-river-dale;
from Lax, a salmon.   Eoradale is written for
Eyrar-dalr—Beach-dale; from Eyrr, a beach.
Rodel, spelled Rodle and Roudil in the same
rental, is cognate with Roeness, Shetland, and
Raudhanes,   Iceland,   and   must   have   been
Raudhi-dalr — Red-dale; from Raudhr, red.
Ranigdale, a wretched place on the shore of
Loch Seaforth, is probably Rannveigar-dalr;
from Rannveig, a proper name.   On the west
side of Lewis there are Dale-Beg—Little Dale,
and Dalemore—Great Dale; and also North and
South Dale.   All these are sharp, little valleys,
and their original has been Dæl—a little dale.
But it has to be remarked that when *dale* pre-
cedes, the combination is of Gaelic origin,
though the word *dail* is borrowed.

Eidh, an isthmus, neck of land.   In 1576
Eidh in Shetland had become Ayth, now Aïth,
but a much greater change took place with
Eidhs-vik, which in 1576 was Aythiswick, but
now Ea-swick and E-swick.   Eidh, in the Orkneys, is often very corrupt.   It remains almost
intact in Aith, Aithstown; less conspicuous in

Ai-sdale; but Haugs-eid has become Hoxa; Eidh-ey, Eday; and Skalp-eidh, Scapa.

Eidh has many strange forms in the Hebrides: Ie, Ey, Y, Ay, Eie, Huy, Ui, Vye, Uiy, Uie, Eye; written in Gaelic it. is Uidh (pron. Oo-ee). Uiy, Eiy, in Taransay, is simply Eidh — isthmus. Branahuie, Stornoway, is better written in the Gaelic form, Braigh na h-Uidhe; where Uidhe represents Eidh, Aith-'isthmus. Bràighe is the Gaelic for upper part, upper end; and Bràigh na h-Uidhe means the farm at ' the upper (nearer) end of the isthmus '; Uie-head occurs again at Vattersay, Barra. The -peninsula of Eye is near Stornoway.

Endi, the end. Mossend, Stornoway, as it stands, is modern English, but it is likely to have been derived from Mos-endi—Mossend; from Mosi, moorland, moss. Tobson; any Scandinavian name beginning with *H* may, when used as a Gaelic word, have an initial *T*, and the *H* deleted to put it in the nominative case; thus Tobson is a Gaelic from of Hóps-endi—the end of the hope or tidal lake.

Ey, an island. Ey, in some form (a, ay, in Gaelic aidh), is the termination of the name of nearly every island in the Hebrides that is smaller than a land, or larger than a holm. Captain Thomas notices only those that are named in the rentals. He says—" There are three islands, in the Outer Hebrides, called

Bernera, for Bjarnar-ey; Björn's-isle, from Björn, a proper name. It is to be noticed, the names of these islands are pronounced by the people, not as they are written in English, but in their Norse forms (*e.g.*) Be-ornar-ay (*vide* 'Princess of Thule'). Besides Scalpa, in Harris, there is another in Skye, and both have snug little harbours; there is also Scalpa, Skálp-eidh, in the Orkneys. Scalpa is for Skalpey, Ship's-isle, from Skálpr, a kind of boat or ship— shallop. There are two Shellays, one belonging to Harris, the other to North Uist. Shellay is the Gaelic pronunciation of Sellay, and this is for Sel-ey, Seal's-isle, from Sel—seal. Ensay is a remarkably fertile island, and well deserves the name of Engis-ey, Meadow (Grassy)-isle; from Engi, a meadow. Scarp is again repeated in Barra as Scarpamutt. Scarp, more properly Scarpay, is for Skarp-ey, Scarped or Cliffy-isle; from Scarpr, scarped. Hermitray is indeter-minate. [It is Hermundarey, or Hermund's-isle.] Taransay, St Taran's island. The ruins of his church are still traceable, and a stone cross from it is in the Museum. A curious legend is related by Martin (West. Isles, p. 48); but I suspect he has inverted the names, and written 'Tarran' for 'Che' (in later copies, 'Keith'), and the contrary. There is a St Tarannan, Abbot of Bangor, commemorated on the 12th June. There are four islands having

the name of Pab-ay, in the Outer Hebrides;
another in Skye; two (Papa) in the Orkneys;
three (Papa) in Shetland; and one (Papey) in
Iceland.   The name is very interesting, for it
indicates that Culdees, Céli-dé, Servi-Dei, were
located there before the devastation by the
Northmen.   Pabay, Pabbay, for Pap-ey,
Priest's-isle; from papi—priest.''

Fjördhr, a firth, bay.   This word fjördhr
takes many forms in the Hebrides—-such as
"port, fort, forth, furt"; and by aspiration
becomes in Gaelic orthography fhurt; hence
written phonetically "ort, ord, irt, urd," etc.
In the Orkneys and Shetland it is "firth."

"*Resort* on the west, and *Erisort* on the east
side, divide the mountains from the lower
(though anything but level) part of Lewis.   I
believe them to be the same word.   On looking
into the history of the word, it is found written
' Eriford, Erisport, Iffurt (error for Isfurt),
Herrish—Arisford ' with the Gaelic Loch prefixed.   These words plainly represent Herris-
firth."   Such is Captain Thomas's idea   We
have already remarked on the name Snizort and
Knoydart.   Further, there are Gruinard (grein-
fjordhr, the split-firth), Moidart (Módha, a large
river, loam, vapour), Enard, Eport, Skiport
(ship-firth), etc.

PART III.

FOLLOWING the alphabetical order of the chief
Norse words which enter into the topography of
the Western Isles, we came, at the end of our
last article, to the word fjördhr, or firth; and
its appearance in the names of places, after six
hundred years of Gaelic pronunciation, as ard,
ort, and port, though extremely puzzling to an
outsider, is just what we might expect from the
laws that regulate aspiration and accentuation
in Gaelic. It is the rarer words which precede
these Gaelic terms that puzzle the student of
place names. Thus Gruinard has been variously explained as green-firth, split-firth, and
shallow-firth (Norse, Grunna-fjördhr), and the
latter is doubtless the correct derivation in the
case of the Islay Gruinart, for shallowness does
characterise the firth there.

    We left, in our last number, an important
word out of our alphabetic list, in our eagerness
to discuss its compound form, bólstadhr. This
is the simple ból, which means a building or
farm. Thus the Icelandic Kirkjuból appears as
the Sutherlandshire Kirkiboll and the Tiree
Kirkapool. The island of Tiree, indeed, shows
a plethora of these bols, but in the deceptive
form of poll or pool—there are Crossapoll

(Cross-town), Barrapoll (Barley-town), Hellipoll (Helgi, holy), and Vassipoll. In Islay there is Corsopoll, and in Coll, Crossipoll (both Cross-town), and there is Harrapool in Strath, Skye, a name which must be connected with the Norse Harrastadhir, discussed in connection with Harris. Sutherlandshire presents, among others, Eriboll (Beach-town) and Skibo (Skelbol, Shell-town); and Ullapool shows the same word combined with a personal name (Ulli).

Resuming our alphabetical list of the most general Norse names, and still relying largely on Captain Thomas, the first we take up is *Fell*, *fjall*, the Norse for hill. It appears in Gaelic terminally, as bhal, val, and even in the good Gaelic form of Mheall, which has the same meaning. Compare Coinn-mheall in Sutherlandshire. It is the commonest name for a hill in the Outer Hebrides, and, as its force is now lost, the prefixing of the Gaelic Beinn (hill) duplicates the sense. "It seems at first unaccountable that the lakes and hills in the uninhabited parts of these islands should have retained their Scandinavian names to this day. But, in fact, the whole country was divided for a pasture among the town-lands of the coast, and about midsummer nearly all the people removed with their herds to the moors, so that the most desolate spots were yearly inhabited and depastured; and it is from this cause that so many

of the place-names have been remembered.
Copeval in Harris is for Kúpu-fell, Bowl
(shaped)-fell; from Kupádhr, bowl-shaped con-
vex "—(Captain Thomas).   Goatfell in Arran
is unmistakable.

  Gardhr, an enclosure, garth.   In the " Com-
playntes " of Shetland, 1576, gardhr becomes
garth or gar, seldom goird, gord, gorde.   In
the " Old Rental " of the Orkneys (1503),
gardhr is represented by garth, which in 1593
has generally become gair, and is now commonly
ger or gar.   In the Hebrides, Gardhr is compli-
cated by the Gaelic gàrradh (garden), a word
borrowed from the English, and also by the
native Gaelic word garadh, copse, den, which
appears in the names of one or two glens (Glen-
Garry).   As in the case of *dail*, when Garry is
prefixed the name is Gaelic.   Names of farms
which appear to be Scandinavian are—Croi-
garry, for Kraer-gardhr, that is, Kros'-garth;
from Kró, a pen; here the place which at first
was only a sheep-fold has become settled; Asmi-
garry, for Asmundar-gardhr, that is, Osmund's
garth or farm; there is another Oshmigarry in
Skye.   The mutations to which the proper name
is subject is shown by the Orcadian " Asmundar-
vágr," which passes in 1503 to " Osmundwall,"
and at last appears as " Osnawall."   Tims-
garry may be Tuma-gardhr; where Tumi is
Thomas.   Rusigarry, Rushigarry, in Bernera,

Harris, has been Hrís-gardhr, Bush-girth; from Hrís, a shrub, brushwood. Trumsgarry, in North Uist, may be for Thrums-gardhr, that is, Thrum's, or Slow man's garth.

Gil, a narrow glen with a stream in it, appears terminally very often. In Skye we have rivers and streams named Varra-gill, Vikis-gill (Wick-gill), Oisgil (Oyce-gill), and possibly the place names Galtrigil (Hog's-gill) and Crisi-gill (Cross-gill) may belong to the same word. The word Udrigill, which appears so often in connection with points and capes, could easily be explained phonetically as Ytri-gil or Further-gill, if the physical features of the places always suited. In Arran, we have Scaftigill (Shaft-gill) and Catacol (Cat or Ship's gill); and in Islay, as a farm name, Giol. Tralagill in Assynt is doubtless Troll's gill.

Gisl, a hostage, bailiff, and a person's name. The name is not found in the Orkneys, nor in Shetland, but it is not uncommon in Iceland (Gislakot, Gislabeer, etc.). Gisla, in Uig, Lewis, is certainly formed from this word, and may be a proper name. The terminal part may be á, water, or hlé, shelter, or hlídh, slope.

Gnípa, a peak. This word occurs in the Orkneys, in Gal-neap; Neep, in Shetland; Nipa, in Iceland. In this case, the Scandinavian form is better preserved in Lewis than in the northern

7

islands, as it is written and pronounced Kneep, but its Gaelic form, Críp, is rather confounding. There is a Greepe in Skye, not far from Dunvegan.

Gras, grass; pl. grös.   We find Gresmark, Grashól, in Iceland; Grassfield, Girsigarth, in Shetland; Grassholm, Girsa, in the Orkneys; and Grasabhaig, a Gaelic form of Grasa-vík, Grasswick, in Uig, Lewis.   The name of Gress, Stornoway, stands for grös—pastures; and a hint for the reason of the name may be found in Macculloch, who says, " A body of limestone occurs at Gres " (p. 194, Vol. I., Western Isles).

Gröf, a pit.   There are Gröf and grafirgill, in Iceland; Graven, Graveland, Kolgrave, in Shetland; and Grawine, in the Orkneys.   In the Hebrides there is Graffnose, in South Uist; Grafirdale — erroneously spelt Cravodale—in Harris; and Gravir, in Lochs of Lewis; it stands for Grafir, pits, ravines.

Heimr, an abode, a village.   This word is rare in Lewis, but it appears to occur in Borsam, Harris; and the ancient form may have been Börrs-heimr or Bas-heimr.   (Captain Thomas).

Hóll, a hill, hillock.   This term, although not common, appears to occur in Ärnol, Barvas; for Arnar-hóll, Orns-hill, where Orn, gen. Arnar, is a proper name, though the noun örn means an eagle, that is, the English erne.   In Lionel, Barvas, we have Lín-hóll, Flax-hill.

Kjós, a deep, hollow place. There are several places named Kjós in Iceland; and Keotha, in Shetland, may be the same word; but it is surprising to find in Keose, Lochs, Lewis, the name so well preserved. It occurs again on the east side of Loch Seaforth.

Klettr, a rock, cliff. In the Orkneys, a precipitous, detached holm is called a Clett; while, in Lewis, clet is applied to any rough, broken-faced hill. It is one of the most common names for a hill in Lewis. Inaclete is probably cognate with Ingyebuster, Orkneys; Ingasten, Shetland; and Einganes, Engamyrr, Iceland; for Engjaklettr, that is, clet of the meadow. Enaclete is also for Engja-klettr. Hacklete is certainly Hár-klettr, high-clet. Breaclet is paralleled by Braebost, Skye; Breaquoy, Orkneys; Breidharhlídh, etc., Iceland, and stands for Breidhar-klettr—that is, Broad-clet. Diraclet, Harris, is cognate with Jura; with Duirinish, Skye, Deerness, Orkneys. There are no Dyr commemorated in Shetland; for Dyra-klettr is for Deer's-clet; Dyr means an animal, a deer. Breasclet may be Breidhar-ás-klettr—Broad-ridge-clet.

Kollr, a top summit. Kollr, in Iceland, is represented by Coal, in Shetland, and, perhaps, by Colsettr, Orkneys. It is Coll, in Lewis; otherwise Koll, Kolle, for Kollr.

Kross, a cross.   There are ten places with
this name, Kross, in Iceland; and three (Corse,
Cross, Crose), in the Orkneys; and in Shetland
it appears in various forms in combination.
Besides Cross, in Barvas, there is Crossbost in
Lochs, Lewis.   Crossapoll, in various forms,
has already been noticed in regard to Tiree,
Coll, and Islay.

Mùli, a jutting crag.   This as Mull, Moul, is
in common use in the northern islands, and is
not infrequent in Lewis; but it does not enter
into the name of a farm except in Clashmeil,
Harris, which may be Klas-mùli, and cognate
with Klasbardhi, Iceland.   Joyce is wrong (p.
383) in deriving Mull in the Mull of Galloway
and Mull of Kintyre from Mael, Gaelic, a bare
promontory; it is from Norse Mùli, a high, bold
headland, and not implying " bareness."   Other
mulls are the Mull of Deerness and the Mull of
Papa Westray in the Orkneys; Blue Mull in
Unst, Shetland; Mùlin (thrice), Faeroes; Mùli
(seven times repeated), Iceland.

Nes, a ness or nose.   Ness is a very com-
prehensive topographical term, including not
only the high chalk cliffs of Cape Grinez, but
also the low shingle beach of Dungeness.   It is
usually written *nis* in Gaelic, and pronounced
" nish."   Sometimes " Ness " becomes not
only the name of a " ness " proper, but of a
large district.   The Northmen invariably called

the modern county of Caithness by the name of
Nes, and the northern district of Lewis is known
by the same name, Nes.   There are ten farms
called Nes in Iceland, and Ness occurs both in
the Orkneys and in Shetland.   In the Lewis
Rental the entry is " Fivepenny Ness "; Johnston's map gives " Fivepenny " alone; and the
Ordnance map translates the latter into Gaelic,
" Cuig Peghinnean," Five Pennies.   Aignish
is called by the all-observant Martin, " Eggi-
ness "; and he remarks :—" The shore of Eggi-
ness abounds with little smooth stones, prettily
variegated with all sorts of colours.   They are
of a round form, which is probably occasioned
by the tossing of the sea, which in those parts
is very violent "—(p. 10, West. Isles).   In
Captain Thomas's opinion also, Aignish was
probably named from these egg-shaped pebbles,
thus Aignis would stand for Eggia-ness,
from Norse egg, an egg.   But egg also means
an edge, which equally well explains the
name.   Steinish is represented by Stein-nes in
Iceland; Stennis, Orkneys; and Stennis in Shetland.   The decay of the great conglomerate
has, around Stornoway, left great quantities of
smooth, water-worn boulders and pebbles—
hence Steinish for Stein-nes, from steinn, a
stone.

Arinish, better written Arnish, has its
counterpart in Skye (Arnish); as also Arnisort

(where ort=fjördhr), occurring again in Iceland
as Arnarnes, Arnanes; from Orn, a proper name
meaning eagle, the feminine of which is Orna.
Captain Thomas thus refers to words in Rar :—
" Aaernish is repeated again in South Uist as
Rarnish, and again in Skye, where we have also
Raasay.   Although there is no record of the
roe-deer in Lewis, this name tells us that they
were once there.   Raernish, otherwise Rairnish,
is close to the Birken Isles, and ' roe ' are
included in a contract for protecting the game
in 1628 (p. 190, De. Reb. Alb.).   For Ráar-
ness means Roe-deer's-ness; from Rá, a roe."
Since writing the first part of these papers, Rev.
Mr Mactaggart, of Glenelg, has drawn our attention to the fact that Raasay is sometimes heard
pronounced Raarsa, with an r.   This spelling
we knew of as existing in Dean Munro's work
(1549), but thought it an oddity of his own.   The
word may mean " roe-island," though still the
double genitive in rs is difficult to account for.
We might look on rá as both masculine and
feminine.

We find the meaning of Breinish by com-
paring it with the oft-repeated Brabuster, in the
Orkneys, and Brebuster, in Shetland, which are
contractions of Breidharbólstadhr, Broad-farm,
of which there are ten in Iceland.   Breinish,
then, is for Breidhar-ness, Broad-ness.   Carnish, Uig, appears again as Carnish, North Uist,

and as Carness, in the Orkneys. It seems to be cognate with Kjará and Kjörs-eyri, in Iceland; if so, Carnish stands for Kjarr-ness, Bushy-ness; from Kjarr, copsewood, brushwood. Haroldsen has Kiörr, to mean palus; gen. kiarrar, terra saltuosa, aquatica; this describes both the Carnesses; but the word, in this sense, is not in Cleasby's Norse Dictionary. Callernish is an interesting name and place. It may have been Kjalar-ness; from Kjölr, a keel, a keel-shaped ridge. But the fine Celtic megalithic cross-circle and avenue which stands upon the top of it suggests that the Northmen may have given to the point one of the names of Odin, viz., Kjallarr. Kjalar-nes is a place name in Iceland. Quidinish seems to be cognate with Quidamuir, and Quiderens, in Shetland, and is probably an abbreviation of Kviganda-nes, Quey-nes; from Kviganda, a young cow or bullock. Manish is repeated in Skye; and in the aspirated form of Vanish (in Gaelic, Mhanis) it occurs at Stornoway, Benbecula, and South Uist. In Iceland mán, mána, is a common prefix (mána-vik, mán-á), where máni is a proper name. "An intimate acquaintance with Stockinish enables me to give its etymology; it is Stokki-nes, Stakkness,' from a chasm (stokkr), navigable at high water, which separates the island from the main. Stokkr means the narrow bed of river between two rocks; compare stok-land, an isolated rock.

Mollinginish is in fact two words, Mol Linginish;
where Mol is the Gaelic for beach. Linginish is
for Lyngar-nes, Ling-ness, Heather-ness; from
Lyng, heather.   Hushinish, in Harris, occurs as
Ru Ushinish (an iteration of the idea of cape) in
Lewis, and again in South Uist; and cognate
names are Husabost, in Skye; Housby, in the
Orkneys; Housay, in Shetland.   Húsa-nes, in
Iceland, is identical, meaning ' House-ness ';
from Hús, a house.''—(Captain Thomas).
Grishernish in Skye is for Grísarnes, or pig's
ness.

Oss, that is, *óss*, the mouth or outlet of a
river, oyce.   In Barvas the termination is, no
doubt, oss, *i.e.*, Barv-oss.   The prefix may be
an obscure form of Bára, a wave, billow; but
we do not find any other name like it, and therefore do not receive the usual help from analogy.
In Aros we have the combination of á (water)
and óss; the noun áróss means a river mouth or
oyce in Norse.

Papi, a pope, priest.   The Scottic clerici,
Céli-dé, Servi-Dei, must have been bold and
hardy seamen, for some of them sailed in the
month of January, about the end of the eighth
century (A.D. 795?), to Iceland, and stayed there
till August, and when the island was colonised
by the Northmen in A.D. 874, they found missals,
bells, and crosiers at places on the south-east
coast, which from that circumstance they called

Papyli and Papay.   One of these clerical sailors
informed Dicuil that he had sailed (from Shetland most probably) to the Faeroes in thirty-six
hours, in a four-oared boat.   This, as the
distance is about 180 miles, would give the
moderate rate of five miles per hour.   At that
time hermits had lived there for nearly one
hundred years.   There is neither Papyli nor
Papa in the Faeroes, but they must be commemorated in Vestmann-hafn, though the name
as it stands only indicates the former presence of
the Gael or Westman.   In Shetland, before the
devastation by the Northmen, the Céli-dé or
Culdees were established in Papal, Unst; Papal
Yell; and at Papal Burra; as well as on Papa
Stour, Papa Little, and Papa, in the bay of
Scalloway.   In the Orkneys they were located
at Papley, South Ronaldsha; Paplay, Holm; and
Papdale, at Kirkwall; as also at Papa Stronsay
and Papa Westray.   In the Hebrides the Céli-
dé are commemorated at Payble, North Uist;
Papadill (papa-dalr), Rum; Paible, Harris; and
Pyble (Byble, Bible!), Lewis.   All these forms
are ⌒variations of Papyli, which represents
Papabyli, Papbyli, or Priest's-abode, one labial
absorbing the other.   Besides these, the Servi-
Dei must have been established on Pabbay,
Skye; Pabay, Barra; Pabbay, Loch Boisdale,
South Uist; Pabay, Harris; and on great and

little Pabay, Lewis; the original form being Pap-ey, or Priest's-island.

Rif, a reef in the sea. Reef, as the name of a farm, occurs in Lewis, South Uist, and the Orkneys; and as Ríf, in Iceland; in every case from an adjoining " reef."

Setr (1) a seat, residence; (2) mountain-pastures, dairy-lands. This noun, so common in the names of farms in the northern and western islands, is not to be found at all among the seven thousand in the Icelandic Ny Jardhar-bók. In the Orkneys and Shetland the " setters," which originally were only summer " seats," have become fixed residences and cultivated lands. In Lewis, in mid-summer, the home farms are almost deserted, the men being at the herring fishing, and the women and cattle on the moors. There are thirteen " Shadirs " named in the Lewis Rental; when written in Gaelic the word is Seadair, pronounced shader. There are places of this name in Lewis; Bernera, Harris; and in Skye. In the Orkneys we have seater; in Shetland, setter; in Landnámabók, saetr. Some of the differentiated " setters " of Lewis can be readily resolved. Grimshader is identical with Grymsetter in the Orkneys, Greemsetter in Shetland; and cognate to Grim-stadhir, in Iceland. Grimr is a very common Scandinavian proper name, and the learned editor of the " Icelandic Dictionary " would fain

persuade us that it by no means implies an un-
amiable person. Grimshader, for Grim-setr,
means Grimm's-setter, seat or pasture. Ker-
shader is met with as Cursetter, in the Orkneys;
for Kjör-setr, that is, Copse or Brushwood
setter. Besides Quishader, in Lewis, there is
Quinish, Bernera, Harris; Vallaque, North Uist;
and the far-famed Cuidhrang, in Skye—a Gaelic
spelling of quoyrand, Kvi-rand, round-quoy.
"In the Orkneys," says Captain Thomas,
" quoy is a subsidiary enclosure to the principal
farm, and is the only exception I know of to the
rule which governs Scandinavian names, by
being used as a substantive prefix. Sometimes
a quoy is only a few square yards of land,
enclosed by a rough stone wall, to rear and pro-
tect young cabbage plants; this, in Shetland,
would be called a *cro*. In Shetland we have
' Queys, Quiness,' etc., but the name is not
common; in Iceland, Kvi-ból, Kviar-ness.
Quishader, for Kví-setr, fold or pen setter;
from Norse Kví, a fold, pen. Earshader has
cognate representatives in Air, Irland, in the
Orkneys; Erebie, Sandsair, Ireland, in Shetland; and Eyri; Eyarhus, in Iceland. Earshader, for Eyrar-setr, Beach-setter, from Eyrr,
a gravelly bank, beach. Linshader is the
embarking place for crossing to Callernish, and
may very well be Hlein-setr; from Hlein, a rock
projecting like a pier into the sea; but it is more

probably Lón-setr, that is, Creek-setr; from
Lón, an inlet sea loch.'' Shulisheder, which
appears in the Long Island and in Skye, may be
from Súla, a pillar, a root word which appears in
Sulisker islet (Pillar-skerry), and in the Assynt
mountain name of Súlvein, the pillared hill.

Other shaders are Limshader, Sheshader,
Gurshader, Carishader, Geshader, and Ung-
shader, but their interpretation is not easy, for
the prefixes may be variously resolved.

Uigshader, in Skye, means Wick or Bay
Seat; and Ellishader, the Ellister of Shetland,
may stand for Hellis-setr, or Cave-seat.   Ard-
elester and Ellister, in Islay, have similarly
been explained.

PART IV.

GAELIC and Norse differ widely in their methods
of combining compound words so as to make
up a place-name.   Gaelic places the possessive
genitive second, and the generic term (town,
village, hill, field, etc.), first; Norse places the
genitive first.   It is similar with the qualifying
adjectives—Norse, as English, places the adjective before the noun; Gaelic places it after.
This helps us immensely in deciding upon the
Norse or Gaelic character of a place-name.   For
instance, if val or mheall comes after the parti-

cular possessing noun or the qualifying adjective, we deal here with the Norse fell and not with the Gaelic meall. Thus, Griomabhal (grimfell) would, in Gaelic, be Meall-gruamach. Gaelic has borrowed one or two of the Norse generic terms, notably dail (dale) and sgeir (skerry or insulated rock). When dail or sgeir comes first, the combination is of Gaelic origin; when these words come last we deal with a Norse name. Thus we have Dal-more and Skerry-more, the big dale and skerry, as against Swordale (Sward-dale) and Hasker (High Skerry) of the Norse. We must be specially careful, in dealing with dal and sker, to remember their position in the compound.

The above remarks and cautions have been necessitated by the fact that in pursuing our alphabetical list of Norse generic names in our insular topography, we have come to the word Sker, which so many people who deal in etymology fancy to be a native Gaelic word. It is the Norse sker, a skerry or rock. It is a common word in place-names all round Britain, applied to rocks and skerries; but as entering into farm and town-land names it is rare. We have Vatisker in Lewis, which Captain Thomas referred to the adjoining Vádha-sker, or dangerous skerry. The famous Talisker is probably the hall of the rock (Norse höllr, a hall).

Stadhr, a "stead" or abode.   This word appears in the English steading and homestead. In Iceland stadhr or stadhir forms the termination of 61 local names in the old Landnamabok. In local topography in the northern Isles it means the place on which the dwelling stands. In Shetland, by 1576, stadhr had usually been shortened to sta.   This is frequently now changed to ster.

In Earl Sinclair's rental of his share of the Orkneys (1502), which in part seems to have been copied from an older document, stadhr is represented by "stath," "stayth," "staith." By 1595 "staith," "stayth," had been reduced to "sta," but a real corruption was introduced by "stane," and this has now generally become "ston," "ton," "tonn."   We can trace the whole change in Grims-stadhr, which in 1503 appears as Grymestath; in 1595, Grymston and Grymestan, and which is now written Gremiston.

In Lewis stadhr is not an uncommon generic term.   Skegirsta—the Gaelic form of which is Sgiogarstagh—is the same name as Skeggja-stadhr in Iceland and Skeggestad in Norway, and indicates that Skeggi was located there. Mangarsta, occurring as Mog-stat, Mugstot, Monkstadt in Skye, and as Mangaster in two places in Shetland, was Munku-stadr, and tells us that it was formerly the abode of monks. Mealista is Melastadr; from Melr, *i.e.*, sand-hills

overgrown with bent grass, in Scottish "links."
We have Melbost twice in Lewis; Melsettr in the
Orkneys, and Melby in Shetland. In Iceland
there is Melar, and the same name as in Lewis,
Mel-stadr. All these places are sandy, and
in summer luxuriantly green. The monks of
Mangaster may have joined in spiritual joys with
the Cailleacha Dubha, *i.e.*, nuns, the site of
whose house is still to be seen at Mealista.

There are two "Tolsta" in Lewis, which
may have been Tolu-stadhr, that is, Toli's-stead,
of whom seventeen are named under a great
variety of spelling as pilgrims in the Reichenau
Obituary; but it is strange that neither in Iceland, Shetland, nor Orkney, is any name like
Tolsta found. This would suggest that the name
may really begin with *h*, and be Hol-stadhr,
hollow or low stead. Crowlista or Crolesta may
be for Kró-hlídh-stadhr, or Pen-lea-stead, but
we cannot be certain. Borrowston is possibly
Borgar-stadhr, Burg-stead; the ston originated
in the same manner as the Orkney names from
stadhr considered above. There is no tún,
town, in Lewis, and it is rare in Iceland, being
applied to insignificant places, and equally rare
in Orkney and Shetland, where false analogy and
English influences modified the sta.

In Harris we have Scarista, and there is
another Scarista in Uig, Lewis, not named in the
Rental; these are synonymous with Skára-stadr,

in Iceland. Skári (skorey, in Shetland) is a young gull still in its grey plumage; but it is also a nickname, so that Skára-stadr is not the "stead of a skorey," but the "stead of Skari." This word skári is borrowed into Gaelic as sgáireag with a like meaning (see Mr M'Rury's interesting remarks on this bird in the 3rd volume of the *Highland Monthly*, page 353).

Erista in Uig adjoins some quicksand which has been fatal to horse and driver, and Captain Thomas suggests the root as yrja in sand-yrja, quick-sand, adducing the Icelandic place-name, Irjar. But it is likely the same root word as in Erisort.

Strönd, a strand, coast. It is represented by Strond in Harris, Strand in Shetland, and Strönd in Iceland. Strandabhat appears twice as a lake-name in Lewis; it means strand water.

Troll, a giant, troll; *trylla*, to enchant; *tryllskr*, bewitched. Ballantrushal, properly Baile an Truiseil, a township in the west of Lewis, which takes its name from Cloch an Truiseil, the Trusel-stone. This is a gigantic monolith or standing stone, which, as Captain Thomas remarks, well deserves the title of Tryllskar-steinn, that is, the stone of enchantment, and which has become Tryskall, Tryshall, by metathesis. Doubtless, in Trysil Fiall in Norway the same form is seen. The legend connected with the stone is best related in another place. The sagacity of the topographer is sometimes severely taxed—"L Vnsal Sago" is not to be directly recognised "Trusal Stone," nor does "B Trade" immediately suggest "Baile an Truiseil." That is how maps are made.

Toft, a knoll, or toft or tuft. This is borrowed into Gaelic as a common noun in the form of tobhta, or tota, and it generally means turf. It appears in Lewis as Totta, Totaichean Aulaidh (Olave's Tofts), and in Skye in Totscore.

Tunga, a tongue, tongue of land. This is a very frequent place-name in Northern and Western Scotland. It is frequent in Iceland, and occurs as Toung in both Orkney and Shetland; it is Tong in Lewis, and Teangue in Skye.

Vágr, a creek or bay. It is a troublesome though most important word in topography, for both its *v* and *g* may disappear in Gaelic. In Iceland the word is clear and easy; it is common as a place suffix. In Shetland vagr retains its right sound as "voe," except only in Scalowa, Scaloway, the final *way* being a concession to folk-etymology working on the English "way." Compare Bible Head (Paible), and Europa Point of Lewis. Scaloway stands for skála-vágr, shieling or hall bay, skáli being a hut or hall. The Orkneys have few bays or voes; but here there is a great confusion between vagr and völlr, a field, for both are made to end in "wall"

8

now; nor is the confusion lessened by the fact
that voe and field are almost always adjacent.
Many farms in Orkney end in -wall.   One of
them, Bigswall, is not near the sea, so that vágr
is out of the case.   Nor can we doubt as to
Green-wall being Green-völlr, that is, Green-
field; or Ting-wall, meaning Thing-völlr.   But
there is a parish Walls in Shetland, and another
Walls in the Orkneys, both of which are historically Vágarland; Osmandwall is Asmundar-vágr;
Widewall is Vidhívágr; and Kirkwall, originally
Kirkjuvágr, continues as late as 1525 as Kirke-
vaag.   It is evident, therefore, that in the
Orkneys *wall* may represent either vágr or völlr.
On this point Captain Thomas says :—''Yet it is
with extreme reluctance that I yield to this con-
clusion; there is no difficulty with wall from
völlr, but how, I ask, could vágr come to be
represented by wall?   From whence came the
ll?   Was it that Scottish immigrants finding the
sound of vá represented it in writing by ' wall,'
the *ll* at first being silent?   But the opinion I am
inclined to adopt is that both forms were current;
as noted above, where ' wall ' represents vágr,
a völlr is also present.   Besides Kirkju-vágr,
there was always in fact Kirkju-völlr (Kirkfield),
Kirkwall; and so of the rest.   And the parish
names Walls appear to me to be used in contra-
distinction to the peculiarly mountainous districts of Sandness in Shetland, and Hoy in the

Orkneys; if so they would have been called vellir, Englished by Walls (Vales).   It is true, however, that both ' walls ' are largely inter-sected by ' voes.'   The solution of the question depends upon whether most weight is given to the induction from observation, or to the historical documents.''

In the Hebrides this unfortunate word vágr is plagued by complications of another kind. The Rentals, indeed, record the names of farms with greater purity than in the northern islands, but they have been written by Northern Saxons; v is turned to w, and vágr becomes '' way ''; no doubt, when first written, '' way '' rhymed with '' far,'' but now, in common English speech— from the influence of the written form—it rhymes with '' day.''   But in the native (Gaelic) speech, no word can have an initial v in the nominative case; also if two nouns are combined to form a word, the suffix, if capable, suffers aspiration.   These rules are sometimes strictly followed and sometimes not.   We will take the examples of Carloway, which undoubtedly was Karla-vágr, that is, Carl's bay.   In Karla-vágr, the final r in Norse merely emphasised the pre-ceeding consonant.   When the Gael took posses-sion of the word Karla-vag, they would do, as the northern islanders have done, viz., drop the g, and next they would consider va' to be a noun in the genitive case, and would therefore soften the á to ai, thus sounding " vai," which in Gaelic orthography would be bhaidh, bhaigh, and of which the nominative would be bagh, badh; this, again, translated into English, would be " bay." In this roundabout manner the vágar of Harris have become the " bays." Karla-vágr, reduced to Karla-vai, would be written Carlabhaidh, and Teutonic influence, changing the v or bh to w, brings us to Carlo-way.

Stornoway : this name is repeated (Loch Stornua) in Kintyre. In Iceland there were formerly Stjörnu-stadhr and Stjörnusteinar, but these names are now obsolete. Stornoway—which is spelt in thirteen different ways—has been referred by Captain Thomas to Stjörnu-vágr, Star's-voe; where Stjarna, Star, is a proper name. " The only person I find," adds Captain Thomas, " recorded bearing that name is Oddi, who was so learned in astronomy that he was called ' Stjörnu-Oddi.' He had a remarkable dream, ' Stjörnu-Odda Draumr,' but it appears to have had nothing to do with the stars (Nordiske Old-skrifter, XXVII.). It may be noted that no place on land in Kintyre bears the name of Stor-noway, which disposes of the foolish Gaelic etymology of Sròn-a-bhàigh, Bay-nose." This derivation of the Captain's is unsatisfactory. The root word clearly is Stjörn, steering, the ö of which is stable, and does not change to a. Stornoway, we take it, means " Steerage-bay."

Stimeravay stands for stemdi-vágr, the stopped-up voe, which describes the place. For Carloway, Blaeu's Atlas has Carleywagh; there is no cognate in the Orkney or Shetland Isles, unless Charleston in Aithsting. In Iceland there is Karlafjördhr, that is, Carl's firth, where Karli either means carle or a man's proper name. Flodeway either stands for Fljóta-vágr (stream or flood voe) or Flota-vágr (Fleet's voe).

Vatn, water, lake. This is by derivation the same word as English water and the Greek hudor, hydrant, etc. It is very common in Hebridean place-names, where it appears as bhat or vat. The lake named Langavat or Long-water appears several times; and there are Breidh-bhat (Broad lake), Skára-bhat (Skári's water, see Scarista), Lacsabhat (Lax or salmon), and numerous others. An interesting perversion of vatn appears in Loch Sandwood, in Eddrachillis parish.

Vík, a creek, bay, wick. This appears terminally in Gaelic as bhaig, aig, or ag. A common name is Sandwick, that is, Sand-bay. It is in Iceland, Shetland, and Orkney, in the Long Island, and as far south as Arran, where we have Sannox, a plural form to denote that there are three sand-bays there. Marweg or Marvig appears as Marwick, in the Orkney and Shetland Isles. It comes from már, a sea-gull. The same name may also appear in Maraig or

Marag, which Captain Thomas erroneously refers to vágr, voe. The prefix he explains as myrar or mire (bog) voe. Meavig or Meavag, in Lewis and in Harris twice, is for Mjó-vík, narrow voe. Kerriwick, otherwise Kirvig, has been referred to Kirkju-vík, that is, Kirk-wick. Colivick goes along with Crowlista, explained under stadhr. There is a Cruely in Shetland. The simple form of Vick appears often; we have the town of Wick in Caithness. There are one or two parishes called in Gaelic Uig (Lewis and Skye), that is, Wick. Captain Thomas strangely refers these to the Norse ögr, an inlet or creek, which is a rare name, not found in Orkney or Shetland, and twice in Iceland.

We have now passed in review the principal Norse words that enter into the place-names of the Hebrides. The universality of these names in the Long Island is most remarkable. In considering the Gaelic names, we shall find that the Norse names beat them in Lewis by four to one; and, further, these Gaelic names are importations since the re-occupation of the Islands by the Gael on the fall of the Norse power.

PLACE-NAMES

OF

INVERNESS AND VICINITY

PLACE-NAMES

OF

INVERNESS AND VICINITY

INVERNESS as a town name goes back to the 12th century, possibly further—to Macbeth's time (1057). The name is partly, at least, of Gaelic origin, which proves that the town could not be so called in the time of the Picts, who would have named it Aber-ness, not Inver-ness. The word *inbhir* (Inver) means in Gaelic a confluence, and is by derivation the same word exactly as the English word "infer." The town derives its name, of course, from being at the confluence of the River Ness. The name Ness appears in Adamnan's life of St Columba as *Nesa*; the Norse called it *Nis*; and the modern Gaelic pronunciation and spelling are the same, viz., *Nis*. The word must be referred to an original form *nesta* according to Celtic philological laws, and this Dr Whitley Stokes has equated with the Sanscrit word *nadi*, signifying river.   We may compare also the old Thracian river name Nestos, and possibly the mother of the great mythic King of Ulster, *Nessa*, he being Conchobar Mac Nessa, bears the same name, for she may have been a river goddess.   Rivers were worshipped as deities, as we know from Gildas, and as such names as Dee and Don (Deva, Divona), meaning " goddess," prove.

The name Clachnacuddin stands for Clach nan Cùdainn, or stone of the tubs, a phrase which is explained as referring to the habit of the women carrying water from the river, and of resting their tubs on the stone that now forms the Palladium of Inverness.   Markinch stands for Marc-innis, the horse isle or " inch."   The name is interesting in two ways; firstly, animal names may come before the word *innis*, although Gaelic otherwise insists on all genitive or possessive forms coming last; secondly, the word *innis*, so common all over the country in place names, is now obsolete in the sense of " island," its only meaning in present Gaelic being a shelter for cattle, such as a clump of wood and the like.

The *Haugh* and *Holme*.—The name Haugh is English, or rather Scotch; the word originally possessed an *l*, now lost; Barbour in his *Bruce* writes *halche*, and the Anglo-Saxon form is *healh.* The Haugh is mentioned in a charter, 1361, as Halc; and the Gaelic people still keep up the old *l* in their version of the name, that is, an Talchan. In borrowing English or Scotch words beginning with *h*, the Gaels always introduced a *t;* so we find the Gaelic of Holme, so named from the English *holm*, an island in a river, to be Tuilm.

Ballifeary.—This appears in 1244 as Balnafare, and it is explained as the Gaelic Baile-nafaire, the town of the watching. Similarly, Clachnaharry means the stone of the watching. The town had to place sentinels at these points to give notice of any hostile visit which the restless clans around might think proper to make to the town.

Drummond.—This name is common all over the country. It is the locative case of the word *druim*, a ridge, which had a stem ending in *men* originally.

Bught.—This is the Scotch word *bought,* *boucht,* signifying a bending, a bay, a pen. The root is the Teutonic *bugan*, to bow, which is possibly allied to the Gaelic word *bog*, whence is borrowed the English word *bog.*

Kinmylies.—This appears in 1232 as Kinmyly, and it has been well explained as standing for ceann mìle, mile-end.

Leachkin.—This is the Gaelic word *leacuinn,* a face, hillside; it is really, like Drummond, an oblique case from a nominative *leac*, signifying cheek or face.

Torvean and *Kilvean.*—These are the *tor* or hill and the *kil* or church of St Bean, a saint of the Celtic Church, usually reckoned first bishop of Mortlach (11th century). The name Bean, in Gaelic Beathan, is a derivation of the word *beatha*, life; and it has the same force as the more famous name Macbeth. The saint usually supposed to be meant here is Baithene, St Columba's successor, but in modern Gaelic his name would be Baothan. Dunain means the hill of birds (dùn-ian).

Tomnahurich.—Much fanciful nonsense has been written about the meaning of this name. The favourite derivation is that which refers it to the idea of " boat hill," for the mound looks like an upturned boat. The Gaelic may be written Tom na h-iubhraich; and the dictionaries give the word *iubhrach* as meaning a boat. This, however, is nonsense; there was only one boat called the Iubhrach, and that was the mythic boat of Fergus MacRo, in which he took over to Ireland the sons of Uisnech and Deirdre. The word *iubhrach* simply means a yew wood, and the root word has given some famous place names. The word appears in Gaulish as Eburos, and hence we have the British Eburacum, which is now York (" Yew-town ").

Dochfour.—The first part of the name—Doch —is easy; it is the contracted form of *dabhach*, a tub, and then a measure of land equal to four plough-gates. The latter part—*four*—is an extremely difficult term to unravel. It appears in many place names, but only in Pictland. We meet with Balfour, Pitfour, Delfour, Tillipowrie, Letterfour, &c. It is a maxim in deriving these names that the chief term lies where the accent is on the word, and *four* always carries the accent. This settles that it is a noun and not an adjective; for some people will have it, despite Gaelic phonetics, that *four* is simply the adjective *fuar*, cold. The preserved *f* shows that the word began with *p*, and this again proves the Pictish character of the word; for *p* is not native to Gaelic. I have elsewhere suggested that this word is allied to the Breton *peur*, Welsh *pawr*, a pasture—a derivation which Dr Whitley Stokes, one of our best Celtic philologists, has accepted most cordially.

Abriachan.—This appears in 1239 as Abirhacyn, and in 1334 as Aberbreachy. The name undoubtedly stands for Aber-briachan, the confluence of the Briachan. For the loss of a syllable between *aber* and *briachan*, consider Arbroath and Aberbrothock. One of the *ber*s simply has gone. The stream running into Loch Ness at Abriachan must have originally been called Briachan; it has now two or three names, mostly descriptive of the water—Allt-dubh, Allt-dearg, Allt-liath.   What Briachan may mean it is hard to say; it is evidently Pictish.   The derivations offered for this place-name (Abriachan) have been very numerous; a full account of them is given in the third volume of the Transactions of the Inverness Field Club just issued (pp. 167-171).

In passing beyond the bounds of Inverness and Inverness Parish, a word may be said about Bona, the alternate name to Inverness—the parish of Inverness and Bona.   In 1233 this is spelt Baneth, and two hundred years later as Bonacht, Bonoch.   It has been explained variously as *Bàn-achadh*, white field, and *Bàn-àth*, white ford.   It seems to me that it is a reminiscence of Ptolemy's Banatia, which some authorities place here, and possibly is due to some pedant of the twelfth century.

Petty.—This parish name, in Gaelic Peitidh, is a plural form of the well-known prefix *pet*, so common in Pictland, and meaning a farm or township.

Dores.—This name must be compared to the parish name of Durris in Kincardine, which is nearer the Gaelic pronunciation in form than Dores is.   The name seems allied to the word *dorus*, a door.

Stratherrick.—This is named after the river Farigag, and the name Farigag probably stands for Far-gág, "above the cleft or rift," made up of the preposition *far* or *for* (above) and *gàg*, a cleft or pass.

Urquhart.—This is one of the oldest names in the district. Adamnan (700 A.D.) mentions the glen as Air-chartdan. The first part, *air*, is the preposition *air*, on. The significant part is *cartdan*, or the later cardan, cardainn. This last part appears in two other combinations, viz., Kin-cardine and Plus-carden. The name is undoubtedly Pictish, and therefore we have to look at Welsh, as the nearest of kin to Pictish, for the explanation of the name. The only likely one is *cerddin*, which means the rowan tree. Kincardine might thus mean the " end of the rowan wood "; Urquhart, "by the rowan wood."

Daviot, Moy, &c.—The name Daviot is not unique; it appears in Aberdeenshire as a parish name. The Gaelic is Deimhidh, pronounced *Devidh;* Devy nearly, and answering the old charter form Deveth very well. It seems the exact modern equivalent of the old Welsh tribe-name Demetae, now Dyved; and here again we meet with an old Pictish name. The root *dem* signifies "fixed," "sure." Moy is in Gaelic A' Mhagh, "the plain"; while Dalarossie is simply Dail-Fhearghuis or "Fergus's dale."

Ardersier, Croy.—The former appears in 1227 as Ardrosser, and in 1570 as Ardorsier;

the Gaelic, influenced by folk-etymology, is Ard-na-saor, the cape of the carpenters. It has been explained as Ard-ros-iar, the west cape. The name Croy signifies hard, being from *cruaidh*, hard.

Beauly.—This is a mediæval French name—*beau lieu*, pretty place—introduced by the Vallis Caulium monks in 1232, who founded the Priory. The Gaelic name is A' Mhanachainn, which may be rendered the "Monkery," from *manach*, monk. Kilmorack is the parish name; this means the church of Morag, that is, St Moroc.

Foyers.—This is the name of the land below the falls by the side of Loch Ness. It stands for Fo-thir, that is, "low ground." O'Reilly says *fothir* signifies "good land," but the former meaning is doubtless the correct one here. Fort-Augustus in Gaelic is Kill-Chuimein, the *Kil* of St Cummin, a saint name which occurs more than once, the first being Cummian the Fair, who, about 650, wrote a biography of St Columba.

The county names of Nairn and Ross may claim our attention for a little. The name Nairn primarily applies to the river Nairn, and this has invariably been connected with the word *fearna*, alder wood, despite the phonetic and other difficulties. The names of large rivers and leading features of the country are the oldest of any; they go back to the times of other races and different languages. Names like Dee, Don, Tay, Ness, Nairn, &c., cannot be etymologised from modern Gaelic. We must rise to a higher level, and consider the Celtic tongues as a whole, even falling back upon European root forms to help us. And beyond all this, the name may have been borrowed from a primitive race that used a language that was neither Celtic nor Indo-European. The name Nairn is Celtic, for the termination *rn* is peculiarly so. The root is therefore *na*, possibly *nav*, which possesses the idea of sailing, swimming, floating, and is found in the English word *naval* and the like. The name is Pictish doubtless. So also is the name Ross; this is allied to the Welsh word *Rhos*, a plain, mead, which is very common in Welsh place names.

Dingwall.—This is the Norse *Thing völlr*, field of the thing or meeting—the meeting or paramount place. The name appears in the Isle of Man and in all places under Norse sway now or heretofore.

Strathpeffer.—The river or streamlet named Peffer or Peffery appears three or four times in Pictland; we have two in Haddingtonshire, an Inverpephry in Perthshire, and this one at Strathpeffer. The Gaelic of Strathpeffer is Inbhir-feo'arain; the Feofharan is the stream name, where the first *f* represents the Pictish

9

original *p*, and the second *f*, now aspirated, either an *f* or more probably a *b*. There is a modern Welsh word *pefr* which might suit phonetically, meaning "fair," "beautiful."

Ben Wyvis.—This, in Gaelic, is *Beinn Uais*, the oblique or locative form of Beann Uas; the word *uas* is now obsolete, but it was common once as a personal appellative—Colle Uas being, for instance, King of Ireland in the 4th century, and ancestor of the Macdonalds. The word means "noble," "majestic," and is but a shortened form of the Gaelic word *uasal*, proud.

PLACE-NAMES

OF

INVERNESS-SHIRE

PLACE-NAMES OF
INVERNESS-SHIRE

THE County of Inverness can boast neither of symmetry nor of compactness. It sprawls westwards across the northern neck of Scotland through Skye, diving under sea to re-appear at the far-west sea-bank of the Outer Hebrides. One thing it can boast of, however, among Scottish counties : it is the largest of them. Its area of 4232 square miles—a square land-piece of 65 miles per side—is unsurpassed by any other county in Scotland. And once the Sheriffdom of Inverness extended still further. In the twelfth century it comprehended all the country north of the Grampians, but the thirteenth century saw the rise of the shires of Elgin, Nairn, and Cromarty. For four hundred years thereafter, however, the Sheriffdom of Inverness included Ross, Sutherland, Caithness, and part of Argyle. The present Sheriffdoms of Argyle, Sutherland, and Caithness were constituted in 1631-3 and Ross in 1661, the latter three being pure dismemberments, so to speak, of Inverness Sheriffdom. The County of Inverness was thus finally formed in 1661 curiously by a process of subtraction, but it has kept its then acquired bounds ever since, with certain small adjustments. The irregularity of its northern borders from Harris to Beauly is due to the Mackenzie influence in 1661; that family wanted the clan estates to be all in Ross-shire. A scientific frontier was, therefore, out of the question.

The history of Inverness county is nearly as sporadic in its character as the county itself. There is a separate story for the Isles, a second one for the west coast mainland (Garmoran), and a third story to tell of the province of Moray portion of the county. It is really a great pity that the old province of Moray itself was not made a county—a pity historically, for it was an ecclesiastical and almost a political unit. It included all Inverness east of the Drumalban watershed east of Lochaber, and comprehended also the shires of Nairn, Elgin, and even a part of Banff. Macbeth's family province of Moray further included Easter Ross, disputed with the Norsemen, and its sway at times (11th century) extended over Banff and Buchan, as we can see from the Book of Deer. In the 12th century the old Earls of Moray were suppressed, and native thanes, with incoming Normans, began to take their place (early 13th century); the coast began to be planted with burghs. The great family of Cumming rose to power in Buchan, and early in the 13th century they acquired Lochaber and Badenoch. The Earldom of Moray was again restored by Bruce and given to Randolph, his nephew, inclusive of Lochaber. The Church also occupied vast and valuable property in Moray, but the after history of the Moray portion of Inverness concerns the rise of the Gordons and their struggles with the Earls of Moray and the native clans, and scarcely bears on the place-names, which by this time were mostly fixed. The West Coast portion of Inverness-shire, north of Morvern, and extending to Glenelg—that is, Moydart, Morar, and Knoydart—was called "Garbh-mhorbhairne," in 1343 Garwmorarne, the "Garmoran" of the historians. It and Lochaber formed part of North Argyle, which once extended to Lochbroom. Garmoran belonged to the descendants of Somerled of the Isles, a side branch (probably junior) to the Clan Donald. The heiress of Garmoran married John of Isla in the 14th century, and the property came to the Clanranald branch of the Macdonalds. The Outer Hebrides belonged to the Norse, and therefore to the King of Man and the

Isles; but after 1263, the date of the overthrow
of the Norsemen, Skye and the Long Island fell
as his share of the booty to the Earl of Ross.
Forfeiting them in the wars of David II. and
Edward Balliol, he recovered only Skye, the
outer isles going to his rival, the Lord of the Isles.
The Island Lord next century succeeded also
to the Earldom of Ross, sometime after Harlaw.
This Prince therefore held (say) about 1450,
through himself or his kin of Clanranald, all the
Outer Hebrides, Skye and its adjacent isles, Garmoran and Lochaber (inclusive of Glengarry).
Glenelg belonged to his vassal, Macleod of Harris.
On the break-up of the Lordship of the Isles
(1475-1493), the local chiefs came to the front
—Macleods of Harris and Glenelg, also of Dunvegan, Macneills of Barra, Camerons of Lochaber, and the numerous but powerful branches
of Macdonald—Clanranald (Garmoran and Uist,
with the Glengarry branch further east, soon to
succeed in Knoydart another set of Macdonalds),
the Clan Hugh of Sleat, whence the present Lord
Macdonald, and the disinherited, because ille-
gitimate, Macdonalds of Keppoch, in Brae
Lochaber, whose lands were given to Mackintosh.
The after history of these clans does not concern
our subject; the place names with which we have
to deal were given by the earlier clans, tribes,
and races which had successively possessed the
land prior to the 15th century.

The earliest Celtic nation that established itself in Scotland was the Pictish. They found before them another race or two, one of which was fair and square-headed, and the other dark and long-headed. The Celts arrived in their iron age, possibly in 600 B.C. The language spoken by the previous inhabitants is unknown; the Picts spoke a dialect of Celtic near akin to the Welsh. Some Inverness County names bear out this fact. The test letter between the Brittonic and Gadelic or Gaelic branches of old Celtic is the letter *p;* old Gaelic had no letter *p,* and modern Gaelic developed native *p* within the last five or six hundred years; the many borrowed *p's* in Gaelic do not here count. Gaelic *cuid* is in Welsh *peth* (for older *pett*), a thing; this is the Pictish *pet* or *pit,* a possession or farm—in short, the Gaelic *baile* in meaning. Here Pictish and Welsh show *p* as against Gaelic *c,* which, so far, proves Welsh and Pictish closer allied than Gaelic and Pictish. The *pits* or *pets* in Inverness-shire are not now so numerous as once they were. We have still Pityoulish (Abernethy), Pitchirn (Rowan-ton) and Pittowrie (Alvie), and Pitmean (Middleton, Kingussie), and Pettyvaich (Byre-ton) in Kiltarlity. Balmaglaster of Glengarry was formerly Pit-maglaster or Pittenglassie. Several are obsolete—Pitkerrald (St Cyril's Croft) in Glen-Urquhart, and Pitchalman and Pitalmit in Glenelg. Then there is

Petty, the Parish name, which simply means the "land of farms" or "pets." *Pet* or *Pit* has given way to its equivalent in meaning, *baile*, for two good reasons—the word first, like *aber*, was getting obscure, as not belonging to the ordinary vocabulary; and second, it got mixed up with another word of nearly like sound but obscene meaning. This especially has driven it out.

Another test word is *aber*, a confluence; the Gaelic is *inbhir* or *inver* (root *ber*: *in-fer*); the Gaelic *abar*, now obsolete, having meant a "marsh" (root of *tobar*). The Pictish *aber* had two dialect forms—*aber* and *ober*; the latter alone has survived in modern names as spoken in Gaelic—Obair-pheallaidh (Aberfeldy), Obair-readhain (Aberdeen), &c. Inverness-shire shows five or six of these *abers*: Abertarf, or Mac Vurich's old Gaelic Obair-thairbh, so named from the Tarf or "Bull" river; Aberarder (Laggan and Daviot), Gaelic, Obair-ardair, seemingly "high-water"; Aberchalder (Glengarry), where Calder appears, a name common in Pictland. It first applied to water, the root is *cal*, sound, and the rest seems pure termination -*ent* and -*ar*, the former a participial suffix, the latter an agent one. The name is undoubtedly Pictish. With it may be compared the Gaulish river names Calarona, Callus, and Calla. The fourth name is Abriachan:

in 1239 this was Abirhacyn, and in 1334
Aberbreachy. Seemingly the streamlet entering
Loch-Ness here must once have been called the
Briachan; the curtailed phonetics reminds us of
Arbroath from Aberbrothock.   Abernethy, a
name repeated in Fifeshire, is in Gaelic Obair-
neithich, in 1239 Abyrnithy; the river is the
Neithich.   This has been equated with the Nith
of Southern Scotland, which Ptolemy records as
the Novios or " Fresh " (*nuadh*) stream, Welsh
newydd.   This would make the Pictish phonetics
exceedingly Welsh and somewhat modern; but
it is the best derivation offered.

Two other words come to Gaelic from the
Pictish, and are included in the ordinary vocabulary.   These are ' dul ' or ' dail,' ' a plain of
fallow land, especially by a river-side,' and
' preas,' ' a bush,' but in place-names, ' a
brake.' The word ' dul ' or ' dail ' is exceedingly common as a prefix; as a suffix it shows the
genitive ' dalach,' both in ordinary speech and
places called Ballindalloch.   The word does not
appear in Irish, ancient or modern; but it is
clearly allied to the similarly used word of similar
meaning, W. ' dôl,' pl. ' dolydd,' Corn. and
Bret. ' dol.'   Many place-names in Wales and
Cornwall bear this prefix.   The Perthshire parish
name Dull, G. Dul, bears it in its naked sim-
plicity, and the form ' dul ' is the usual one along
the Great Glen, especially in Glen-Urquhart and

Glen-Moriston. The modern spelling, however,
is almost always ' Dal-' in these last cases. The
Wardlaw MS. (17th century) always writes
' Dul-', however. The root seems to be ' dul,'
and therefore not allied to Eng. ' dale ' or Norse
' dalr '; but it is likely allied to the root ' dul,'
bloom, as in Gaelic ' duilleag.' The word
' preas' is not common in place-names; in the
county we have it in Preas-mucrach (Badenoch),
' Pig-brake place.' The Welsh word allied is
' prys,' brake, evidently allied to the W. ' perth,'
brake, whence the names Perth, Logie-Pert, Lar-
bert, Partick, &c. The root, which is ' qr,' is
that of G. ' crann,' W. ' pren.'

Pictish influence may be seen in the common
use of names rare or practically non-existent in
Irish : *monadh*, hill, as in Monadh-liath; *blàr*, a
plot, free space of ground—Blairour, ' Dun-
plain' (Lochaber), *Blàr*-na-leine (1545) at
the upper end of Loch Lochy; *allt*, a burn,
Aldourie, from the ''Dourag'' burn, while
Dourag itself is from *dobhar*, water; *beinn*, a
hill, Irish *beann*, not much used in Irish place-
names as compared to Gaelic ' beinn ' or ' ben ';
càrn, a hill, cairn, which Welsh also is fond of
for names of hills, though not used in Ireland
similarly—Cairn-gorm, Gealcharn, and others
very numerous; *coire*, a corry or kettle—
Corry Mhadagain, the '' doggie's corry,'' a
use of ' coire ' '' scarcely known in Ireland ''

(Reeves); *srath*, a strath, also a common
Welsh and rare Irish word.   The word
which shows most departure from Gaelic use is
both, a house, but used in Pictland for *baile*.   It
finds an especial development in Inverness
county, particularly along the valley of the Great
Glen—Bunachton, for Baile-Nechtain or Nectan's *baile;* Bochrubin, from old *crùibin*, a paw, a
back-bent hill; Boleskine, in 1227 Buleske, from
both-fhlescáin, "town of the withes," from
flesc, a rod; Bolin (Glengarry), "flax-town";
and Bohuntm (Lochaber), where *hunndainn*
stands for *conntainn*, a confluence.

    The use of 'ràt,' apparently for 'ràth,' a
'fortified residence' originally, in Strathspey
and Badenoch, has also to be noted.   The Welsh
has the word 'rhath,' a clearing or open space,
which seems to be the same word, and which
Professor Rhys regards as borrowed from Gaelic.
The exact extent of the use of 'rat' in Pictland
has not yet been considered, but on the analogy
of Rothiemurchus, we might claim all the names
in Rothie-, as Rothiemay.   Raith in Fife, which
certainly looks like the form that Pictish 'rat'
would assume, is claimed for Scotch 'wreath,' a
pen, as are the several other names of like form.
The matter is considered further on under
Rothiemurchus.

    The first writer who gives any name bearing
on Inverness-shire is Tacitus, who mentions the

Caledonians, and the geographers represent
them as extending into our county. Despite
some difficulties in the classical form of the name
Caledonia on the score of its phonetics not
according with the root—that given being *cald*,
the root of coille, English *holt*, nevertheless the
name Dun*keld* and its Gaelic Dun-chailleann seem
amply to prove that the classic Caledonia means
really as the poet said, " land of the woods "—
the Caledonians being the " Woodlanders."*
Tacitus also records another famous name,
Graupius, which has been misused in MSS., and
appears most often as Grampius, whence comes
the popular form Grampian. Tacitus meant
some hill or hillock near Blairgowrie, but mediæval imagination could fancy that nothing less
could do justice to this great battle than the Gram
pian hills as a background and place of retreat.
The root of Graupius is ' grup ' or, rather,
' gruq,' and means ' hooked,' much as some
hills are called ' sockach,' snouted. Ptolemy,
the Geographer of 120 A.D., mentions the
Vacomagi as the tribe inhabiting the " laigh "

* Dr Stokes separates the old Gaelic Caillen or Calden from
the Classical Caledonius, with its long·*e* between *l* and *d;*
and the Welsh forms old and new (Celidon, Celyddon) are
certainly derived from the classical form, while the English
form Dun-keld shows the Welsh phonetics. The question is
whether the classical form represents the real original; if so
the roots of Caillen and of Caledonia are not the same.

of Moray; the name divides as Vaco-Magi, the latter part being *magh*, a plain, the whole seemingly "Dwellers on the plain." The name is lost. His name for Spey is Tvesis, which seems to have been an attempt at pronouncing Pictish initial *sp*, which in old Gadelic would be *sqv*, and in Welsh *chw*—a troublesome sound. Dr Whitley Stokes explains Spey as Pictish, from the root *sqe*, as in *sgeith*, vomit, the Scotch *spate*, Welsh *chwyd*. The name appears to mean the "spatey, vomiting river," and it has the reputation of being the swiftest of our large rivers. The Spean, on these terms, would stand for *Spēsona*, another stem from the same root. The Varar Estuary of Ptolemy answers to the Beauly Firth, and the River Farrar ideally suits the phonetics. The root may be *var, crooked*. The Island Sketis, or better *Skitis*, which Ptolemy places about 70 miles north-east of Cape Orkas (Dunnet-Head), is probably the Isle of Skye misplaced, a view which commends itself to Muller, Thomas, and Stokes. The latter says that it is "the wing-shaped Island of Skye; Norse, *Skidh*; Irish, *Scii* (dat. case, date 700 in ' Annals of Ulster '), Adamnan, *Scia*; gen. *Sceth* (date 667 in ' Annals of Ulster '), *Scith* (Tigernach, 668); means wing, Ir. *Sciath*, Sciathan." Dr Stokes' derivation is the one usually accepted; the Norse Skídh, which is possibly influenced by "folk-etymology," means a "log," "firewood," "tablet," and is

allied to another Gaelic word *sgiath*, a shield.
It is interesting to note that the Dean of Lismore
refers to the island as " Clar Skeith "—the
Board of Skith, thus showing that the Norse
name of the island was remembered and translated by Clàr. More modern bards have used
the expression Clàr Sgith in regard to Skye.
Thus Rory Mac Vurich in his elegy on Macleod
(published in 1776) says :—

" Dh' fhalbh mo lathaichean éibhinn
O'n thréig sibh Clàr Sgìthe."

In another on John, Sir Rory's son :—

" 'S e 'n Clàr Sgìth an Clàr raibh sgìth."

The earliest charter and record forms of the
name Skye are Skey (1292), Sky (1336), and Ski
in the " Manx Chronicle." Adamnan's ' Ocia '
shows no trace of ' th.' The root is Celtic
Ski, cut, slice, and the whole means the " indented isle." The root *Ski* is still the basis of
Gaelic *sgiath* and Norse Skídh.

Ptolemy's tribes in ancient " North Argyle "
were the Creones, Cerones, and Carnonacae.
The roots *cer*, *cre*, *car*, are here much to the
front, and the root generally means " broken,
rough." Carnonacae especially recalls *càrn*, a
cairn, a favourite name in the district as Càrn,
Càrnan, and Càrnach; to which may be added
the Carron, the ' rough ' river, *Carsona.

The title Hebrides, as applied to the Western Isles, appears first in Hector Boece's " History of Scotland." It is a copyist's blunder for the classical Hebudes or Haebudes, the name given by Pliny to a group of the Western Isles, 30 in number, he says. Ptolemy calls the Western Isles the Eboudae or Ebūdae, five in number, of which two are named Ebūda. This made some writers attempt to identify the two " Uists " with the two Eboudae, but the phonetical difficulties here are too great; besides, the name Uist is, as Professor Munch said, simply the Norse word *i-vist*, a habitation. It has lately been conjectured that Ebouda stands for the Greek article (' e ' or ' æ '), plus Bouda or Boudda, or later Bódda, and is really the old Pictish name of Bute. This would give that island name the meaning of " Victoria Isle."

Adamnan, Abbot of Iona, who died in 704, has left us in his " Life of St Columba " the most important document that we possess bearing on the ancient history of our country. He has recorded seven or eight names belonging to Inverness County. Passing over his Dorsum Britanniae or Drum-Alban, which means the watershed of Argyle and Perth, continued northwards also past the Great Glen, we have the names *Nesa* or Ness, *Scia* or Skye, *Egea* or Eigg, *Airchartdan* or Urquhart, *Artdamuirchol* or Ard-

10

namurchan, *Aporicum Stagnum* or Lochaber,
and, lastly, the river whose Latin name is *Nigra
Dea* (Black Goddess) in Lochaber.   The river
Ness is mentioned four times, three times as
Nesa and once (in the genitive case) as *Nisae*.
We learn also a lesson in topography from
Adamnan—" a 'cute ould observer," as an
Irishman would call him—Loch-Ness he calls the
" Lake of the River Ness "; and it is almost
invariably true, however large the loch or small
the river, that the loch is named after the river
which drains it.   In addition to this, the river
also names the glen through which it flows; and
we shall instantly find that the proud Ben Nevis
is named after the humble nymph who once in
pagan Pictish days ruled over the destinies of the
Nevis stream.   The name *Ness* is, of course,
Pictish; and we need not look at modern Gaelic
as exactly possessing the name in this form.   We
must have recourse to roots : *Nesa*, of Adamnan,
points to Celtic *Nesta* and a root *ned*, which we
find means " water," " wet," German *netzen*,
to wet, *nass*, wet, Sanskrit *nadi*, river.   In old
Greece there was the river Neda and in Thracia
the Nestos, which is practically the " Ness."
But we may go farther; in Ireland they had a
heroic personage called Ness, mother of the
famous demi-god king Conchobar Mac Nessa,
who was, as can be seen, metronymically named.
There are indications in the legends that Ness

was really a river goddess of pagan Ulster; and, if so, we may regard the Pictish "Nessa" or "Ness" as either the same goddess or her Celtic cousin. The Celts were great worshippers of rivers and wells. Gildas before 600 thus refers to the native worship of the early Britons :— "Nor will I invoke the name of the mountains themselves and the hills, or the rivers, to which the blind people then paid divine honour." One text represents Gildas as including the fountains in the above enumeration, and we have in Ausonius (circum 380 A.D.), the Gaulish poet, an invocation to "Divona, fons addite divis," that is, "Divona, fountain dedicated to the Gods"; for the name meant "Goddess," and is the same as appears in the Ptolemæic name for Aberdeen—Devana, which is still the Gaelic name of the river Don (Dian or Deathan), and which still abides in the -deen of Aberdeen. The river name Dee also means "Goddess"; and we see from Adamnan that a river in Lochaber was called Nigra Dea or Black Goddess. Adamnan also mentions as in or on the Dorsum Britanniae the Lake of Loch-dae, and it has been well con- jectured that Loch-dae is the Gaelic or Pictish of Nigra Dea, for lóch means "dark" and dae means "Goddess." In short, the river meant is the Lochy in Lochaber. There are at least four other rivers of this name : Lochay, entering the west end of Lochtay; Lochy in Glenorchy,

entering the Orchy above Dalmally; Lochy, or
Burn of Brown, which acts for a short distance
as the boundary of Abernethy parish and Inverness county, and which joins the Avon at Inverlochy near Kirkmichael; and Lochy with Glen-
Lochy at the head of Glenshee.

We may, however, suspect more river names
to have been " Goddess " river names. This is
undoubtedly the case with the " Earns," of
which we have at least three or four : the Perthshire *Earn*, the Inverness-shire *Find-horn*, or
White Earn, and the Banffshire *Deveron*, or
Doveran (oldest charter form Duff-hern) or Black
Earn; and there is the Earn of Auldearn.   The
Earn of Strathdearn is called in Gaelic *Eire*, and
its genitive is *Eireann*, the same in pronunciation
as the name for Ireland, and it is the same as the
name Erin of Ireland.   Eire was one of the last
Tuatha-dé-Danann queens of Ireland, to which
she left her name; she was, in short, one of the
last pagan female deities worshipped in Ireland.
Ptolemy calls Ireland " Ivernia," and the Celtic
form of the name is restored as " Iverjo," or,
possibly, a pre-Celtic *Piverio* (stem Piverion),
which has been equated with the Greek land-
name of Pieria, famed as the haunt of the muses.
The root, in that case, would mean " rich, fat,"
and would scarcely apply to a river name.
Adamnan's Evernilis, for " Irish," makes the
whole matter doubtful, and at present we must

confess ourselves beaten to explain the name
" Eire " or " Eireann "—" another injustice to
Ould Ireland?"*   I am inclined to include with
these Goddess names also the name Nevis, the
local Gaelic of which is *Nibheis*.   This points to
an early Pictish form—*Nebestis* or *Nebesta*, the
latter possibly.   The root *neb* or *nebh* is also
connected with clouds and water, and gives us
the classical idea of Nymph, root *nbh*—the
fairies of Greece and Rome.   The nymph Nebestà,
then, gave her name to, or found her name
in, the River Nevis, and gave her name to Glen-
Nevis, and it again to the famous Ben, which
again renders Inverness-shire unique, not merely
among Scottish but among British counties, by
having as one of its glories the highest hill in
Britain.   Loch Nevis also lends proof to the
argument that Nevis really denotes water originally.   There was a river in ancient Spain called
the *Nebis*, now *Neyva*, which may also show the
root.

Before leaving the river Ness and the other
" Goddess " rivers of the district, I have to

---

* The root ' pi ' means " fat " and " drink," " water,"
" flow," and is no doubt the ultimate root of these ' erin '
names, a stem ' pi-vo ' intervening, which is found in the
Gaelic name of Iona, that is I, older Eo, Ii, Hii, from nom.
' Piva,' loc. ' Pivi.'   The rivers Esk, Ptolemy's Iska, are from
*pid-ska, root *pid*, *pi-d*, spring, well, Grk. *pid-ax*, fountain.
So likely Islay and Isla are from *pi-la*.

explain that there is another and more popular, possibly more poetic, derivation of the name Ness than the one I have offered. Once upon a time, the story goes, the Great Glen which now lies under the waters of Loch Ness was a beautiful valley, filled with people and plenty. In the bottom of the vale was a spring of magic virtue, but there was a *geas* or taboo connected therewith. Whenever the stone on the well was removed and the water drawn, the stone had immediately to be replaced or else something dreadful was to take place. One day a woman came to the well, leaving her child playing on her hut floor; but while at the well she heard her child scream as if it had fallen into the fire. She rushed to the house to save her child, and forgot to replace the stone over the well. The well overflowed at once, and soon filled the long valley. The people escaped to the hills and filled the air with lamentations, crying, "Tha *loch nis* ann; tha *loch nis* ann"—there is a lake there now. The lake remained, and from that agonised cry is still known as *Loch-Nis*.

Four other names in Adamnan still remain for us briefly to discuss—*Egea, Aporicum, Artdamuirchol,* and *Airchartdan*. His "Egea" Insula is the island of Eigg, the *g* of which we should expect to be aspirated nowadays, but here, as in the Ptolemaic Ebouda for Bute, and Adru for Ben Edair (Howth), the double sound

of the consonant is not brought out in the old
spelling. *Egea* is for *Eggea,* and now it is in
Gaelic *Eige,* old Gaelic genitive *Ega* or *Eca.* It
is glossed or explained in a mediæval MS. as
" fons " or fountain, but the name seems to be
the modern Gaelic *eag,* a notch. The island is
notched, and so appears in approaching it.
There is another " Egg " island off Glenelg, like
in appearance. The Aporicum Stagnum or
Stagnum Aporum—that is, the " Aporic lake "
or " lake of Apors "—it is twice mentioned—
is, of course, Lochaber. It is usual to regard
the *aber* here as the Pictish prefix denoting
" confluence," and, no doubt, " Loch of the
Confluence " of the Lochy with the Linne Dhubh
(Black " Pool or Sea-loch ")—Loch Linnhe—is
possible; but the Gaelic *aber,* a marsh, seems
really to be the origin of the name, especially in
view of Adamnan's plural *Aporum* or *Abers.*
" Loch of the Marshes," therefore, is the meaning of Lochaber. Artdamuirchol or Artdaib
Muirchol is described as a " rough and stoney
district "; it is known still as the Garbh-
chrìochan, and in the old charters we saw it was
called Garmoran or Garbh-Morvern or " Rough
Morvern "—Morvern itself being in older Gaelic
" Na Morbhairne " (genitive). In 1475 the
records spell the name as " Morvarne "; it cannot be *Mór Earrainn* (Great Portion), as often
explained, or *Mór Bheannaibh;* it is rather like

Mór-bhearnaibh, " Great Gaps or Hill-passes."
Coming back to Artdamuirchol, the predecessor
of Ardnamvrchane (1515), or now Ardnamurchan, we can easily divide the word into
arda or *ardaibh* (accusative and locative plural
of *ard,* high, height), and *muirchol.* This last
Bishop Reeves explained as " Sea-hazel."
Muir, sea, undoubtedly forms part of the word.
There is no personal name of the form *Mur-chol;*
so that Dr Reeves is probably right in his
" hazel " derivation.   Lastly, we have Adamnan's Airchartdan, which, of course, is Glen-
Urquhart, the older " Wrchoden," and the
modern " Urchadainn."   There is an Urquhart
in Cromarty, and another in Moray.   The name
is a compound : *Air-card-an,* the first element
being the prefix *air,* on, beside.   The second
part, *card* or *cardin* appears in the oft-repeated
Kincardine.   It is clearly Pictish, and as Welsh
cardd (older *card*) means " brake," we may
take it that the Pictish means " wood, forest, or
brake."   Urquhart, therefore, means " Wood-
side," as Kincardine means " Woodend."   Cf.
Welsh name Argoed, for ' ar-coed,' ' At Wood.'
The word ' cardden ' is also found in Drum-
chardine, older Drumcharding (1514), the former name of Lentran.

   Let us now glance at the county from an
ecclesiastical standpoint.   There are thirty-five
parishes in Inverness-shire, some of which 'it

shares with its neighbours.   Inverness town is
in the territorial parish of Inverness and Bona;
Bona refers especially to the Dochfour end of the
parish, and is supposed to mean the ferry there
crossing the Ness, called "Bàn-àth" or
"White-ford."   In 1233 the parochial name
was spelt Baneth, and two hundred years later
Bonacht (for Bonath).   The prefix *cill*, the
locative of *ceall*, a church, appears in only four
of the parishes, though it is otherwise common.
Kil in Scotland almost invariably prefixes a
saint's name; it is the *ceall* of some saint.   There
are two or three exceptions, and the first on our
list is one of them : Kilmallie, Kilmalyn in 1296,
Kilmale, 1532, means the church of Màillie, but
there is no saint of that name, and it cannot be,
as is often supposed, a pet corruption of Màiri or
Mary.   All *cills* dedicated to St Mary are Kil-
moires or Kilmuirs, Moire being the real old
Gaelic for St Mary, the name Màiri being of late
Scoto-French origin.   In Kilmallie parish is the
river Maillie and Invermaillie; we have also
Kilmaly (1536), or Culmaly (1512), and Cul-
malin (1471) as the old name of Golspie parish;
the stream at Golspie appears to have no name
save Golspie Burn, so that it may have been
called Maillie.   There is a Dalmally in Glen-
orchay, with an Allt-Maluidh running through
it.   There is Polmaly ('màilidh') in Glen-
Urquhart, with Allt-Phuill running into it, which

must have been Allt-maly. Màilidh is a stream name; in Ireland Máilli is a personal name; but further than this I cannot go at present. Killin in Stratherrick, on Lochtayside, and at the upper end of Garve, means "White-church" (*cill-fhinn*), and is not, therefore, named after any saint any more than Kilmallie. In regard to the northern Killin there is the proverb—

> "Cill-Fhinn, Cill-Duinn
> 'S Cill-Donainn—
> Na trì Cilltean is sine an Albainn."

Kilvaxter, in Kilmuir of Skye, means the *cill* of Baxter, which got its name from the trade of somebody connected with it and the monastery of Monkstadt. Kilmore in Sleat means the Cella Magna or Great Church; there is a Kilmore in Glen-Urquhart. Kilmonivaig, Kilmanawik (1449), is the church of St Mo-naomhóc or "my saint" Naomhan. Kilmorack, Kilmorok (1437), seems dedicated to a St Moroc; the name has long puzzled ecclesiastical students, but the form Mawarrock, a saint's name connected with Lecropt parish, at once suggests Mo-Bharróc, and we get the well-known St Barr or Barre, more fully Barr-finn or "White-head." There were several saints of the name, as also the name Finnbarr, the same name reversed, which was also curtailed to Barr, Findan, and Munn (Mo-Fhindu). The St Barr of Barra Isle was Finnbarr, whose day was on the 25th September. Moroc's day was the 8th November. Kilmuir, in Skye, means St Mary's Church, but the original name was Kilmaluok (1538)—Moluoc's or Lughaidh's Church, a favourite saint. Kiltarlity was in 1234 Kyltalargy, in 1280 Keltalargyn; the saint is a Pictish one—Talorgan, "Fair-browed one."

We have already discussed, in other connections, Abernethy, Ardnamurchan, Boleskine, and Abertarff, Cawdor (under the name Aberchalder, Cawdor being Caldor in 1394), Petty, Uist, Barra (that is Barr's *ey* or isle, mixed Norse and Gaelic), and Urquhart. Ardersier is in its oldest form Ardrosser (1226); it seems to mean Ard-rois-ear, "East-point-height," as against Ros-marky opposite it. The present pronunciation is Ard-na(n)-saor, 'Carpenters' Point'; but 'saothair,' a promontory or passage covered at high water, has been suggested. This word is common on the West Coast. Taking the Skye parishes together, we find Bracadale spelt much the same in 1498—Bracadoll; the Gaelic is Bràcadal; the name contains the common term *breac* or *brac*, slope, almost the same force as Gaelic *sliabh*, and it comes from the Norse *brekka*, a slope, English *brink*. Sleat, in 1389 and 1401 Slate, comes from the Norse *slétta*, a plain, *sléttr*, level. It is the only decently level part of Skye. Strath is a curtailment of Strathordail; it is a hybrid of Gaelic *Srath* and *Sword-dale* or "Sward-dale," both Norse elements, usually Suardal in pronunciation. It is a very common name, this Swordale. Duirinish, in 1498 Dyurenes, stands for Norse "Deer's ness or head." It is the same as Durness in Sutherland. Snizort is Snesfard in 1501; it possibly stands for Norse Snaesfjord or "snow-firth." Portree doubtless gets its name of "King's Port" from James V.'s punitive visit to the Isles in 1540.

Alvie parish, about 1350 Alveth and Alway, presents a well-known name, which appears elsewhere as Alva, Alvah, Alves, and Alyth, which, save Alves, show an old form Alveth. It seems a Pictish stem *alvo*, an extension of the root *al*, rock. Daviot is another old word evidently Pictish, for its old form Deveth (1206-33) is clearly the same as the British tribal name Demetæ of South Wales, now Dyfed. The root is *dem*, sure, strong, Gaelic *deimhin*. Croy and Dalcross formed an old parish. The former is from the adjective ' cruaidh,' hard. Dalcross is a corruption for what Shaw gives as Dealg-an-Ross or Dalginross, a name which appears in Athole and Strathearn. It means ' spit of the ridge or promontory,' for ' ros ' can be used inland, as in Abernethy—Ruigh-da-ros, ' Shiel of the two points.' Dunlichity or Flichity is an alternate name for the parish; this is Flechate in 1560, and comes from *flichead*, moisture, a derivative from *fliuch*, wet. Dores, about 1350 Durrys, is in Gaelic Durus; this word meant in the old language "a gloomy wood" (*dubhras*), an epithet that would well suit the Inverness-shire Dores, if only the phonetics were more satisfactory. The name is Pictish—its termination ('-as') favours this idea, and hence the root is ''dur,' strong—'a strong hold,' it seems to mean. It has also been taken to mean 'dorus,' a door or opening; the roots in any case are the same. There is a Durris in Banchory parish. Duthil, about 1230 Dothol, has been explained by Lachlan Shaw, the historian, as the *tuaitheal* or north-side of Creag-an-fhithich, while the Deshar or *deiseil* is on the south side. This also is the local derivation, and it seems right enough. Glenelg, Glenhelk in 1282, means "noble glen," or properly the "glen of the noble (*elg*) river." The root *elg* is also in Elgin. Kingussie, Kinguscy (1103-11), is in Gaelic Cinn-ghiùthsaich, "Head of the fir-forest"; *cinn*, or *kin*, as a prefix, is the locative of *ceann*. Kirkhill, a modern name, comprises the old parishes of Wardlaw (Wardelaw in 1203-24, an English name, meaning "Beacon-hill") and Farnua (Ferneway in 1238). The latter name means the "place of alders" in Gaelic, and Shaw, who so explains it, adds that alders "abound there,"

which they have done till lately.   Laggan is for
Lagan-Choinnich or " St Cainneach's hollow,"
and in the old records it appears as Logynkenny
(1239).   The church was then up at the end of
Loch Laggan.   Moy is the locative of *magh*,
plain, and Dalarossie is in Gaelic Dail-Fhearghuis, the Dulergusy of 1224-42, the " dale of
St Fergus," to whom the chapel there was dedicated.   Rothiemurchus is in modern Gaelic
Ràt-a-mhurchais, which in 1226 is just the same,
Ratemorchus, beside Rathmorcus.   The prefix
ràt is a common one, confined, however, to Pictland; it is an extension of *ráth*, an enclosure or
farm building, but whether the termination is
due to Pictish influence or not can hardly be
said; for in several cases *d* ends local suffixes,
both in Ireland and Scotland (Irish *kealid* from
caol, and *croaghat* from *cruach*; Scotch Bialaid
in Badenoch, from *bial*, mouth).   In fact *ràt*
takes the place of *ràth* in Pictland; and beside it
we may no doubt place *rà'ig* or *ràthaig* as in
Raigmore and Raigbeg of Strathdearn, although
the old forms show here an internal *v* : Ravoch-
more; also Kil-ravock, which is now pronounced
Kill-ra'ag.   The main body of the word Rothiemurchus seems a personal name, possibly
Muirgus, " Sea-choice," allied to Fergus and
Murchadh.   The local derivation here is Ràt-
mhóir-ghiuthais, ' Rath of the big fir(s),' and is

· not to be despised on the score of phonetics, and certainly not as to the facts.

The island parishes, besides Skye, comprise the Small Isles and the Outer Hebrides. Only Eigg now remains to Inverness-shire. Muck (Eilean-nam-muc or " Pig Isle "), Canna (Porpoise Isle, old Gaelic *cana*, porpoise), and Rum (origin unknown) belong now to Argyle. St Becan, from ' bec,' ' beag,' little, seems to have died in Rum (gen. Ruimm) in 676, if we can judge what the Irish annals and martyrologies say correctly. Eigg has been already considered. So, too, have the Uists and Barra. Harris was in 1546 *Hary*, 1546 *Harige;* Dean Munro (1549) calls it " the Harrey." The Gaelic is *Na h-Earra*, which gave the English form " the *Herries* " and Harris or " the Harris." There is Harris in Rum and Islay, Herries in Dumfries, and Harray in Orkney. It is usual to explain *Na h-Earra* as " the heights," and both in Harris and in Islay this admirably suits, but the Norse words, whence the name undoubtedly comes, cannot be easily fitted in. The Norse for " high " is *hár*, plural *havir*, especially the comparative *haerri*, higher (" The Higher Ground " as compared to low-lying Lewis).

The Church has supplied many other than purely parish names. Saints' names, generally wit the prefix *cill*, are abundant, and saints' wells, as well as saints' isles, are common. St Columba is first favourite, something like a score of places being connected with his name in such forms as Cill-cholumchille (Kil-columkill) or Cill-choluim, Tobair-Cholumchille, and Eilean-Cholumchille; and Portree bay was named after him originally. The next in importance of dedication is the Virgin Mary; Kilmuir or Kilmory are the usual forms in English of the name. There are two in Ardnamurchan, Kilmory and Kilvorie, Kilmuir in North Uist, and Kilmuir in Skye as a parish, and in Duirinish, with several other places. St Bridget, the "Mary of the Gael," has two or three Kilbrides in the county—as in Strath, South Uist, and Harris. St Maolrubha, older Maelruba, appears in place names as Molruy, Morruy, and Maree (as in Loch-Maree). His centre in Scotland is Applecross; here he died in 721. He seems to have been a favourite in Skye; there is Kilmaree in Strath, and Cill-ashik was of old Askimolruy or "Maelruba's Ferry"; Kilmolruy in Bracadale, and Ardmaree in Berneray. In Skye also Moluag or St Lughaidh has some dedications—Kilmaluock in Trottarness and in Raasay; there was a croft Mo-luag at Chapelpark, near Kingussie, whence the latter name. St Comgan is celebrated in Ardnamurchan and Glenelg—Kilchoan; and he was the special patron of the old Glengarry family.

St Cuimine the Fair, the 7th century biographer of Columba, seems to have been celebrated at Glenelg, Kirkton (Kilchuimen, 1640). But we have his name certainly in Cill-chuimen of Fort-Augustus. St Donnan gave Kildonnan to Eigg and South Uist. The Pictish saint Drostan, who is misrepresented as a pupil of St Columba's, was patron of Alvie; his chapel is still seen in ruins at Dunachton, and there is, or was, in Glen-Urquhart a croft named after him—Croit-mo-chrostan; and seemingly the patronymic M'Rostie (Perthshire) comes from Drostan under Lowland influence. Another Pictish saint was Kessoc, whose name at least is borne by the ferry of Kessock (Kessok, 1437). The name Kessoc or Kessan is from 'ces,' meaning 'spear' in Gaelic, but what it meant in Pictish it is impossible to say. Tarlagan, the Pict, had a 'kil' on the north of Portree bay, besides being the patron saint of Kiltarlity (Ceilltarraglan). Adamnan appears rarely; Tom-eunan of Insh is named after him, and a croft of his existed in Glen-Urquhart. Such names as Kilpheder, Kilmartin, Kilaulay (Olave), Kilchalman, Kilcrist (now Cill-chrò, or "pen kirk," in Gaelic, in Strath), Pitkerrald (Cyrill), and Kilmichael in Glen-Urquhart, Killianan (Finan) in Glengarry, Ardnamurchan and Abriachan, and others can only be mentioned.

11

A most interesting . ecclesiastical name is
Annaid; it occurs very often in Inverness county,
from Killegray of Harris to Groam of Beauly.
Achnahannet is common, and there are Teampull
na h-Annaid, Clach na h-Annaid, and Tobair na
h-Annaid.   It means in old Gaelic a patron
saint's church; it is rare, however, in Ireland,
and seems in Scotland to denote the *locale* of the
pioneer anchorites' cells, that is, their *clachans*
and little oratories, often away in a *diseart* (Lat.
Desertum) or desert (island or remote place).
The name Clachan is common on the West Coast
and in the Isles; it means, firstly, the monk's or
anchorite's bee-hive stone cell—built where
wood and wattle were scarce, so that on the
eastern mainland there are no *clachans.*   The
word developed into the meaning of oratory or
kirk, and, from the cluster of *clachans* making a
monastic community, into '' village,'' which is
its only meaning in the Lowlands.   There are
three in Kilmuir (Skye), for example; one at
least in N. Uist, which is countenanced by Kallin
or Ceallan (Kirkie) and Kirkibost ('' Kirkton '')
there.   *Réilig* is now an old Gaelic word for
church-yard, and from Lat. *reliquiae;* it appears
in the Aird and near Beauly as Ruilick.   *Team-*
pull and *Seipeal* (Chapel) give many names:
Tigh-an-Teampuill or Temple-House in Glen-
Urquhart, and Pairc-an-t-seipeil (Chapel-park)
in Badenoch, for example.   The church officials,

too, have naturally left their mark : Balnespick
is Bishop's-ton; Paible is from the Norse Papyli
or Papa-byli, " Pope or Priest's town," a Gaelic
Bail'-an-t-sagairt, and Papay is "Priest's Isle";
Mugstad or Monkstead of Skye is the half Norse
representative of Bal-vanich in Benbecula, which
is half Gaelic (*manach*, monk, from Lat.
monachus). In the same island is Nunton or
Ballenagailleich (1549). There is no Appin in
Inverness-shire—Abbacy or Abbey-land, but
there is "A' Mhanachainn," the *Monkery*, the
the Gaelic name for Beauly, itself from the Lat.
Bellus Locus or "Beautiful Place," a name no
doubt bestowed on it—and rightly—by the early
13th century monks.

We shall now notice the District names not
already considered, as we have considered Lochaber, Morvern, Strathdearn, &c. The Aird
explains itself; it is the high ground of Kirkhill
and Kiltarlity. Glenmoriston is a difficult name;
the river, of course, gives the name, and it is
usually explained as for *Mór-easan*, "river of
great water-falls." It is Pictish, no doubt, and
points to a Celtic *Môr-est-ona*. Stratherrick, the
older Stratharkok and Stratharkeg, comes from
the river Farigag, which means " lower ravine"
river (Gaelic *far*, below, and *gàg*, cleft). *Far* is
a common prefix in northern Pictland—Farleitir
("lower slope"), Farraline ("lower linn"),
Farr ("lower place"), &c. Strathnairn derives

its name from the Nairn River; this river name
is Pictish, likely old Naverna, the same root and
partial stem as we have in the Naver of Sutherland, Ptolemy's Nabaros. The root is *nav* or
snav, flow, swim, Gaelic *snàmh*; and we may
compare the Welsh Nevern as a parallel form to
Nairn.   Badenoch is the Gaelic Bàideanach; the
root is *bàide*, submerged, from *bàth*, drown.   In
Ireland there is Bauttogh in Galway, " a marshy
place," and the river Bauteoge, running through
swampy ground.   Passing over Lochaber as
already discussed, we come to the ancient lordship of Garmoran, the Clanranald land, bounded
on the south by Loch Shiel and on the north by
Loch Hourn, as the poet says in the Dean of
Lismore's Book (1512)—

> Leggit derri di vurn
> eddir selli is sowyrrni

—" An end of merriment between Shiel and
Hourn."   Adamnan's Sale is the above Shiel,
but the Sorn is a later name given by the Gael,
who had by the time they reached it adopted the
Latin ' furnus,' whence ' sorn,' a furnace, undoubtedly comes.   Loch Hourn is ' Furnace
Lake '—Lochshuirn, which may be compared
with the Lochalsh name Coire na Sorna, the one
a masculine, the other a feminine genitive, both
genders being shown in the the early language,
as is not uncommon in the case of a borrowed

word. The lordship of Garmoran, to which
Skene devoted an extraordinary chapter in his
"Highlanders of Scotland," under the fancy
that it was an earldom, and about which he is
silent in "Celtic Scotland," comprised Moydart,
Morar, and Knoydart. The name, spelt in 1343
Garmorwarne, means 'Rough Morvern,' and
Morvern means 'Great Passes'—Mór-bhearna;
the modern Gaelic has adopted the name Garbh-
chrìochan, or 'Rough-bounds,' instead. The
Morvern furthers south may be regarded as
adjacent, and perhaps part of the same name;
if not, then it also is bisected well enough by its
own 'bearn' or pass of Lochs Tacnis, Loch
Arienas, and, we may add, Loch Aline, with
their respective streams, to entitle it to a
separate but singular Mór-bhearn.   M'Vurich
calls it in the gen. sing. fem. 'Na Morbhairne';
the oldest charter spelling is Morvern as now
(1390), and Morvarne (1475). The name Moydart, G. Mùideard, was spelt Mudeworth in
1343, Modoworth in 1372, and Mudewort in
1373. The name is difficult as to derivation; it
is Norse by its ending '-ard,' '-ort,' which is
for 'fjord.' Like Knoydart and Sunart, it likely
comes from a personal name, here Mundi, and
for the phonetics compare the island names
Gometray and Hermitra, from Godmund and
Hermund, and the personal name Tormoid from
Thormund.   Better still is the Thrond of

Trotternish for comparison. Sunart, in 1372 Swynwort, and in 1392 Swynawort, is Sveinn's fjord; while Knoydart (Cnudeworth in 1343) stands for Knut's or Canute's fjord. Arisaig, in 1309 Aryssayk, is the Norse *arós-vík*, the bay of the river mouth (*arós*, river-mouth, whence Aros, the place name). Morar was in 1343 Morware, Mordhowor, 1517 Moroyn, Mac Vurich's old Gaelic Móiróin, which last points to *Mór-shrón* or "Great nose" (promontory) as the meaning of the word; but Morar or Morwar stands for Mór-bharr,' Great-point.' Glengarry takes its name from the river Gareth (about 1309). There is another Garry in Perth, and the Yarrow is the same name, while allied by root are the English rivers "Yair" and "Yare" (Yarmouth), and also the French "Garonne," classic Garumna. The root is *garu*, or Gaelic *garbh*, *rough*. In Skye we have Trotternish, Waternish, and Minginish districts. Trotternish is in 1549 both Trouteruesse and Tronternesse, either with a *u* or with *n* in the main syllable. Mac Vurich (17th century) gives the then Gaelic as , "Tróntarnis "; it stands for Norse "Throndarnes " or "Thrond's Headland." Waternish is the Icelandic "Vatnsness" or "Water-ness." Minginish—Myngnes in 1498, Mygnes in 1511, and Myngynnes in 1549—contains the prefixed element *ming*, which appears in the island names Mingulay and Mingay, and Mingarry, where in every case the Gaelic has no ' ng ' sound at all. Mingarry is Mioghairidh (Mewar, 1493, and Meary, 1505, but Mengarie, 1496). The word here prefixed seems to be ' mikil,' ' great,' whose accusative is ' mikinn,' ' mikla,' ' mikit ' in the three genders. Hence Minginish means Rudha-Mór of Gaelic, which it is.

The Norsemen, who held the Isles for some 450 years, have left a deeper impress on the place-names there than the Gael. Of the names usually printed on maps, in directories, or in the Valuation Rolls for the Outer Hebrides, four are Norse to the Gaelic one; that is, the proportion is four-fifths Norse and one-fifth Gaelic. In Skye the proportion is not so heavily against Gaelic; practically the two languages are equal. Of the names on the Valuation Roll, 60 per cent. are Norse as against 40 per cent. that are Gaelic. The coast-line of Garmoran is also considerably Norse, though nothing like the proportion in Skye; and as we go inland the Norse names get fewer. There are no Norse names in Lochaber; so we may conjecture that that district was free of the Norse yoke. Norse names abound in Easter as well as in Wester Ross, and they can be traced south to the Beauly valley, where we have Eskidale ("Ash-dale") and Tarradale on the Beauly River. Further south we do not find any trace of the Norse power in place names; nor is it likely that they ever had any conquest

or sway south of Beauly, despite their own assertions, in their sagas, that they possessed also
Moray.   The Norse power in Scotland at its
strongest extended over Caithness, Sutherland,
Ross, Argyle, and Galloway, with, of course, the
Western Isles.   This was about 980 to 1050.
Gaelic slowly regained its hold in the Isles after
the rise of Somerled and the other patriarchs of
the Clan Donald in the latter part of the 12th
century; but Gaelic in its re-conquest left the
Norse nomenclature of the country practically
intact.

The most prominent Norse words borrowed
are those for island (*ey*), hill (*fjall*), *vík*
or -aig, bay, *nes* or *nish*, headland, *dalr*
or -*dale*, a vale, a dale; *fjördhr*, sea-loch
or firth (fjord), or -*ord*, -*ard*, and the various
words for township, farm or settlement (*setr*,
stadr, *bólstadr* and *ból* or -*bo*).   The termination -*ay* and -*a* of the island names is the Norse
ey, isle.   Beginning with the isles about Harris,
we have Berneray, or "Bjorn's Isle"—Bjorn
either meaning "bear" or being a personal
name, which last it likely is.   Fladda, so commonly repeated, means "flat isle"; Soay, also
repeated often, is for Saudha-ey or "Sheep-
isle"; Isay, "Ice-isle"; Taransay, St Taran's
Isle; Ensay, "meadow (*engi*) isle"; Killegray,
"Kellach's Isle," the Kellach being the Irish
"Cellach" or "Kelly" (Warrior), borrowed

early by the Norse, and now known in the name
MacKillaig; Lingay, "Heath Isle"; Scalpay,
"Shallop" or "Ship Isle"; Rossay, "Horse
Isle"; Eriskay, "Eric's Isle." Oransay and
Orasay, of which names there are a great number
of isles, is from *orfiri*, ebb or shallow, and means
that the island is one at full tide only; Pabbay,
"Pope or Priest's Isle"; Sandray is "Sand
Isle"; Benbecula is only partly Norse; the
Gaelic is Beinn-a-bhaodhla, and really means
"Height of the Ford," from Gaelic *faodhail*,
"a ford," itself borrowed from the Norse *vadill*,
"a shallow or ford." Rasay or Rarsay
(Rairsay, 1526, Rasay and Raarsay in 1549)
seems to be 'Rár-áss-ey,' 'Roe-ridge-isle.'

The hills in the isles generally end in -*val*.
This is the Norse *fjall*, fell or hill. The name
Roine-val is common; this is Hraun-fell, a rocky-
faced hill; the island Rona is also from *hraun*,
"rocky-surfaced isle." Horne-val is "horn-
fell"; Helaval is "flagstone fell"; and so on.
Layaval in South Uist, and Laiaval in North Uist,
may be equated with Ben Loyal in Sutherland;
perhaps for 'Leidhfjall,' 'levy or slogan hill.'
Mount Hecla in Mingulay has the same name as
the famous burning mountain in Iceland, which
means 'hooded shroud.' Blavein in Skye is for
Blá-fell, 'Blue-fell.'

The sea-lochs in -*ord*, -*ard*, -*art* are too
numerous even to make a selection from; and

the same may be said of the *nesses* or headlands (Norse *nes*). I must pass over also the townships with their *bols*, *bosts*, and *stas*. An odd change is undergone by *hólmr*, an islet (in a bay or river), a holm; this may appear either as terminal -*am*, or -*mul*, or -*lum*. We have Heistamul and Hestam, both from *hestr*, horse; the famous Eilean Beagram is probably Bekraholmr, "Ram-holm"; Lamalum is "Lambholm," and Sodhulum is from *saudhr*, sheep. Airnemul is Erne-holm—"Eagle-holm." Lianimul no doubt means "flax-holm." *Os* means "river-mouth, oyce"; we have it in the Skye Ose and Glen-ose, and in Aros. Hoe and Toe are not uncommon, and we have Howmore in S. Uist; this is Norse *haugr*, burial mound, howe. Torgabost shows *horgr*, a heathen place of worship, and also Horogh (Castlebay).

There is a marked difference between the Island and West Coast topography and the eastern mainland in the common names of hills, dales, lochs, and rivers; in the west we have *cleit*, *stac*, *sgùrr*, *sgeir*, and *gil*, all Norse; in the east *càrn*, *meall*, *creag*, *monadh*, and *gleann*. In the east *coire*, *srath*, *sliabh*, as against the terminal *dal* and *breac* and *gil* of the Isles. Then the absence of terms for wood is most marked in the west, *sco*, terminal for *skógr*, a shaw, appearing only in Skye, as Birkisco, Grasgo, &c. In the east, wood is very common in the nomenclature. The bird names also differ much, even when not Norse, from the Gaelic Mainland. We have *orri*, N. moorfowl, also a nickname, in Oreval, hills in Harris and Uist; *mar*, sea-mew, in Maraig, ' Sea-mew bay '; *örn*, *eagle*, in Arnamul, ' Eagle-head ' (Mingulay), and Arnaval (Skye); *kráka*, crow, Crakavick, ' Crow-wick ' (Uist); *hrafn* or *hramn*, raven, Ramasaig, ' Raven-bay ' (cf. Ramsay, Ramsey); and Geirum, ' Auk-holm ' (Barra).

The mainland *baile*, farm or township, is often represented in the Inverness-shire isles by Norse *setr*, a stead, shieling. The latter name appears alone as Seadair (Gaelic) or Shader (English) in Bernera and Skye. Uigshader means ' Ox-ton ' (compare Uisgeval and Uisgneval, hills); Roishader, ' Horse-ton '; Marishader ' Mare-ton '; Herishader, ' Lord's-ton '; Sùlishader, ' Pillar-ton ' or ' Solan-goose-ton '— it is not far inland—all in Skye; which, however, prefers *bost* (N. *bólstadhr*), as Húsabost, ' House-stead '; Eabost (' Eidh ' or isthmus?); Colbost (pronounced Cyalabost), ' Keel-ton '; Heribost, ' Lord's-ton '; Orbost, ' Orri's-ton '; Breabost, ' Broad-ton '; Skeabost, ' Skidhi's-ton,' as in Skibo (old Scythebol); Carbost, ' Kari's-ton.' The Norse *gardr*, a garth or house and yard, which appears elsewhere on Norse ground, is represented in the Western Isles and Mainland by its diminutive *gerdhi*, which has been adopted into Gaelic as *gearraidh*, the land between machair and moor. It is common in place-names in its Gaelic use—Gearadu, 'Black-garth,' in N. Uist; Geary (Duirinish); Garrymore (Bracadale), Garrafad (Kilmuir), and Gairidh-Ghlumaig (Kilmuir). Terminally it is *garry*, and is very extensively used with Norse names—Osmigarry, from Osmund; Calligarry, from Kali; Grimagarry, from Grimm; Shageary, 'Sea-garth' (Sagerry, 1541); Flodigarry, 'Float or Fleet garth' (though Gaelic has long *o*); Biggary, 'Barley'; Mugeary, 'Monk's garth' (?); and Mosgaraidh, 'Moss'—all in Skye. In N. Uist there are Hougheary (howe), and Trumsgarry (Thrum's); in Benbecula, Creagarry may be Gaelic, as may be Crogarry there, though *kró* may be Norse borrowed from Gaelic (a pen); Mingarry (Benbecula) is 'mickle-garth.' In S. Uist appears Stelligarry, the first portion of which is pronounced 'staol,' and is found in Stulay isle; it is Norse, pointing to *steil*, *steyl*, *stadhil* or *stagil*, but these forms are either non-existent or cannot be used in place-names, save the last, as in Stagley, 'rock-isle.' Seemingly we have here a corruption of the proper name Stulli or Sturla. The Norse has borrowed besides *kró* the imporant word airigh, shieling, originally as *aerg* or *erg*, as in Asgrims-aergin, in the Orkney Saga, where it is explained that *erg* is Gaelic for *setr*. Asgrims-erg now appears

as Askarry, even Assary (Caithness), where we
have also Halsary (Hall), Dorrery, Shurrery
(Shureval, ' Pig-hill,' in S. Uist), etc.   In Duirinish we find Soarary, ' Sheep shiel '; in Ardnamurchan, Smirisary, ' Butter shiel,' and Brunary
(Brunnary, 1498), an ' Airigh an tobair '; in
Glenelg, Beolary and Skiary; in N. Uist, Obisary,
' Bay or Hope '; Aulasary, ' Olaf's '; Risary,
' Copse-wood '; Dùsary, Vanisary, and Hòrisary;
in S. Uist, Vaccasary and Trasary (Thrasi); and
others.

Some of the more interesting land and farm
names may be glanced at.   The Norse ounce
and penny lands—especially the latter—have left
their mark. The *tirung* or ounce-land is equated
with the Mainland *davoch* or *doch*, four plough-
gates, whose fourth is the common name Kerrow
(*ceathramh*, fourth).   The Norse for this last
phonetically was *fjordhungr*, fourthing or farthing, which appears in the place-name Feòirlig, the
phonetics being the same as for *birlinn*, a galley
(N. *byrdhingr*).   It meant ' farthing land.'   The
ung was old Gaelic, and existed in Ung-an-ab,
the abbot's ounce-land, in N. Uist in 1561.   The
pennyland gives many names : Pein-chorran
(Portree), from *corran*, point, the masculine
form of *corrag*.   This *corran* is a very common
name in the Isles, and appears as Corran simply
several times, as at Ballachulish.   The usual explanation of ' bay ' is absurdly wrong, therefore,

from *corran*, a sickle, supposed metaphorically to mean 'bay,' which it does not. Of course these 'corrans' often guard sickle-shaped bays, and hence the mistake. Other penny-lands are —Penifiller, 'Fiddler's'; Pensoraig, 'Primrose' (? or N. 'Saur-vík,' ' Mud-bay'); Pein-more (big); Peiness (waterfall); Peinaha; Peinlich; Leiphen (half-penny); and Pein-gown (smith)—all in Skye. Peinavaila is the romantic form which ' Peighinn-a'-bhaile ' takes in Benbecula. Pen-inerin in S. Uist stands for ' Peighinn an aor-ainn '—where mass was said. In Pictland *davoch* or *doch* is the commonest land-measure: Dochgarroch, ' D. of the rough-land '; Doch-four, of which presently; and Lettoch, near Beauly, is ' Half-davoch,' like the Aberdeen-shire Haddo and Haddoch. The terminal ele-ment *-fùr* enters largely into the names of Pict-land—Balfour, Inchfur, Dalfour, Dochfour, Pit-fur (very common), Tillifour and Tillifourie (Tough), and Trinafour (Perthshire). The form with *f* is clearly an aspirated *p*; the word is *púr*, which seems to exist in diminutive form in Purin (Fife), older Pourane, Porin (G. Pòrainn) in Strathconan, and Powrie near Forfar. The Book of Deer has the aspirated Fúrené, repre-sented now by Pitfour in Deer. The *p* proves the word to be Pictish; and it is possible that the root is *par*, as in Welsh *pawr*, pasture, Breton *peur*. The ultimate root is *qer*, as in *preas*,

crann, and perhaps *craobh*.   In Inverness we
have Dochfour, Dochgarroch, and Delfour.

The words *gart*, corn, *goirtean*, cornfield,
allied to English *garden* and Norse *gardhr*, appear in Boat of Garten and minor places.   Cluny
is a very common name; the Gaelic is Cluanaigh,
a locative of *cluanach*, meadowy place, from
cluan, a mead.   In Badenoch the nom. or acc.
is found in A' Chluanach, west of Kincraig.
Longart, a shieling, camp, is now obsolete, save
in place-names; it is met with in Dail-an-longairt,
Coire-an-Longairt, and Badenlongart (1773,
Gaick)—all in Badenoch.   The old word was
longphort, ' ship-port,' or harbour, encampment, which, with a dialect pronunciation of
long as ' low,' gives *lùchairt*, a palace.   Tarbert
means isthmus, from *tar*, across, and root *ber*,
bring, bear.   Drummond presents the full stem
of *druim*, back (dromann, dromand), and does
not stand, as usually said, for Druim-fhinn,
white ridge, still less for Fionn's ridge.   Strath-
glass presents the old word *glais*, stream, which
we have in Inveruglas, the confluence of the
Duglas or Dark-stream (now nameless); this is
also found in Southern Scotland, and has given
the famous family name.   The word *leacainn*,
a cheek, hill face or side, gives Leachkin, at
Inverness, and elsewhere, generally with an
epithet.   The diminutive *sidhean*, a fairy knoll,
gives Bailintian and many names else; the simple

sìdh appears in Ben Tee, of Glengarry, and is found elsewhere for conical hills, as in Schiehallion, 'Hill of the Caledonians,' with which the name Dunkeld and Rohallion, near Dunkeld, are to be compared. The *làirig* is given in the dictionaries as a "plain, hill, sloping hill," somewhat contradictory meanings; but the real meaning is found in the place-names, and that meaning is 'pass.' In Old Irish we have *làarc*, a fork or 'gobhal.' Finnlarig, both in Duthil and at Killin, means 'Fair Pass,' as Rev. J. Maclean, Grandtully, etymologises the Perthshire name. In Rothiemurchus we have Larachgrue or Lairig-dhrù, probably the pass of Druie river (root *dru*, flow, as in Gaulish Druentia), which the Ordnance Map, with its wonted perversity, names Lairg Gruamach. The place-name Elrick is common in the county, and there must be over a hundred such in Scotland; it is from the obsolete *eileirig*, locative of *eileireag*, which meant the *cul-de-sac* bounded by fallen trees and other obstructions into which the deer were driven, and one side of which was formed of a hill, on the face of which the hunters took their place and shot the deer. These hills and places are called Elrick, Eldrick, Elrig, and Ulrig; 'eileir' is given in the dictionaries as a 'deer path,' no doubt from the root *eln* in *eilid*, hind. It is sometimes explained as *iolairig*, a knoll on which eagles rested, which is not likely.

The ' bordlands ' of the royal and other castles
appear in Gaelic as *borlum*, whence Borlum,
near Fort-Augustus, also the old name for Ness
Castle, whence the famous and notorious Borlum
family got its name.   There is Borlum in Skye,
and elsewhere.

We will finally consider some interesting indi-
vidual names, and begin with the furthest west,
which is St Kilda.   This name is one of those
known   as   ' ghost   names '—a   geographer's
blunder.   In Gaelic the island is called *Irt* or
Iort, which means in old Gaelic ' death '; it is
likely that the ancient Celts fancied this sunset
isle to be the gate to their earthly paradise, the
Land-under-the-waves, over the brink of the
western sea.   The Dutch map-makers of the
17th century are responsible for St Kilda or
Kilder.   There were some wells near the village
famous   for   their   virtues—Tobar-nam-buadh,
and there was a Tobar-Kilda among them—one
or all of them retaining the Norse name for well,
which is *kelda*, corrupted into St Kilder's Well
in the 17th century.   Kelda is known in the
North of England on Norse ground as *kild*, as in
Kildwick, Kilham (Domesday Chillum), and
Halikeld, ' Holy-well.'   The well-names got
mixed with the true name of the island on the
maps.   The Dutch were active herring fishers in
the western seas in 'he 17th century, and to

12

them we owe more curiosities than St Kilda—
doubtless the Minch is due to them, the Gaelic of
which is A' Mhaoil, the Moyle, also the old Irish
name for the sea between the 'Maoil' of Kintyre
and Ireland.

Rodel, *o* long, stands for Norse Red-dale,
from the colour of the soil.

Lee, in N. Uist, Ben Lee, Skye, N. *hlídh*,
slope.

Lochmaddy, from *madadh*, a shellfish there.

Heisker, Hellisker, 1644, N. 'Rocky skerry.'
Munro in 1549 calls it Helskyr na gaillon (nuns).

Stoney-bridge, in S. Uist, G. Staoni-brig, is
for N. Stein-brekka, 'stone-slope.'

Boisdale, N. Bugis-dalr, 'Slight bay dale.'

Dorlin, Ardnamurchan, G. *doirling*,' isthmus.

Glenfinnan, G. Gleann-Fìonain, named after
St Fìnan, Ellan-Finan having been the old name
of Ardnamurchan parish. St Finan lived in St
Columba's time, is called of 'Swords in Leinster,' and was latterly a leper, taking the
infection for penance. His name appears in
Abriachan and Glengarry in Killianan. He is
not to be confused with St Finnan (short *i*, from
finn, white); as the following triplet on the last
Glengarry shows, the quantity of the *i* is long :—

> 'S ann 'na laighe 'n Cill Fhìonain
> Dh' fhàg sinn biatach an fhìona,
> Làmh a b' urrainn a dhìoladh.

Inveraros, in Raasay, is a good case of hybrid; for *arós* is the Norse for inver.

Point of Ayre, in Raasay, is derived from *eyrr*, a gravelly beach, connected in Britain with headlands; we have it in Snizort as Eyre (Ire, 1630), and Ken-sal-eyre or Kinsale (sea-end) of Eyre. There is a Point of Ayre on the north-east coast of Man; and we may perhaps conjoin the Heads of Ayr in the county of that name, and perhaps the county name.

Idrigill, which appears twice as a promontory in Skye, with Udrigle in Gairloch, stands for Ytri-kollr, 'Further or Outer Hill.' It is not connected with *gil*, a ravine.

Bealach Colluscard (Kilmuir) is interesting again as showing tautology, for Collu-scard means Pass of the Hill (kollr), N. *skardhr*. It is again repeated in Bealach na Sgairde in Portree, with somewhat ugly emphasis.

Armadale is Norse, meaning 'bay-dale.'

Skulamus (Strath) seems to be for Skúli's moss, while Strolamus must be for Stúrli's moss (for *ú* as *ó*, compare Knoydart, which has a liquid also).

Broadford is a modern name, not Norse.

Talisker, G. Tallasgar, N. T-hallr-sker, 'Sloping rock.'

Eist (Duirinish), a Chersonese, is from *hestr*, horse, that is, 'horse-shaped.' Otherwise, as in Eilean Heist, it really means 'Horse'-isle.

Greshornish (Duirinish), pronounced Gris-innis now usually, is for Grice or Pig Ness.

Rigg (Snizort) and Digg (G. Dìg) are respectively from Norse *hryggr*, ridge, and *dìk*, a ditch.

Duntulm is the *dùn* of the *hólmr*, islet.

Staffin, 'The Staff,' from N. *stafr*, a staff, applied to basaltic and other pillared rocks, as in Staffa (basalt isle) and Dunstafnage (Dun-staffynch, 1309), Dun-stafa-nes.

Loch Arkaig (Lochaber), river Arkaig, from Celtic root *arc*, dark, W. *erch*, dusky; Loch Arklet, Stirling.

Corpach, 'place of bodies.' Here, it is said, the bodies carried to Iona for burial rested to await sailing.

Banavie, Banvy (1461); compare Banff, Bamff, also Banba, an old name for Ireland, from *banbh, a pig*. For meaning, compare Mucrach and Muckerach (Kilmorack), Pres-Mucrach, *mucrach* meaning 'Place of Pigs.'

Fersit, Farset (Bleau), from obsolete *fearsaid*, sandbank at the mouth of a river, whence also Belfast.

Fassfern, G. Fasaidh-fearn, 'Abode or stead of the alders.'

Glen-quoich, Glen of the Cuaich river, the river of *cuachs* or bends. It is a common river name.

Loch Oich; Oich points to a Celtic Utaka, root *ut*, dread , 'awesome.'

Vinegar Hill, Gaick, is in Gaelic ' A Mhìn Choiseachd,' the easy walking.   The English is a fancy name.

Ettridge is for Eadar-dha-eas, ' Between two falls.'   Nessintullich, Essintullich (1645), is for ' Water-fall of the hillock.'   Phoines is for Fo 'n eas, ' Below the fall.'   So with Phoineas in Kiltarlity.

Coylum Bridge; Gaelic, Cuing' leum, ' Narrow leap,' which it is.

Achnacoichen (Rothiemurchus), ' Field of the Owls '; so in Lochaber—Achnacochine, in 1509 Auchancheithin.

Rothiemoon (Abernethy), G. Ràt a' mhòin, ' Rath or stead of the peat-moss.

Pityoulish, in Abernethy, older Pitgaldish, is Pictish in prefix, root, and termination (-ais). The root word is *geall*, pronounced like the word for ' promise.'   It is found in many river names : Geldie Burn, running into Upper Dee; Abergeldie; Innergeldie near Comrie; Innergelly in Fife (river Gelly); perhaps Lochgelly there; Glen-geoullie near Cawdor; Allt Gheallaidh at Dalnacardoch and Knockando.   The root is *geld*, as in Norse *kelda*, a well, Ger. *quelle*, already mentioned in connection with St Kilda. A shorter form of the root is found in G. *geal*, a leech, root *gel*, water.   Compare Welsh Abergele.

Granish (Duthil), G. Grèanais (Grèn-), for older Grànais, apparently from *gràin*, abhorrence; but likely Pictish, denoting 'rough place,' from the same root and stem. The place figures largely in Druid lore and writings on account of its stone circles, and is consequently called Grianais, 'Sun-place,' which does not agree with the modern pronunciation.

Aviemore, G. Agaidh-mhór; there is also Avinlochan, the Avie of the loch. Gallovie, as in G. Gealagaidh and present Blairgie, was writtetn in 1603 as Blairovey—both in Laggan. *Agaidh* may be Pictish; compare Welsh *ag*, cleft, opening, Gaelic *eag*.

Craigellachie, whence the war cry of the Grants, has its name from *eileach*, place of rocks, rock, old Gaelic *ail*, rock. It is a much be-bouldered and rock-ribbed bare hill.

Morile (Strathdearn), G. *Móir'l*, seems to stand for a Pictish Mor-ialon, 'Large clearing,' Welsh *ial*, open space. Hence, too, Balmoral.

Kyllachy, G. Coileachaigh, 'Place of moor cocks.'

The Cuigs of Strathdearn, or fifth parts, are famous: "Is fheàrr aon chóige' an Eireann na cóig chóige' an Strath-Eireann"—"Better is one fifth in Ireland than the five fifths in Strathdearn." The Irish fifth is a province, such as Ulster. The 'Cuigs' were—Cùig-na-fionndruinich ('Bronze Place,' perhaps a smith's place), Cùig-na(n)-scàlan (tents or huts), Cùig-na-sìth (fairy hill, near is the Sìdh-bheinn, the Schiphein of the charters), Cùig-na-fearn (alders), and, likely, Cùig-na-muille (mill).

Scaniport, 'Cleft of the Ferry,' over the Ness.

Foyers, old Foyer, for old Gaelic *fothir*, good land, evidently 'low-lying land,' as the land of Foyers along Lochness is.

Allt-saidh (Glen-Urquhart), 'Burn of the hound (female).'

Fort-Augustus, from William Augustus, Duke of Cumberland, so named by General Wade, circ. 1730.

Fort-William, the fort built at Auchintore (Bleaching-field) for William of Orange; also Maryburgh for the village, from Mary, his consort; then Gordonsburgh, from the dukes of Gordon, who disliked 'Orange'; and Duncans-burgh, on the 'passing' of the Gordons, from Sir Duncan Cameron of Fassfearn; and now finally settled as Fort-William.

Fort-George, built in 1748, takes its name from the King. The original Fort-George was the Castle of Inverness.

Essich, Essy in 1456, a locative of *easach*, water-fall stream, rapidly falling stream. The name exists in Strathbogie, Forfar, and Moray.

Castle Heather presents an interesting ' ghost name.' Further back it was Castle-leather, older Lathir, and we find the Lordship of Leffare (1456) applied to the district along the slope there. It comes from *leathair*, a side, found in Leathair nam Manach, at Beauly, ' Monks' Side of the Valley,' ' Monks' Hillside '—the Kilmorack district east of Breakachy Burn. In the west, we have An Leathair Mhorairneach and An Leathair Mhuileach—the coastland of Morvern and of Mull.

Culloden, Cullodyn in 1238, present Gaelic Cùil-fhodair, ' Fodder-nook,' by popular etymology. It really comes from *lodan*, a pool, and means ' Back of Pool,' or ' Nook of Pool.' As in many similar cases, there is quite a shower of ' cuils ' near Culloden, going over the Nairn valley, ending with Cuil-chuinneig, ' Nook of the wooden pail,' apparently. It was here that Prince Charles' staff was stationed before the battle.

Brochnain is for Bruach 'n-eidheinn, ' Ivy Bank.'

Tomnahuirich, Gaelic of 1690 Toim-ni-húrich, ' Hillock of the Yew-wood.' The Wardlaw MS. gives both Tomnihurich and Tom ni Fyrich. This last may account for the derivation of the name from Tom-na-fiodhraich, *fiodh-rach* being alleged to mean ' wood ' (A. Mackenzie in Inverness Field Club Trans., III., p. 11).

Erchless, a *quoad-sacra* parish, (H)erchelys in 1258, Ercles, 1403, Arcles, 1512, appears to stand for *air-glais*, On the Glass—the river Glass passes through the Mains of Erchless. Compare the neighbouring Urray from *Air-ráth*, On-fort or Repaired Fort, and Urquhart and Urchany of Beauly and Nairn (air-canach). The Gaelic is Air-ghlais.

Glen Affric takes its name, as does the loch, from the river Affric, which has the old female name Afric or Oirig (Euphemia), and which comes from *ath-breac*, somewhat-speckled, from *breac*, speckled, a trout. Here it was no doubt a water-nymph's name.

Glen-Convinth and Convent, which was an old parish, appears in old records as Conveth and Conway, and in Gaelic the name is Confhadh-aich, which, applied to the river, means ' noisy, stormy,' from *confhadh*, storm.

Lovat, older Loveth, seems a Pictish word (root *lu*, stem *lu-vo*, mud) translated into Gaelic as A' Mhor'oich, the sea-side plain or swamp.

Two districts of Inverness-shire have had their names discussed in detail, and both can be relied upon as much as any work done in this paper. The districts are Badenoch, which is considered in the Transactions of the Gaelic

Society of Inverness, Vol. XVI., pp. 148-97,
and Urquhart and Glenmoriston, the place-names
of which are fully discussed in Dr Mackay's
work, "Urquhart and Glenmoriston," pp. 571-
85.

BADENOCH:
ITS HISTORY, CLANS
AND PLACE-NAMES

MAP OF
BADENOCH
BY
R. GORDON of STRALOCH
1641–48.

BADENOCH:

ITS HISTORY, CLANS, AND PLACE-NAMES

THE LORDSHIP OF BADENOCH.

BADENOCH is one of the most interior districts of Scotland; it lies on the northern watershed of the mid Grampians, and the lofty ridge of the Monadhlia range forms its northern boundary, while its western border runs along the centre of the historic Drum-Alban. Even on its eastern side the mountains seem to have threatened to run a barrier across, for Craigellachie thrusts its huge nose forward into a valley already narrowed by the massive form of the Ord Bain and the range of hills behind it. This land of mountains is intersected by the river Spey, which runs midway between the two parallel ranges of the Grampians and the

Monadhlia, taking its rise, however, at the ridge
of Drum-Alban.   Badenoch, as a habitable
land, is the valley of the Spey and the glens that
run off from it.   The vast bulk of the district is
simply mountain.

In shape, the district of Badenoch is
rectangular, with east-north-easterly trend, its
length averaging about thirty-two miles, and its
breadth some seventeen miles.   Its length along
the line of the Spey is thirty-six miles, the river
itself flowing some 35 miles of the first part of
its course through Badenoch.   The area of
Badenoch is, according to the Ordnance Survey,
551 square miles, that is, close on three hundred
and fifty-three thousand acres.   The lowest
level in the district is 700 feet; Kingussie, the
" capital," is 740 feet above sea-level, and
Loch Spey is 1142 feet.   The highest peak is
4149 feet high, a shoulder of the Braeriach
ridge, which is itself outside Badenoch by about
a mile, and Ben Macdui by two miles.   Mountains and rivers, rugged rocks and narrow glens,
with one large medial valley fringed with cultivation—that is Badenoch.   It is still well
wooded, though nothing to what it once must
have been.   The lower ground at one time must
have been completely covered by wood, which
spread away into the vales and glens; for we find
on lofty plateaux and hill sides the marks of
early cultivation, the ridges and the rigs or

feannagan, showing that the lower ground was not very available for crops on account of the forest, which, moreover, was full of wild beasts, notably the wolf and the boar.   Cultivation, therefore, ran mostly along the outer fringe of this huge wood, continually encroaching on it as generation succeeded generation.

The bogs yield abundant remains of the once magnificent forest that covered hillside and glen, and the charred logs prove that fire was the chief agent of destruction.   The tradition of the country has it that the wicked Queen Mary set fire to the old Badenoch forest.   She felt offended at her husband's pride in the great forest—he had asked once on his home return how his forests were before he asked about her. So she came north, took her station on the top of Sron-na-Bàruinn—the Queen's Ness—above Glenfeshie, and there gave orders to set the woods on fire.   And her orders were obeyed. The Badenoch forest was set burning, and the Queen, Nero-like, enjoyed the blaze from her point of vantage.[1]   But many glens and nooks escaped, and Rothiemurchus was left practically intact.   The Sutherlandshire version of the story is different and more mythic.   The King of Lochlann was envious of the great woods of Scotland; the pine forests especially roused his jealous ire.   So he sent his *muime*—it must

1 Queen Mary ravaged Huntly's lands, and burnt the woods.

have been—a witch and a monster, whose name was Dubh-Ghiubhais, and she set the forests on fire in the north. She kept herself aloft among the clouds, and rained down fire on the woods, which burnt on with alarming rapidity. People tried to get at the witch, but she never showed herself, but kept herself enveloped in a cloud of smoke. When she had burned as far as Badenoch, a clever man of that district devised a plan for compassing her destruction. He gathered together cattle of all kinds and their young; then he separated the lambs from the sheep, the calves from the cows, and the young generally from their dams; then such a noise of bleating, lowing, neighing, and general Babel arose to the heaven that Dubh-Ghiubhais popped her head out of the cloud to see what was wrong. This was the moment for action. The Badenoch man was ready for it; he had his gun loaded with the orthodox sixpence; he fired, and down came the Dubh-Ghiubhais, a lifeless lump! So a part of the great Caledonian forest was saved among the Grampian hills.

Modern Badenoch comprises the parishes of Laggan, Kingussie and Insh, and Alvie; but the old Lordship of Badenoch was too aristocratic to do without having a detached portion some-where else. Consequently we find that Kincar-dine parish, now part of Abernethy, was part of the Lordship of Badenoch even later than

1606, when Huntly excambed it with John of Freuchie for lands in Glenlivet. Kincardine was always included in the sixty davachs that made up the land of Badenoch. The Barony of Glencarnie in Duthil—from Aviemore to Garten and northward to Inverlaidnan—was seemingly attached to the Lordship of Badenoch for a time, and so were the davachs of Tullochgorum, Curr, and Clurie, further down the Spey, excambed by Huntly in 1491 with John of Freuchie. On the other hand, Rothiemurchus was never a part of Badenoch, though some have maintained that it was. The six davachs of Rothiemurchus belonged to the Bishops of Moray, and at times they feued the whole of Rothiemurchus to some powerful person, as to the Wolf of Badenoch in 1383, and to Alexander Keyr Mackintosh in 1464, in whose family it was held till 1539, when it passed into the hands of the Gordons, and from them to the Grants.

Badenoch does not appear in early Scottish history; till the 13th century, we never hear of it by name nor of anything that took place within its confines. True, Skene, in his *Celtic Scotland*, definitely states that the battle of Monitcarno was fought here in 729. This battle took place between Angus, King of Fortrenn, and Nectan, the ex-king of the Picts, and in it the latter was defeated, and Angus

13

shortly afterwards established himself on the Pictish throne. We are told that the scene of the battle was "Monitcarno juxta stagnum Loogdae"—Monadh-carnach by the side of Loch Loogdae. Adamnan also mentions Loch-dae, which Columba falls in with while going over Drum Alban. Skene says that Loch Insh —the lake of the island—is a secondary name, and that it must have originally been called Lochdae, that the hills behind it enclose the valley of Glencarnie, and that Dunachton, by the side of Loch Insh, is named Nectan's fort af)ter King Nectan. Unfortunately this view is wrong, and Badenoch must give up any claim to be the scene of the battle of Monadh-carno; Lochdae is now identified with Lochy, and Glen-carnie is in Duthil. But Dunachton is certainly Nectan's fort; whether the Nectan meant was the celebrated Pictish King may be doubted. Curiously, local tradition holds strongly that a battle was fought by the side of Loch Insh, but the defeated leader was King Harold, whose grave is on the side of Craig Righ Harailt.

From 729, we jump at once to 1229, exactly five hundred years, and about that date we find that Walter Cumyn is feudal proprietor of Badenoch, for he makes terms with the Bishop of Moray in regard to the church lands and to the " natives " or bondsmen in the district. It has been supposed that Walter Cumyn came into

the possession of Badenoch by the forfeiture and
death of Gillescop, a man who committed some
atrocities in 1228—such as burning the
(wooden) forts in the province of Moray, and
setting fire to a large part of the town of Inverness.   William Cumyn, Earl of Buchan, the
justiciar, was intrusted with the .protection of
Moray, and in 1229 Gillescop and his two sons
were slain.   Thereafter we find Walter Cumyn
in possession of Badenoch and Kincardine, and
it is a fair inference that Gillespie was his predecessor in the lordship of Badenoch.   The
Cummings were a Norman family; they came
over with the Conqueror, and it is asserted that
they were nearly related to him by marriage.
In 1068, we hear of one of them being governor
or earl of Northumberland, and the name is
common in English charters of the 12th century,
in the early part of which they appear in Scotland; they were in great favour with the
Normanising David, and with William after him,
filling offices of chancellors and justiciars under
them.   William Cumyn, about the year 1210,
married Marjory, heiress of the Earldom of
Buchan, and thus became the successor of the
old Celtic Mormaers of that district under the
title of Earl of Buchan.   His son Walter
obtained the lordship of Badenoch, as we saw,
and, a year or two after, he became Earl of
Menteith by marrying the heiress, the Countess

of Menteith. He still kept the lands of
Badenoch, for, in 1234, we find him, as Earl of
Menteith, settling a quarrel with the Bishop of
Moray over the Church lands of Kincardine.
Walter was a potent factor in Scottish politics,
and in the minority of Alexander III. acted
patriotically as leader against the pro-English
party. He died in 1257 without issue. John
Comyn, his nephew, son of Richard, succeeded
him in Badenoch; he was head of the whole
family of Comyn, and possessed much property,
though simply entitled Lord of Badenoch. The
Comyns at that time were at the height of their
power; they could muster at least two earls, the
powerful Lord of Badenoch, and thirty belted
knights. Comyn of Badenoch was a prince,
though not in name, making treaties and kings.
John Comyn, called the Red, died in 1274, and
was succeeded by his son, John Comyn, the
Black, and in the troubles about the kingly
succession, at the end of the century, he was
known as John de Badenoch, senior, to distin-
guish him from his son John, the Red Comyn,
the regent, Baliol's nephew, and claimant to
the throne, whom Bruce killed under circumstances of treachery at Dumfries, in 1306.
Then followed the fall and forfeiture of the
Comyns, and the lordship of Badenoch was
given, about 1313—included in the Earldom of

Moray—to Thomas Randolph, Bruce's right-hand friend.

The Cummings have left an ill name behind them in Badenoch for rapacity and cruelty.

Their treachery has passed into a proverb—

"Fhad bhitheas craobh 's a choill
Bithidh foill 'sna Cuiminich."

Which is equally smart in its English form—

"While in the wood there is a tree
A Cumming will deceitful be."

It is in connection with displacing the old proprietors—the Shaws and Mackintoshes—that the ill repute of the Cummings was really gained. But the particular cases which tradition remembers are mythical in the extreme; yet there is something in the traditions. There is a remembrance that these Cummings were the first feudal lords of Badenoch; until their time the Gaelic Tuath that dwelt in Badenoch had lived under their old tribal customs, with their *tòiseachs*, their *airés*, and their *saor* and *daor* occupiers of land. The newcomers, with their charters, their titles, and their new exactions over and above the old Tuath tributes and dues, must have been first objects of wonder, and then of disgust. The authority which the Cummings exerted over the native inhabitants must often have been in abeyance, and their rents more a matter of name than reality. However, by making it the interest of the chiefs to side with them, and by granting them charters, these initial difficulties were got over in a century or two. It was under this feudalising process that the system of clans, as now known, was developed.

Earl Randolph died in 1332, and his two sons were successively Earls of Moray, the second dying in 1346 without issue, when "Black Agnes," Countess of Dunbar, succeeded to the vast estates. The Earldom of Moray, exclusive of Badenoch and Lochaber, was renewed to her son in 1372.[1] Meanwhile, in 1371 Alexander Stewart, King Robert's son, was made Lord of Badenoch by his father, as also Earl of Buchan; and in 1387 he became Earl of Ross through his marriage with the Countess Euphame. His power was therefore immense; he was the King's lieutenant in the North (*locum*

---

[1] Sir W. Fraser, in his "History of the Grants," says:—"After the forfeiture of the Comyns, Badenoch formed a part of the earldom of Moray, conferred on Sir Thomas Randolph. In 1338, however, it was held by the Earl of Ross, and in 1372, while granting the Earldom of Moray to John Dunbar, King Robert II. specially excepted Lochaber and Badenoch." Sir W. Fraser's authority for saying that Badenoch was in the possession of the Earl of Ross must be the charter of 1338 granting Kinrara and Dalnavert to Melmoran of Glencharny; but a careful reading of that document shows that the Earl of Ross was not superior of Badenoch, for he speaks of the services due by him to the "Lord superior of Badenoch." Besides, in 1467, when Huntly was Lord of Badenoch, we find the Earl of Ross still possessing lands there, viz., Invermarkie, which he gives to Cawdor as part of his daughter's dowry.

tenens in borealibus partibus regni) ; but such
was the turbulence and ferocity of his character
that he was called the "Wolf of Badenoch."
He is still remembered in the traditions of the
country as "Alastair Mór Mac an Righ"—
Alexander the Big, Son of the King—a title
which is recorded also in Maurice Buchanan's
writings (A.D. 1461, Book of Pluscarden), who
says that the wild Scots *(Scotis silvestribus)*
called him "Alitstar More Makin Re." Naturally enough he gets confused with his famous
namesake of Macedon, also Alastair Mór, but the
more accurate of tradition-mongers differentiate
them easily, for they call Alexander the Great
"Alastair Uabh'rach, Mac Righ Philip"—Alexander the Proud, son of King Philip." This
epithet of *uabh'rach* or *uaibhreach* appears as
applied to Alexander the Great in that beautiful
mediæval Gaelic poem that begins—

"Ceathrar do bhi air uaigh an fhir
Feart Alaxandair Uaibhrigh :
Ro chansat briathra cen bhréicc
Os cionn na flatha ó Fhinnghréicc."

Translated—

Four men were at a hero's grave—
The tomb of Alexander the Proud;
Words they spake without lies
Over the chief from beauteous Greek-land.[1]

1 See "Dean of Lismore," p. 84; Ranald Macdonald's Collection, p. 133, and *Highland Monthly*, II., p. 376. (The
above is from a British Museum MS.).

The Wolf of Badenoch's dealings with his inferiors in his lordship are not known; but that he allowed lawlessness to abound may be inferred from the feuds that produced the Battle of Invernahavon (circ. 1386), and culminated in the remarkable conflict on the North Inch of Perth in 1396. We are not in much doubt as to his conduct morally and ecclesiastically. He had five natural-born sons—Alexander, Earl of Mar, Andrew, Walter, James, and Duncan—a regular Wolf's brood for sanguinary embroilments. He had a chronic quarrel with Alexander Bur, Bishop of Moray, which culminated in the burning of Elgin Cathedral in 1390. But in nearly every case the Bishop, by the terrors of the Curse of Rome, gained his point. In 1380, the Wolf cited the Bishop to appear before him at the Standing Stones of the Rathe of Easter Kingussie (apud le *standand stanys* de le Rathe de Kyngucy estir) on the 10th October, to show his titles to the lands held in the Wolf's lordship of Badenoch, viz., the lands of Logachnacheny (Laggan), Ardinche (Balnespick, &c.), Kingucy, the lands of the Chapels of Rate and Nachtan, Kyncardyn, and also Gartinengally. The Bishop protested, at a court held at Inverness, against the citation, and urged that the said lands were held of the King direct. But the Wolf held his court on the 10th October : the Bishop standing " extra curiam "—outside the court, *i.e.*, the Standing Stones—renewed his protest, but to no purpose. But upon the next day before dinner, and in the great chamber behind the hall in the Castle of Ruthven, the Wolf annulled the proceedings of the previous day, and gave the rolls of Court to the Bishop's notary, who certified that he put them in a large fire lighted in the said chamber, which consumed them. In 1381, the Wolf formally quits claims on the above-mentioned church lands, but in 1383 the Bishop granted him the wide domain of Rothiemurchus—" Ratmorchus, viz., sex davatas terre quas habemus in Strathspe et le Badenach "—six *davochs* of land it was. The later quarrels of the Wolf and the Bishop are notorious in Scotch History : the Wolf seized the Bishop's lands, and was excommunicated, in return for which he burnt, in 1390, the towns of Forres and Elgin, with the Church of St Giles, the maison dieu, the Cathedral, and 18 houses of the canons. For this he had to do penance in the Blackfriar's Church at Perth. He died in 1394, and is buried in Dunkeld, where a handsome tomb and effigy of him exist.

As the Wolf left no legitimate issue, some think the Lordship of Badenoch at once reverted to the Crown, for we hear no more of it till it was granted to Huntly in 1451. On this point Sir W. Fraser says :—" The Lordship of Badenoch was bestowed by King Robert II. upon

his son, the 'Wolf of Badenoch,' in 1371, and
should have reverted to the Crown on the Lord
of Badenoch's death in 1394.   But there is no
evidence in the Exchequer Rolls, or elsewhere,
of any such reversion, and Badenoch seems to
have been retained in possession by the Wolf of
Badenoch's eldest son, who became Earl of Mar.
. . . Alexander, Earl of Mar, and his father,
were therefore the successors of the Comyns as
Lords of Badenoch.''

The Lordship of Badenoch was finally
granted to Alexander, Earl of Huntly, by James
II., by charter dated 28th April, 1451, not in
recompense for his services at the Battle of
Brechin, as is generally stated, but upwards of a
year before that event.   The great family of
Gordon and Huntly originally came from near
the Borders.   They obtained their name of
Gordon from the lands of Gordon, now a parish
and village in the west of the Merse, S.W.
Berwickshire.   There, also, was the quondam
hamlet of Huntly, a name now represented there
only by the farm called Huntlywood.   The
parish gave the family name of Gordon, and the
hamlet of Huntly gave the title of Earl or
Marquess of Huntly.   Sir Adam de Gordon was
one of Bruce's supporters, and after the forfeiture of the Earl of Athole he got the lordship
of Strathbogie, with all its appurtenances, in
Aberdeenshire and Banff.   The direct male

Gordon line ended with Sir Adam's great-grand-
son and namesake, who fell at the battle of
Homildon Hill in 1402, leaving a daughter
Elizabeth, who married Alexander Seaton,
second son of Sir W. Seaton of Winton.   Her
son Alexander assumed the name of Gordon,
and was created Earl of Huntly in 1449.   His
son George was Lord Chancellor, founded
Gordon Castle, and created the Priory of
Kingussie (Shaw's *Moray*).   The Gordons were
so pre-eminent in Northern politics that their
head was nicknamed "Cock of the North."
In 1599, Huntly was created a Marquis, and in
1684 the title was advanced to that of Duke of
Gordon.   George, the fifth and last Duke of
Gordon, died in 1836, when the property passed
into the possession of the Duke of Richmond and
Lennox, as heir of entail, in whose person the
title of Duke of Gordon was again revived in
1786, the full title being now Duke of Richmond
and Gordon.

Save the Church lands, all the property in
Badenoch belonged to Huntly either as superior
or actual proprietor.   The Earl of Ross
possessed lands in Badenoch under the lord
superior in 1338, which he granted to Malmoran
of Glencarnie : the lands were Dalnavert and
Kinrara, and the grant is confirmed about 1440,
while in 1467 we find the Earl of Ross again
granting the adjoining lands of Invermarkie to

the Thane of Cawdor, in whose name they
appear till the seventeenth century, when Invereshie gets possession of them.   The Laird of
Grant, besides Delfour, which he had for three
centuries, also held the Church lands of Laggan
and Insh, that is, "Logane, Ardinche, Bally-
naspy," as it is stated in 1541, and he is in
possession of them for part of the seventeenth
century.   Mackintosh of Mackintosh has in feu
from Huntly in the sixteenth century the lands
of Benchar, Clune, Kincraig, and Dunachton,
with Rait, Kinrara, and Dalnavert.   The only
other proprietor or feuar besides these existing
in the 16th century seems to have been James
Mackintosh of Gask.   The Macphersons, for
instance, including Andrew *in* Cluny, who
signed for Huntly the "Clan Farsons Band." of
1591, are all tenants merely.   We are very
fortunate in possessing the Huntly rental of
Badenoch for the year 1603.   Mackintosh appears as feuar for the lands above mentioned,
and there are two wadsetters—Gask and Strone,
both Mackintoshes.   The 17th century sees
quite a revolution in landholding in Badenoch,
for during its course Huntly has liberally granted
feus, and the proprietors are accordingly very
numerous.   Besides Huntly, Mackintosh, and
Grant of Grant, we find some twenty feus or
estates possessed by Macphersons; there was a
Macpherson of Ardbrylach, Balchroan, Benchar,

(in) Blarach, Breakachie, Clune, Cluny, Corranach, Crathie, Dalraddy, Delfour, Etteridge, Gasklyne, Gellovie, Invereshie, Invernahaven (Inverallochie), Invertromie, Nuid, Phones, and Pitchirn. There was a Mackintosh of Balnespick, Benchar, Delfour, Gask, Kinrara, Lynwilg, Rait and Strone—eight in all. Four other names appear once each besides these during the century—Maclean, Gordon of Buckie, Macqueen, and Macdonald. The total valuation of Badenoch in 1644 was £11,527 Scots, in 1691 £6523, and in 1789 it was £7124, with only seven proprietors—Duke of Gordon, Mackintosh, Cluny, Invereshie, Belleville, Grant of Grant (Delfour), and Major Gordon (Invertromie). The "wee lairdies" of the previous two centuries were swallowed up in the estates of the first five of these big proprietors, who still hold large estates in Badenoch, the Duke of Gordon being represented by the Duke of Richmond since 1836. Only one or two other proprietors on any large scale have come in since—Baillie of Dochfour, Sir John Ramsden, and, we may add, Macpherson of Glentruim. The valuation roll for 1889-90 shows a rental of £36,165 11s 7d sterling.

CLAN CHATTAN.

In the above section we discussed the political history of Badenoch, under the title of the "Lordship of Badenoch," and in this section we intend to deal with the history of the native population of that district. Badenoch was the principal seat of the famous and powerful Clan Chattan. The territory held by this clan, however, was far from being confined to Badenoch; for at the acme of their power in the 15th century, Clan Chattan stretched across mid Inverness-shire, almost from sea to sea—from the Inverness Firth to near the end of Loch-eil, that is, from Petty right along through Strathnairn, Strathdearn, and Badenoch to Brae-Lochaber, with a large overflow through Rothiemurchus into Braemar, which was the seat of the Farquharsons, who are descendants of the Shaws or Mackintoshes of Rothiemurchus. The Clan Chattan were the inhabitants of this vast extent of territory, but the ownership or superiority of the land was not theirs or their chiefs', and the leading landlords they had to deal with were the two powerful Earls of Huntly and Moray. From them, as superiors, Mackintosh, chief of Clan Chattan, held stretches of land here and there over the area populated by the clan, and his tribesmen were tacksmen or feu-holders of the rest, as the case might be, under Moray or Huntly.   It was rather an anomalous position for a great Highland chief, and one often difficult to maintain.   Major (1521) describes the position, territorially and otherwise, of the Clans Chattan and Cameron in words which may be thus translated :—" These tribes are kinsmen, holding little in lordships, but following one head of their race (caput progenei—ceann cinnidh) as chief, with their friends and dependents."   The lordships were held, alas! by foreigners to them in race and blood.

The Clan Chattan were the native Celtic inhabitants of Badenoch.   There are traditional indications that they came from the west—from Lochaber, where the MS. histories place the old Clan Chattan lands.   The same authorities record that, for instance, the Macbeans came from Lochaber in the 14th century, " after slaying the Red Comyn's captain of Inverlochy," and put themselves under the protection of Mackintosh; and this is supported by the tradition still preserved among the Rothiemurchus Macbeans, whose ancestor, Bean Cameron, had to fly Lochaber owing to a quarrel and slaughter arising from the exaction of the " bó ursainn," or probate duty of the time.   It may be too bold to connect this eastern movement of Clan Chattan with the advancing tide of Scotic conquest in the 8th century, whereby the Pictish

kingdoms and the Pictish language were overthrown. That the Picts inhabited Badenoch is
undoubted : the place names amply prove that,
for we meet with such test prefixes as Pet
(Pitowrie, Pictchirn, Pitmean) and Aber (Aberarder), and other difficulties of topography un-
explainable by the Gaelic language. As in most
of Scotland, we have doubtless to deal, first,
with a pre-Celtic race or races, possibly leaving
remnants of its tongue in such a river name as
Feshie, then the Pictish or Caledonian race of
Celtic extraction, and, lastly, the Gaelic race
who imposed their language and rule upon the
previous peoples. The clan traditions are supported in the matter of a western origin for the
Clan Chattan by the genealogies given in the
Edinburgh 1467 MS., which deduces the chief
line from Ferchar Fota, King of Dalriada, in the
7th century.

The name Cattan, like everything connected
with the early history of this clan, is obscure,
and has, in like manner, given rise to many
absurd stories and theories. As a matter of
course, the classical geography of Europe has
been ransacked, and there, in Germany, was a
people called Chatti, which was taken as pronounced Catti; but the *ch* stands for a sound like
that in lo*ch*. The name appears as Hesse for
Hätti. It was never *Katti*, be it remembered.
Yet the Catti are brought from Germany to

Sutherlandshire, which in Gaelic is Cataibh, older Cataib—a name supposed thus to be derived from the Catti. Cataibh is merely the dative plural of *cat* (a cat), just as Gallaibh (Caithness) is the same case of Gall (a stranger, Norseman). The Cat men dwelt in Sutherlandshire; why they were called the Cats is not known. Clan Chattan is often said to be originally from Sutherland, but, beyond the similarity of name, there is no shadow of evidence for the assertion. Others again, like Mr Elton, see in the name Catan, which means, undoubtedly, " little cat," relics of totemism; this means neither more nor less than that the pre-Christian Clan Chattan worshipped the cat, from whom, as divine ancestor, they deemed themselves descended. We might similarly argue that the Mathesons—Mac ¡Mhath-ghamhuin or Son of the Bear—were a " bear " tribe, a fact which shows how unstable is the foundation on which this theory is built. In fact, animal names for men were quite common in early times. The favourite theory—and one countenanced by the genealogies—connects the Clan Chattan, like so many other clans, with a church-derived name. The ancestor from whom they are represented as deriving their name is Gillicattan Mór, who lived in the 11th century. His name signifies Servant of Catan,

14

that is, of St Catan; for people were named after saints, not directly, but by means of the prefixes Gille and Maol. At least, that was the early and more reverent practice. That there was a St Catan is evidenced by such place names as Kilchattan (in Bute and Lung), with dedication of churches at Gigha and Colonsay. His date is given as 710, but really nothing is known of him. This is probably the best explanation of the name, though the possibility of the clan being named after some powerful chief called Catan must not be overlooked. The crest of the cat is late, and merely a piece of mild heraldic punning.

It is only about or after 1400 that we come on anything like firm historical ground in the genealogy and story of our chief Highland clans. This is true of the Grants and the Camerons, and especially true of the Clan Chattan. Everything before that is uncertainty and fable. The earliest mention of Clan Chattan—and it is not contemporary but fifty years later—is in connection with the fight at the North Inch of Perth in 1396, and here historians are all at sixes and sevens as to who the contending parties really were. The battle of Invernahavon (1386?) and the fight at Clachnaharry (1454) are mere traditions, and the battle in 1429 between Clan Chattan and Clan Chameron, in which the former nearly annihilated the latter, is recorded by a writer nearly a century later (1521). In fact, the first certain contemporary date is that of Mackintosh's charter in 1466 from the Lord of the Isles, where he is designated Duncan Mac-kintosh, "capitanus de Clan Chattan," and next year as "chief and captain" of Clan Chattan, in a bond with Lord Forbes. Henceforward, Clan Chattan is a common name in public history and private documents. It comprised in the period of its comparative unity (circ. 1400-1600) some sixteen tribes or septs: these were the Mackintoshes, Macphersons, Davidsons, Cattanachs, Macbeans, Macphails, Shaws, Farquharsons, Macgillivrays, Macleans of Doch-garroch, Smiths, Macqueens, Gillanders, Clarks, &c. Of this confederation, Mackintosh was for, at least, two centuries "captain and chief," as all documents, public and private, testify. These two centuries (circ. 1400 to 1600) form the only period in which we see, under the light of history, the Highland clans in their full development.

The 17th century made sad havoc in the unity of Clan Chattan. Huntly, ever an enemy to Mackintosh, "banded" in 1591 the Mac-phersons to his own person, and, by freely granting charters to them, made them independent, and detached them from Mackintosh. Macpherson of Cluny claimed to be head of the Macphersons, and in 1673 styled himself

" Duncan M^cpherson of Cluney for himself, and
taking burden upon him for the heall name of
M^cphersons and some others called old Clan-
chattan as cheeffe and principall man thereoff,"
in a bond with Lord Macdonell of Morar.   In
support of this claim, the Macphersons appealed
to the old genealogies, which represented Mackintosh as getting the Clan Chattan lands by
marriage with the heiress in 1291, and which
further showed that Cluny was the heir male
descendant of the old Clan Chattan chiefs.   The
case in its solemn absurdity of appeal to
genealogies reminds one of a like appeal placed
before the Pope in the claims of King Edward
upon the throne of Scotland.   He claimed the
Scottish crown as the direct successor of Brutus
and Albanactus, who lived in Trojan times,
every link of genealogy being given, while the
Scots repelled this by declaring that they were
descended from Gathelus husband of Scota,
daughter of the Mosaic King of Egypt; and here,
too, all the genealogical links could have been
given.   Neither doubted the genuineness of
each others' genealogies!   So with the Mackin-
tosh-Macpherson controversy about the chiefship of Clan Chattan.   They each accept each
others' genealogies without suspicion or demur.
And yet the manufacture of these and 'like
genealogies was an accomplished art with Gaelic
seanachies whether Irish or Scottish.   We even

see it going on under our very eyes. The early
chiefs of Lochiel are the *de Cambruns* of the
13th and 14th century records—lists and other
documents — impressed into the Cameron
genealogy, which is doubtless correctly given in
the 1467 MS.   Again, the Macpherson
genealogy in the Douglas Baronage is in several
cases drawn from charters granted to wholly
different families. Dormund Macpherson, 12th
chief, gets a charter under the great seal from
James IV.; but the charter turns out to be one
granted to a Dormund M'Pherson in the Lordship of Menteith, not of Badenoch! John, 14th
of Cluny, who " was with the Earl of Huntly at
the battle of Glenlivet," as the veracious
chronicler says, to add a touch of realism to his
bald genealogical account, gets a charter of the
lands of Tullich, &c., lands which lie in Strathnairn, and he turns out to be a scion of the well-
known family of Macphersons of Brin!
Similarly John, 15th of Cluny, is son of the
foregoing John of Brin; and Ewen, 16th of
Cluny, who gets a charter in 1623 of the lands
of Tullich, &c., is a cousin of Brin. Donald,
17th of Cluny, who gets a charter in 1643, turns
out to be Donald Macpherson of Nuid. And all
this time another and a correct genealogy of the
Cluny family had been drawn up by Sir Æneas
Macpherson towards the end of the 17th century, which must surely have been known to the

writer.[1] During all the period of 14th to 16th chief here given, there was only one man in Cluny, and his name was Andrew Macpherson, son of Ewen.

The name Mackintosh signifies the son of the *tòiseach* or chief, which is Latinised by O'. Flaherty as "capitaneus seu praecipuus dux." The Book of Deer makes the relationship of *tòiseach* to other dignitaries quite plain. There is first the King; under him are the *mormaers* or stewards of the great provinces of Scotland, such as Buchan, Marr, and Moray; and next comes the *tòiseach* or chief of the clan in a particular district. The two clans in the Book of Deer are those of Canan and Morgan, each with a *tòiseach*. This word is represented oftenest in English in old documents by *thane*, which, indeed, represents it with fair accuracy. *Tòiseach* is the true Gaelic word for "chief," but it is now obsolete, and there is now no true equivalent of the word "chief" in the language at all. And here it may be pointed out that the word chief itself was not at once adopted or adapted for this particular meaning of chief of a Highland clan. As we saw, the word at first employed was "captain," then "captain and chief," "captain, chief, and principal man," "chief and principal," &c.,

---

1 See Mr Fraser-Mackintosh's *Dunachton*, pp. 46-49, for a full *exposé* of this remarkable piece of manufacture.

the idea finally settling down as fully represented
by the word " chief " in the 16th century.
Skene's attempt to argue that captain denoted a
leader temporarily adopted, leading the clan for
another, or usurping the power of another,
while chief denoted a hereditary office, is con-
demned by his own evidence, and by the weight
of facts.   Besides, words do not suddenly spring
into technical meanings, nor could chief acquire
the definite meaning applicable to Highland
chiefship, but by length of time and usage for
this purpose.   Hence arose the uncertainty of
the early terms applied to the novel idea presented by Highland clans.   The word *clan* itself
appears first in literature in connection with
Clan Chattan, or rather Clan Qwhewyl, at the
North Inch of Perth, where Wyntown speaks of
" Clannys two."   The Gaelic word *clan* had to
be borrowed for want of a native English term;
why should we then wonder at the idea of
tòiseach being rendered first by captain, and
latterly by chief?

The Mackintosh genealogies, dating from the
17th century, represent the family as descended
from Macduff, *thane* of Fife, as they and Fordun
call him.   Shaw Macduff, the second son of
Duncan, fifth Earl of Fife, who died in 1154, in
an expedition against the people of Moray in
1160, distinguished himself, and received from
the King lands in Petty, and the custody of

Inverness Castle. Here he was locally known
as Shaw Mac an Tòiseich, "Shaw, the son of
the Thane." He died in 1179, and was succeeded by (2) Shaw, whose son was (3)
Ferchard, whose nephew was (4) Shaw, whose
son was (5) Ferchard, whose son was (6) Angus,
who in 1291 married Eva, heiress of Clan
Chattan, and thus got the Clan's lands in
Lochaber. So far the genealogy. It is a pretty
story, but it sadly lacks one thing—verisimili-
tude. Macduff was not *tòiseach* of Fife. In
the Book of Deer he is called *comes*, the then
Gaelic of which was *mormaer*, now *moirear*.
Shaw Macduff would infallibly, as son of the
Earl of Fife, have been called Mac Mhoireir.
With those who support this Macduff genealogy,
no argument need be held; like the humorist of
a past generation, one would, however, like to
examine their bumps. The statement that the
Mackintoshes were hereditary constables of
Inverness Castle is totally baseless and false.
At the dates indicated (12th century) we believe
that the Mackintoshes had not penetrated so far
north as Petty or Inverness, and that we should
look to Badenoch as their place of origin, and
their abode at this time. Unfortunately documents in regard to the early history of Badenoch
are rare, but an entry or two in the Registrum
of Moray Diocese may help us. In 1234,
Walter Comyn, Earl of Monteith, comes to an

agreement with the Bishop of Moray, in regard
to Kincardine, and Fercard, son of Seth, is a
witness, and in the very next document, also
one of Walter Comyn's, of the same date, appears a witness called Fercard " Senescalli de
Badenoch," that is " steward of Badenoch."
We are quite justified in regarding him as the
person mentioned in the previous document as
Fercard, son of Seth. Now, one translation of
tòiseach is steward or seneschal—the person in
power next the *mormaer* or earl. We may,
therefore, conclude that this Ferchard was
known in Gaelic as Ferchard *Tòiseach*. Similarly
in 1440 we meet with Malcolm Mackintosh, chief
of the clan, as " ballivus de Badenoch," a title
of equal import as that of seneschal. We
should then say that the Mackintoshes derived
their name from being toiseachs of Badenoch, the
head of the old Celtic clan being now under the
new non-Celtic mormaer or earl Walter Comyn.
The ease with which the name Mackintosh might
arise in any place where a clan and its *tòiseach*
existed explains how we meet with Mackintoshes, for instance, in Perthshire, who do not
belong to the Clan Chattan. Thus there were
Mackintoshes of Glentilt, which was held as an
old thanage, and whose history as such is well
known. Similarly we may infer that the Mackintoshes of Monivaird were descendants of the
old local Toiseachs or Thanes. The Mackintosh

genealogists have of course annexed them to the Clan Chattan stock with the utmost ease and success.   In 1456, John of the Isles granted to Somerled, his armour bearer, a davoch of the lands of Glennevis, with *toiseachdorship* of most of his other lands there, and in 1552 this grant is renewed by Huntly to "dilecto nostro Donaldo MacAlister M'Toschd," that is, Donald, son of Alister, son of Somerled, the toiseach or bailif, named in 1456.   This shows how easily the name could have arisen.

Skene, while unceremoniously brushing aside the Macduff genealogy, advances hypothetically a different account of the origin of the Mackintoshes.   In 1382, the Lord of Badenoch is asked to restrain Farchard Mac-Toschy and his adherents from disturbing the Bishop of Aberdeen and his tenants in the land of Brass or Birse, and to oblige him to prosecute his claim by form of law.   Skene thinks that Farchard, whom he finds in the 1467 MS. as one of the "old" Mackintoshes, was descended from the old thanes of Brass, and that hence arose his name and his claim.   Being a vassal of the Wolf's, he was a Badenoch man too. Rothiemurchus was a thanage, and the con-nection of the Mackintoshes with it was always close.   Alexander Keir Mackintosh obtained the feudal rights to Rothiemurchus in 1464, and a few years later he styles himself "Thane of

Rothiemurchus.'' Skene then suggests that Birse and Rothiemurchus might have anciently been in the hands of the same *tòiseach* or thane, and that from him the Mackintoshes got their name. We have suggested that the name arose with Ferchard, son of Seth or Shaw, who was *tòiseach* under the Earl Walter Comyn in 1234, and his name appears in the 1467 MS. genealogy as well as in the Mackintosh genealogies.

That a revolution took place in the affairs of Clan Chattan, with the overthrow or extrusion of the direct line of chiefs, in the half century that extends from about 1386 to 1436, is clear from two sources—first, from the 1467 MS., and, second, from the Mackintosh history. The latter acknowledges that Ferquhard, 9th chief, was deposed from his position, which was given to his uncle Malcolm. The reason why he had to retire was, it is said, the clan's dissatisfaction with his way of managing affairs; but the matter is glossed over in the history in a most unsatisfactory manner. If this was the Ferchard mentioned in 1382 as giving trouble to the Bishop of Aberdeen, it is most unlikely that he was an incapable man; in fact, he must have been quite the opposite. He is doubtless the same person, for he is given also in the 1467 MS. genealogy. But further confusion exists in the Mackintosh account. Malcolm, 10th Mackintosh, who dies in 1457, is grandson through William 7th (died

1368) of Angus who married Eva in 1291, the
three generations thus lasting as chiefs from
1274 to 1457, some 183 years! Malcolm was
the son of William's old age, and his brother,
Lachlan 8th, was too old to take part in the
North Inch fight in 1396, sixty years before his
younger brother died! This beats the Fraser
genealogy brought forward lately by a claimant
to the Lovat estates. It is thus clear that there
is something wrong in the Mackintosh genealogy
here, corresponding doubtless to some revolution in the clan's history. And this is made
clear when we consult the Edinburgh Gaelic MS.
of 1467, which gives the genealogies of Highland clans down till about 1450. Here we
actually have two genealogies given, which
shows that the chiefship of the Mackintoshes or
Clan Gillicattan was then either in dispute or a
matter of division between two families. We
print the two 1467 lists with the Mackintosh MS.
genealogy between them, in parallel columns,
supplying dates where possible :—

1467 MS.	*Mackintosh History.*	*1467 MS.*
William and Donald	(12) Ferchar (d. 1514)	Lochlan
William	(9) Ferchar (11) Duncan (d. 1496)	Suibne
Ferchar (1382)	(8) Lachlan & (10) Malcolm (d. 1457)	Shaw
William	(7) William (d. 1368)	Leod
Gillamichol	(6) Angus (d. 1345)	Scayth (1338)
Ferchar (1234)	(5) Ferchar (d. 1274)	Ferchard
Shaw	(4) Shaw (d. 1265)	Gilchrist
Gilchrist	William	Malcolm
Aigcol	(2) Shaw (d. 1210)	Donald Camgilla
Ewen	(1) Shaw (d. 1179)	Mureach
——	Macduff (d. 1154)	Suibne
	Earl of Fife	Tead (Shaw)
Neill		Nachtain
Gillicattan ?]		Gillicattan

The similarity between the 1467 first list and that of the Mackintosh history is too striking to be accidental, and we may take it that they purport to give the same genealogy. There are only two discrepancies from about 1400 to 1200 between them. Ferchar 9th is given as son of Lachlan in the Mackintosh history, whereas the 1467 list makes him son of William, not grandson. The 6th Mackintosh in the one list is Gillamichael, and in the other he is called Angus. Perhaps he had borne both names, for Gillamichael means "servant of St Michael," and might possibly be an epithet. Mr Fraser-Mackintosh has drawn the writer's attention to a list of names published in Palgrave's " Documents and Records " of Scottish History (1837); this is a list of some ninety notables who, about 1297, made homage or submission to Edward I., and among them is Anegosius Maccarawer, or Angus Mac Ferchar, whom Mr Fraser-Mackintosh claims as the 6th of Mackintosh. There are only two other " Macs " in the list, and Maccarawer is, no doubt, a Highlander, and possibly a chief, and, perhaps, the chief of Mackintosh.[1] In any case, in the middle of the 15th century, the direct line of Mackintoshes was represented by William and Donald, sons of William, whereas the chief *de facto* at the time

[1] Angus McErchar here is chief of the Lamonts in Argyle.

was undoubtedly Malcolm Mackintosh.   How
he got this position is a question.

The second list in the 1467 MS. is a puzzle.
Mr Skene called it the genealogy of the " old "
Clan Chattan : *Why*, is not clear.   Scayth, son
of Ferchard, is mentioned in 1338 as the late
Scayth who possessed a " manerium " at the
" stychan " of Dalnavert.   Mr Skene thinks
that he was of the Shaws of Rothiemurchus, and
that this is their genealogy; and this may be
true, but what comes of his earlier theories in
regard to the Macphersons as being the " old "
family here represented?   Theories held in
1837 were abandoned in 1880; but in this Mr
Skene could hardly help himself, considering the
amount of information that has since appeared
in the volumes of such Societies as the " Spalding Club," bearing on the history of the
Moravian clans, and especially on that of Clan
Chattan.

The turmoil in the Clan Chattan, which
changed the chiefship to another line, must be
connected more especially with the events which
took place when King James came North, in
1427, when part of the clan stood by the King
and part by the Lord of the Isles.   We find in a
document preserved in the Kilravock papers,
that King James grants a pardon to certain of
the Clan Chattan, provided they really do attach
themselves to the party of Angus and Malcolm

Mackintosh; and this shews that Malcolm, who was afterwards chief, stood by the king, and received his favours. Angus possibly was his brother, for a depredating rascal of the name of Donald Angusson, supported by Lachlan "Badenoch," son of Malcolm, evidently Lachlan's cousin, gives trouble to various people towards the end of the century. In any case, Malcolm Mackintosh emerged from the troubles that were rending the clan victorious, and his son Duncan was as powerful a chief as lived in the North in his day.

How much the Clan Battle at Perth, in 1396, had to do with the changes in the Clan Chattan leadership it is hard to say. It is accepted as certain that the Clan Chattan had a hand in the fight, for the later historians say so, and the contemporary writer Wyntoun mentions the chiefs on both sides, and one of these bears the name of Scha Ferchar's son, which is an unmistakeably Mackintosh name. He says, in Laing's edition :—

> "Tha thre score were clannys twa,
> Clahynnhé Qwhewyl, and Clachinya;
> Of thir twa Kynnys ware the men,
> Thretty agane thretty then.
> And thare thai had thair chifftanys two,
> Schir Ferqwharis sone wes ane of tha,
> The tothir Cristy Johnesone."

The two clans here pitted against one another
are the clans Quhele or Chewil, and Clan Ha or
Hay, or, according to some, Kay. Boece has
Clan Quhete, which Buchanan and Leslie im-
prove into Clan Chattan.

As so much theorising has taken place upon
this subject already, and so many positive
assertions have been made, it may at present
serve the interests of historic science if we can
really decide what clan names the above cannot
stand for. First, there is Clan Quhele or
Chewil. This clan is mentioned in 1390 as Clan
Qwhevil, who, with the Athole tribes, made a
raid into Angus, and killed the Sheriff. They
are mentioned again in an Act of Parliament in
1594 as among the broken clans, in the following sequence—Clandonochie, Clanchattane,
Clanchewill, Clanchamron, &c. What clan
they really were is yet a matter of dispute. The
form *Chewill* points to a nominative, Cumhal or
Cubhal, or Keval, but no such name can be
recognised in the Clan Chattan district, or near
it. Dughall or Dugald has been suggested, and
the family of Camerons of Strone held as the
clan referred to. But this, like so much in the
discussion of this subject, forgets some very
simple rules of Gaelic phonetics, which are not
forgotten in the spoken language, and in the
English forms borrowed from it. *Feminine
names ending in n never aspirate an initial d of*

the next word. We have Clan Donnachie, Clan Donald, Clan Dugald, and so on, but never Clan Yonnachie or Yonald, or such. Similarly, Clan Hay or Ha *cannot stand for Clan Dai or David-sons.* Let these simple rules of Gaelic phonetics be understood once for all, and we have made much progress towards a solution of the difficulty. The word *Qwhevil* evidently commences with a *C.* Skene suggests it is for Caimgilla, " one-eyed one," the epithet of Donald, Mureach's son, in the 1467 pedigree. But the *m* of *cam* is never aspirated. Again, as to *Ha* or *Hay.* The Clan Cameron are called, in the 1467 MS. and other places, the " Clann Maelanfhaidh," the clan of the " servant of Storm," a name preserved in the Macgillony of Strone, which originally was Mac Gille-anfhaidh, equivalent to Mael-anfhaidh in meaning.

The name, however, that best suits the English form is that of Shaw or Seadh, that is, Seth. There is really a difficulty about Mael-anfhaidh and his clan. The form ought to be either Clann-anfhaidh, which Wyntoun would give as Clahinanha or Clahan-anna, or it would be Clann Mhael-anfhaidh, a form which could not be mis-taken, were it handed down. The most popular theory at present is that the combatants were the Camerons and Mackintoshes, who were enemies

15

for three centuries thereafter; the Mackintoshes were represented by the name of Clan Chewill, the chief being Shaw, son of Ferchar, of the Rothiemurchus branch, while the Camerons were the Clan Hay, with Gilchrist Mac Iain as chief. This is practically Skene's view, and it is the position taken up by Mr A. M. Shaw, the historian of the Mackintoshes. But the phonetics point to a struggle in which the Shaws were the chief combatants, the other side being Clan Kevil, and, on weighing all sides of the question, we are as much inclined to believe that it was the beginning of that struggle in the clan, which is represented by two lines of pedigree, and which latterly gave the chiefship even to a junior branch of one of the lines.

How does the claim of the Cluny Macphersons for the chiefship of Clan Chattan stand in relation to these historic facts? They do not appear at all in the historical documents, but tradition in the seventeenth and eighteenth centuries had enough to tell of their share in the crisis. At the battle of Invernahaven, fought against the Camerons, the Macphersons of Cluny claimed the right under Mackintosh as chief, but he unfortunately gave this post of honour to the Clan Dai or Davidsons of Invernahaven; and the Macphersons retired in high dudgeon. The battle was at first lost to Clan Chattan, but the Macphersons, despite anger, came to the rescue, and the Camerons were defeated. Then ensued a struggle, lasting ten years, for superiority between the Macphersons (Clan Chattan) and the Davidsons, the scene of which, in 1396, was shifted to the North Inch of Perth. These, the Macpherson tradition says, were the two clans that fought the famous clan fight. The Macphersons claim to be descended from Gillicattan Mór, progenitor of the Clan Chattan, by direct male descent, and every link is given back to the eleventh century, thus (omitting "father of")—Gillicattan, Diarmid, Gillicattan, Muirich, parson of Kingussie, whence they are called Clann Mhuirich, father of Gillicattan and Ewen Ban, the former of whom had a son, Dougal Dall, whose daughter Eva, "the heiress of Clan Chattan," married Angus Mackintosh in 1291, and thus made him "captain" of Clan Chattan; Ewen Ban was the direct male representative, then Kenneth, Duncan, Donald Mor, Donald Og, Ewen; then Andrew of Cluny in 1609, a real historic personage without a doubt. In this list, not a single name previous to that of Andrew can be proved to have existed from any documents outside the Macpherson genealogies, excepting only Andrew's father, Ewen, who is mentioned in the Clanranald Red Book as grandfather of the heroic Ewen, who joined Montrose with three hundred of Clans Mhuirich and Chattan. The direct Gillicattan genealogy is

given in the 1467 MS., and, such as it is, it has
no semblance to the Macpherson list. The fact
is that the Macpherson list previous to Ewan,
father of Andrew, is purely traditional and
utterly unreliable. The honest historian of
Moray, Lachlan Shaw, says—"I cannot pre-
tend to give the names of the representatives before the last century. I know that in 1660
Andrew was laird of Clunie, whose son, Ewan,
was father of Duncan, who died in 1722 without
male issue." By means of the Spalding Pub-
lications, the Synod of Moray Records, and
other documents, we can now supplement and
add to Lachlan Shaw's information, though not
much. Macpherson of Cluny is first mentioned
in 1591 when Clan Farson gave their "band"
or bond to Huntly. He is then called "Andrew
Makfersone in Cluny," not *of* Cluny, be it ob-
served, for he was merely tenant of Cluny at that
time. This is amply proved by the Badenoch
rental of 1603, where we have the entry—
"Clovnye, three pleuches . . . Andro
McFarlen (*read* Farsen)[1] tenant to the haill."
In 1609, Andrew had obtained a herit-
able right to Cluny, for then he is
called Andrew Macpherson *of* Cluny in
the bond of union amongst the Clan
Chattan, "in which they are and is astricted
to serve Mackintosh as their Captain and Chief."

1 The MS. has *farsen;* "Farlen" is a misprint.

Huntly had for long been trying to detach the Clan from Mackintosh by "bands," as in 1591 and in 1543, and by raising the tenants to a position of independence under charter rights, which were liberally granted in the seventeenth century, and which proved fatal to the unity of Clan Chattan. But it was a wise policy, nationally considered, for in 1663-5, when Mackintosh tried to raise his Clan against Lochiel, some flatly refused asking *cui bono;* others promised to go if Mackintosh would help them to a slice of their neighbour's land, and Macpherson of Cluny proposed three conditions on which he would go—(1) if the Chiefs of the Macphersons hold the next place in the Clan to Mackintosh; (2) lands now possessed by Mackintoshes and once possessed by Macphersons to be restored to the latter; and (3) the assistance now given was not of the nature of a service which Mackintosh had a right to demand, but simply a piece of goodwill. When Mackintosh was in 1688 proceeding to fight the "last Clan battle" at Mulroy against Keppoch, we are told that the "Macphersons in Badenoch, after two citations, disobeyed most contemptuously." Duncan Macpherson, the Cluny of that time, had decided to claim chiefship for himself, and in 1672 he applied for and obtained from the Lord Lyon's Office the matriculation of his arms as Laird of Cluny Macpherson, and only true representative of the ancient and honourable family of Clan Chattan. Mackintosh, on hearing of it, objected, and got the Lord Lyon to give Macpherson " a coat of arms as cadets of 'Clan Chattan.' " The Privy Council in the same year called him " Lord of Cluny and Chief of the Macphersons," but Mackintosh got them to correct even this to Cluny being responsible *only* for "those of his name of Macpherson descendit of his family," without prejudice always to the Laird of Mackintosh. In 1724 Mackintosh and Macpherson came to an agreement that Mackintosh, in virtue of marrying the heiress of Clan Chattan in 1291, was Chief of Clan Chattan, Macpherson renouncing all claim, but there was a big bribe held out to him—he received the Loch Laggan estates from Mackintosh. In this way the egging on of Huntly, the reputation gained by the Macphersons in the Montrose wars and otherwise, and an absurd piece of pedigree, all combined to deprive Mackintosh of his rightful honour of Chief, and also of a good slice of his estate ! The renown gained by the Clan Macpherson in the Jacobite wars, compared to the supineness of the Mackintosh Chiefs, gained them public sympathy in their claims, and brought a clan, altogether unknown or ignored until the battle of Glenlivet in 1594, to the very front rank of Highland Clans in the eighteenth century. We see the

rise of a clan and its chiefs actually take place
in less than a century and a half, and that, too,
by the pluck and bravery displayed by its chiefs
and its members.

PLACE NAMES OF BADENOCH.

The Ordnance Survey maps, made to the
scale of six inches to the mile, contain for
Badenoch some fourteen hundred names; but
these do not form more than a tithe of the names
actually in use or once used when the glens were
filled with people, and the summer shealings
received their annual visitants.   Every knoll
and rill had its name; the bit of moor, the bog
or *blàr*, the clump of wood (*badan*), the rock or
crag, the tiny loch or river pool, not to speak of
cultivated land parcelled into fields, each and
all, however insignificant, had a name among
those that dwelt near them.   Nor were the
minute features of the mountain ranges and far-
away valleys much less known and named.   The
shealing system contributed much to this last
fact.   But now many of these names are lost,
we may say most of them are lost, with the loss
of the population, and with the abandonment of
the old system of crofting and of summer migra-
tion to the hills.   The names given to those
minute features of the landscape were and are
comparatively easy on the score of derivation,

though sometimes difficult to explain historically. For instance, Lub Mhàiri, or Mary's Loop, is the name of a small meadow at Coilintuie, but who was the Mary from whom it got its name?

Of the fourteen hundred words on the Ordnance Maps, we may at once dismiss three-fourths as self-explanatory. Anyone with a knowledge of Gaelic can explain them; or any-one not so endowed but possessed of a Gaelic dictionary can by the use of it satisfactorily un-ravel the mystery of the names. Of the remain-ing fourth, most are easy enough as regards derivation, but some explanation of an historical character is desirable, though often impossible of being got. One of the most interesting names under this last category is that of Craig Righ Harailt, or the Crag of King Harold, which stands among the hills behind Dunachton; yet there is absolutely nothing known about this Scandinavian chief; even tradition halts in the matter. There are only some six score names where any difficulty, however slight, of deriva-tion can occur, and it is to these names that this paper will mostly devote itself. The oldest written or printed form of the name will be given, for often the difficulty of deriving a place-name yields when the oldest forms of it are found. We have fortunately some valuable documents, easily attainable, which throw light on some obscure names. Among these are the

Huntly Rental for the Lordship of Badenoch for 1603,[1] and Sir R. Gordon of Straloch's map of Braidalbane and Moray, which was published in Blaeu's Atlas in 1662, and which contains a full and intelligent representation of Badenoch. The Badenoch part of this map is reproduced along with this paper for the sake of illustrating it. It was made about the year 1640.

First, we shall deal with the name of the district and the names of the principal divisions of it, and thereafter consider the nomenclature of the leading features of the country, whether river, loch, or mountain, following this with a glance at the names of farms and townships, and at the other points of the landscape that may seem to require explanation. The name of the district first claims our attention.

Badenoch.—In 1229 or thereabouts the name appears as Badenoch in the Registrum of Moray Diocese, and this is its usual form there; in 1289, Badenagh, Badenoughe, and, in King Edward's Journal, Badnasshe; in 1366 we have Baydenach, which is the first indication of the length of the vowel in *Bad-*; a 14th century map gives Baunagd; in 1467, Badyenach; in 1539, Baidyenoch; in 1603 (Huntly Rental), Badzenoche; and now in Gaelic it is *Bàideanach*. The favourite derivation, first given by Lachlan

---

[1] Spalding Club Miscellany, vol. iv.

Shaw, the historian of Moray (1775), refers it to *badan*, a bush or thicket; and the Muses have sanctioned it in Calum Dubh's expressive line in his poem on the Loss of Gaick (1800)—

"'S bidh mùirn ann an Dùthaich nam Badan"
(And joy shall be in the Land of Wood-clumps).

But there are two fatal objections to this derivation; the *a* of Badenoch is long, and that of *badan* is short; the *d* of Badenoch is vowel-flanked by "small" vowels, while that of *badan* is flanked by "broad" vowels and is hard, the one being pronounced approximately for English as *bah-janach*, and the other as *baddanach*. The root that suggests itself as contained in the word is that of *bàth* or *bàdh* (drown, submerge), which, with an adjectival termination in *de*, would give *bàide*, "submerged, marshy," and this might pass into *bàidean* and *bàideanach*, "marsh or lake land." That this meaning suits the long, central meadow land of Badenoch, which once could have been nothing else than a long morass, is evident. There are several places in Ireland containing the root *bàdh* (drown), as Joyce points out. For instance, Bauttagh, west of Loughrea in Galway, a marshy place; Mullanbattog, near Monaghan, hill summit of the morass; the river Bauteoge, in Queen's County, flowing through swampy ground; and Currawatia, in Galway, means the

inundated *curragh* or morass.   The neighbouring district of Lochaber is called by Adamnan
Stagnum Aporicum, and the latter term is likely
the Irish *abar* (a marsh), rather than the Pictish
aber (a confluence); so that both districts may be
looked upon as named from their marshes.   The
divisions of Badenoch are three—the parishes of
Alvie, Kingussie and Insh, and Laggan.

   Alvie.—Shaw says it is a " parsonage dedicated to St Drostan."   Otherwise we should
have at once suggested the 6th century Irish
saint and bishop called Ailbe or later Ailbhe,
whose name suits so admirably, that, even despite the Drostan connection, one would feel inclined to think that the parish is named after St
Ailbhe.   In the middle of the 14th century the
parish is called Alveth or Alwetht and Alway,
and Alvecht about 1400, in 1603 Alvey and
Aluay, and in 1622 Alloway.   The name, with
the old spelling Alveth, appears in the parish of
Alvah in Banffshire, and no doubt also in that of
Alva, another parish in Stirlingshire.   Shaw
and others connect the name with *ail* (a rock),
but do not explain the *v* or *bh* in the name.
Some look at Loch Alvie as giving the name to
the parish, and explain its name as connected
with the flower *ealbhaidh* or St John's wort, a
plant which it is asserted grows or grew around
its bank.   The learned minister of Alvie in Dis-
ruption times, Mr Macdonald, referred the name

of the loch to *Eala-i* or Swan-isle Loch, but unfortunately there is no Gaelic word *i* for an island, nor do the phonetics suit in regard to the *bh* or *v*. The old Fenian name of Almhu or Almhuinn, now Allen, in Ireland, the seat of Fionn and his Féinn, suggests itself, but the termination in *n* is wanting in Alvie, and this makes the comparison of doubtful value.

Insh.—Mentioned as *Inche* in the Moray Registrum in 1226 and similarly in 1380 and in 1603. The name is derived from the knoll on which the church is built, and which is an island or *innis* when the river is in flood. Loch Insh takes its name from this or the other real island near it. The parish is a vicarage dedicated to " St Ewan," says Shaw; but, as the name of the knoll on which the church stands is Tom Eunan, the Saint must have been Eònan or Adamnan, Columba's biographer, in the 7th century. The old bell is a curious and rare relic, and the legend attached to it is one of the prettiest told in the district. The bell was stolen once upon a time, and taken to the south of the Grampians, but getting free, it returned of its own accord ringing out as it crossed the hills of Drumochter, " Tom Eònan! Tom Eònan."

Kingussie.—In Gaelic—*Cinn-ghiubhsaich*— " (at) the end of the fir-forest "; *cinn* being the locative of *ceann* (head) and *giubhsach* being a

" fir-forest." The oldest forms of the name are Kynguscy (1103-11?), Kingussy (1208-15), Kingusy (1226), Kingucy (1380), Kingusy (1538), and Kyngusie (1603). It is a parsonage dedicated to St Columba (Shaw). According to Shaw, there was a Priory at Kingussie, founded by the Earl of Huntly about 1490. The Prior of Kingussie was the tenant of the Church croft in 1565— *Reg. of Moray*, p. 450.

Laggan.—" A mensal church dedicated to St Kenneth " (Shaw). The name in full is Laggan-Choinnich, the *lagan* or " hollow of Kenneth." The present church is at Laggan Bridge, but the old church was at the nearest end of Loch Laggan, where the ruins are still to be seen. It is mentioned in 1239 as Logynkenny (R.M.), and Logykenny shortly before, as Logachnacheny and Logykeny in 1380, Logankenny in 1381 (all from R.M.), and Lagane in 1603 (H.R.). The Gaelic word " lagan " is the diminutive of " lag," a hollow.

We now come to the leading natural features of the country, and deal first with the rivers and lochs of Badenoch. A loch and its river generally have the same name, and, as a rule, it is the river that gives name to the loch. A prominent characteristic of the river names of Badenoch, and also of Pictland, is the termination *ie* or *y*. We meet in Badenoch with Feshie, Trommie, Markie, and Mashie, and not far away are

Bennie, Druie, Geldie, Garry, Bogie, Gaudie, Lossie, Urie, and several more. The termination would appear to be that given by Ptolemy in several river names such as Nov-*ios*, Tob-*ios*, Libn-*ios*, &c., which is the adjectival termination *ios;* but it has to be remarked that the modern pronunciation points to a termination in *idh*, Zeuss's primitive *adi* or *idi;* Tromie in Gaelic is to be spelt Tromaidh, and Feshie as Feisidh. We first deal with the so-called "rapidest river in Scotland."

The *Spey.*—The Highlanders of old had a great idea of the size of the Spey, and also of the Dee and Tay. There is a Gaelic saying which runs thus :—

> Spé, Dé, agus Tatha,
> Trì uisgeachan 's mò fo'n athar.

This appears in an equally terse English form—

> The three largest rivers that be
> Are the Tay, the Spey, and the Dee.

"The river Spey is spoken of as 'she,' and has the character of being 'blood thirsty.' The common belief is that 'she' must have at least one victim yearly."—W. Gregor, *Folklore*, III., 72. In Norse literature the name appears as Spæ (13th century); we have the form Spe in the "Chronicles" (1165); Spe (1228, &c.); Spee (Bruce's Charter to Randolph) and Spey (1451 and 1603). But the Spey is regarded as repre-

senting physically and etymologically Ptolemy's
river Tvesis or Tvæsis. Dr Whitley Stokes says .
—"Supposed to be Ptolemy's Tvesis; but it
points to an original Celtic *squêas*, cognate with
Ir. *scéim* (vomo), W. *chwyd* (a vomit). For
the connection of ideas, cf. Pliny's Vomanus, a
river of Picenum. The river name Spean may
be a diminutive of Spe." The changing of an
original *squ* to *sp*, instead of the true Gaelic form
sg or *sc*, indicates that the name is Pictish. The
Spean is doubtless a diminutive arising from a
form *spesona* or *spesana*.

The *Dulnan;* in Gaelic *Tuilnean*, Blaeu's
map *Tulnen*. It falls into Spey near Broomhill
Station. The root is *tuil*, flood; the idea being
to denote its aptness to rapid floods.

Feshie; Gaelic *Feisidh*. Its first appearance
in charters is about 1230, and the name is
printed *Ceffy*, evidently for *Fessy*. If it is
Celtic, its earliest form was *Vestia*, from a root
ved, which signifies "wet," and which is the
origin of the English word *wet* and *water*. That
Feshie is Celtic and Pictish may be regarded as
probable when it is mentioned that in Brecon-
shire there is a river Gwesyn, the root of the
name being *gwes* (for *vest*), meaning "what
moves" or "goes." ·

Tromie; Gaelic *Trom(a)idh*. In 1603 it is
called Tromye. The Gaelic name for dwarf
elder is *troman*, which appears in Irish as *trom*

or *tromm*, with genitive *truimm*.   It gives its
name to Trim in Meath, which in the 9th century was called Vadum *Truimm*, or Ford of the
Elder-tree.   Several other Irish place-names
come from it.   In Badenoch and elsewhere in
the Highlands, we often meet with rivers named
after the woods on their banks.   Notably is so
the case with the alder tree, Fearna, which
names numerous streams, and, indeed, is found
in old Gaul, for Pliny mentions a river called
Vernodubrum.   Hence Tromie is the Elder-y
River; while Truim, which is probably named
after the glen, Glen-truim—"Glen of the
Elder "—takes its name from the genitive of
tromm.   Compare the Irish *Cala-truim*, the
hollow of the elder.   Glen-tromie is the first
part of the long gorge that latterly becomes
Gaick, and, in curious contrast to the ill fame
of the latter in poetry, it appears thus in a well-
known verse :—

> Gleann Tromaidh nan siantan
>   Leam bu mhiann bhi 'nad fhasgath,
> Far am faighinn a' bhroighleag,
>   An oighreag 's an dearcag,
> Cnothan donn air a' challtuinn,
>   'S iasg dearg air na h-easan.

Guinag, Guynack, Guinach, or *Gynach* (pronounced in Gaelic *Goi(bh)meag*), falls into the
Spey at Kingussie.   It is a short, stormy streamlet.   All sorts of derivations have been offered;

the favourite is *guanag*, pretty, but, unfortunately, it does not suit the phonetics of *Goi-neag*. The name points to primitive forms like *gobni-* or *gomni-*, where the *o* may have been *a*, and the latter form, read as *gamni-*, would give us the root *gam*, which in old Gaelic means "winter." Hence the idea may be "wintry streamlet." Compare Coire Ghoibhnidh in Rosskeen—W. J. Watson, *Place Names of Ross and Cromarty*.

The *Calder*: in Gaelic *Cal(l)adar*. This river and lake name recurs about a dozen times in Pictland and the old Valentia province between the Walls, and there is a Calder river in Lancashire. Cawdor and its Thanes probably give us the earliest form of the word, applied to the Nairnshire district. This is in 1295 Kaledor; in 1310, Caldor; and in 1468, Caudor. But the Gaelic forms persist in other places, as in Aber-*Callador* (1456) in Strathnairn. These forms point to an older *Cal-ent-or*, for *ent* and *ant* become in Gaelic *ed* or *ad*, earlier *et* or *at*. In the Irish Annals mention is made of a battle, fought, it is supposed, in the Carse of Falkirk, called the battle of Calitros, and certain lands near Falkirk were called in the 13th century Kalentyr, now Callendar. Not far away are several Calder waters. Compare also Callater burn, Aberdeenshire, pronounced as spelt; in

16

1564, Auchinquhillater, a farm, now Auchalter; Calder river in Renfrewshire. The root is evidently *cal* (sound, call), as in Latin *Calendae*, and English *Calendar*, borrowed, like the Gaelic equivalent word *Caladair*, from the Latin *Calendarium*.

The *Truim*. See under the heading of Tromie.

The *Mashie; Masie* (1603), in Gaelic *Mathaisidh*, pronounced *Mathisidh*. Strathmashie is famous as the residence of Lachlan Macpherson, the bard, the contemporary and coadjutor of James Macpherson of Ossianic renown. The bard's opinions of the river Mashie are still handed down; these differed according to circumstances. Thus he praised the river :—

> Mathaisidh gheal, bhoidheach gheal,
> Mathaisidh gheal, bhoidheach gheal,
> Bu chaomh leam bhi laimh riut.

But after it carried away his corn he said :—

> Mathaisidh dhubh, fhrògach dhubh,
> Mathaisidh dhubh, fhrògach dhubh,
> Is mór rinn thu chall orm.

The derivation of the name is obscure. *Mathaisidh* could come from *mathas*, goodness, but the meaning is not satisfactory. We might think of *maise*, beauty, but it has the vowel short in modern Gaelic, though Welsh *maws*, pleasant, points to a long vowel or a possible contraction in the original.

The *Markie;* Gaelic *Marcaidh.* Streams and
glens bearing the name Mark and Markie occur
in Perthshire, Forfarshire, and Banffshire. The
first tributary of the Feshie is Allt Mharkie, at
the mouth of which was of old Invermarkie, an
estate held by the Campbells of Cawdor in the
15th and 16th centuries. The root is doubtless
marc, a horse.

The *Pattack;* in Gaelic *Patag.* This river,
unlike those which we have hitherto dealt with,
does not flow into the Spey, but into Loch
Laggan, after making an extraordinary *volte
face* about two miles from its mouth. First it
flows directly northwards, and then suddenly
south-westwards for the last two miles of its
course. Hence the local saying—

> Patag dhubh, bhalgach
> Dol an aghaidh uisge Alba

(Dark, bubbly Pattack, that goes against the
streams of Alba).

We find Pattack first mentioned in an agreement
between the Bishop of Moray and Walter Comyn
about the year 1230, where the streams
"Kyllene et Petenachy" are mentioned as
bounding the church lands of Logykenny. The
Kyllene is still remembered in Camus-Killean,
the bay of Killean, where the inn is. The
Kyllene must have been the present Allt Lairig,

or as the map has it, Allt Buidhe; while Petenachy represents Pattack, which in Blaeu's map
appears as Potaig.   The initial *p* proves the
name to be of non-Gaelic origin ultimately, but
whether it is Pictish, pre-Celtic, or a Gaelicised
foreign word we cannot say.

Alt Lowrag lies between Lochan na h-Earba
and Loch Laggan.   It means the "loud-sound-
ing (*labhar*) one."

The *Spean;* in Gaelic *Spithean*.   See under
Spey.

We have now exhausted the leading rivers,
but before going further we may consider the
names of one or two tributaries of these.
Feshie, for instance, has three important
tributaries, one of which, Allt Mharkie, we have
already discussed.   Passing over Allt Ruaidh
as being an oblique form of Allt Ruadh, "red
burn," we come to the curious river name

Fernsdale; in Gaelic *Fearnasdail*.   The
farms of Corarnstil-more and Corarnstil-beg,
that is, the Corrie of Fernsdale, are mentioned
in 1603 as Corearnistaill Moir and Corearinstail
Beige, and in 1691 the name is Corriarnisdaill.
Blaeu's map gives the river as Fairnstil.   The
first portion of the name is easy; it is *Fearna*,
alder.   But what of *sdail* or *asdail?*   The word
astail means a dwelling, but "Fern-dwelling"
is satisfactory as a name neither for river or
glen.   The tributary of the Fernsdale is called

Còmhraig; in Blaeu *Conrik.* Comhrag
signifies a conflict; but in Irish and early Gaelic
it signified simply a meeting whether of road and
rivers, or of men for conflict. There are
several Irish place-names Corick, situated near
confluences. Doubtless this stream took its
name from its confluence with Fernsdale.

On Feshie we meet further up with Allt
Fhearnagan, the stream of the alder trees; then
Allt Gabhlach, which the Ordnance map
etymologises into Allt Garbhlach, the stream of
the rugged place. This may be the true derivation; it is a big rough gully or corrie with a
mountain torrent tumbling through it.

Allt Lorgaidh is named after the mountain
pass or tract which it drains (*lorg, lorgadh,*
track, tracing), and which also gives name to
the prominent peak of *Carn an Fhidhleir
Lorgaidh,* the Fiddler's Cairn of Lorgie, to
differentiate it from *the* Fiddler's Cairn which
is just beyond the Inverness-shire border, and
not far from the other one.

The *Eidart,* Blaeu's *Eitart,* with the neighbouring streamlet of Eindart, is a puzzling
name. The Gaelic is *Eideard* and *Inndeard*
according to pronunciation.

We now come to the lochs of Badenoch.
Loch Alvie is bound up with the name of Alvie
Parish, discussed already. Loch Insh is the
Lake of the Island, just as Loch-an-eilein, in

Rothiemurchus, takes its name from the castle-island which it contains; but *eilean* is the Norse word *eyland*, Eng. *island*, borrowed, whereas *innis* of Loch Insh is pure Gaelic. In Gaick, along the course of the Tromie, there are three lakes, about which the following rhyme is repeated :—

> Tha gaoth mhór air Loch an t-Seilich
> Tha gaoth eil' air Loch an Dùin;
> Ruigidh mise Loch a' Bhrodainn,
> Mu'n téid cadal air mo shùil.

The rhyme is supposed to have been the song of a hunter who escaped from demons by stratagem and the help of a good stallion on whose back he leapt. The first loch is called Loch an t-Seilich, the lake of the willow, and the third of the series is Loch an Dùin, the loch of the Down or hill, the name of the steep crag on its west side. The intermediate lake is called Loch Vrodain, Gaelic Bhrodainn, which Sir R. Gordon in Blaeu's map spells as Vrodin. The Ordnance map etymologises the word as usual, and the result is Loch Bhradainn, Salmon Loch; but unfortunately the *a* of *bradan* was never *o*, so that phonetically we must discard this derivation. There is a story told about this weird loch which fully explains the name mythically. A hunter had got into possession of a semi-supernatural litter of dogs. When

they reached a certain age, all of them were
taken away by one who claimed to be the true
owner, who left with the hunter only a single
pup, jet black in colour, and named Brodainn.
Before leaving it with the hunter, the demon
broke its leg.   Brodainn was therefore lame.
There was a wonderful white fairy deer on Ben
Alder, and the hunter decided he should make
himself famous by the chase of it.   So he and
Brodainn went to Ben Alder, on Loch Ericht
side; the deer was roused, Brodainn pursued it,
and was gaining ground on it when they were
passing this loch in Gaick.   In plunged the deer,
and after it Brodainn dashed; he caught it in
mid-lake, and they both disappeared never more
to be seen!   Hence the name of the lake is
Loch Vrodin; the lake is there, the name is
there, therefore the story is true!   The word
brodan represents E. Ir. *brot-chú*, a mastiff
Welsh *brathgi;* from *brod*, good, " a broth of a
boy."   Loch-Laggan takes its name from the
lagan or hollow which gave the parish its name,
that is, from Laggan-Chainnich or Lagan-
Kenny, at the northern end of the loch.   There
are two isles in the lake connected with the old
kingly race of Scotland.   King Fergus, whoever
he was, had his hunting lodge on one, called
Eilean an Rìgh, and the other was the dog-
kennel of these Fenian hunters, and is called
Eilean nan Con.   The considerable lake or lakes

running parallel to, and a mile to the south-
east of Loch Laggan are called Lochan na
h-Earba — the lakes of the roe. Loch
Crunachan, at the mouth of Glen-Shirra, has an
artificial island or *crannog* therein; the word is
rather Crunnachan than Crunachan by pronunciation. A Gordon estate map of 1773 calls
it the "Loch of Sheiromore," and distinctly
marks the crannog. Taylor and Skinner's
Roads maps, published in 1776 by order of Parliament, give the name as *L. Crenackan*. The
derivation, unless referable to *crannog*, is doubtful. Loch *Ericht*, the largest lake in Badenoch,
is known in Gaelic as Loch Eireachd. Blaeu
calls it Eyrachle (read Eyrachte). The lake is
doubtless named from the river Ericht, running
from it into Loch Rannoch. Another river
Ericht flows past Blairgowrie into the Isla, nor
must we omit the Erichdie Water and Glen
Erichdie in Blair Athole. The word *eireachd*
signifies an assembly or meeting, but there is an
abstract noun, *eireachdas*, signifying "hand-
someness," and it is to this last form that we
should be inclined to refer the word.

Let us now turn to the hills and hollows and
dales of Badenoch. Many of these place-names
are called after animals frequenting them. The
name of the eagle for instance is exceedingly
common in the form of *iolair*, as Sròn an Iolair,
eagle's ness, &c. We shall begin at the north-

east end of the district, and take the Monadh-lia
or Grey Mountain range first. "Standing
fast" as guard between Strathspey and
Badenoch is the huge mass of

Craigellachie, which gives its motto to the
Clan of Grant—"Stand fast: Craigellachie!"
The name reads in Gaelic as Eileachaidh, which
appears to be an adjective formed from the
stem *eilech*, or older *ailech*, a rock, nominative
ail. The idea is the stony or craggy hill—a
thoroughly descriptive adjective.

The *Moireach;* Gaelic *A' Mhor'oich*, for
A' Mhormhoich, is an upland moor of undulating
ground above Ballinluig. On the West Coast,
this term signifies flat land liable to sea flooding.
It is also the real Gaelic name of Lovat.

Carn Dubh 'Ic-an-Deòir is on the Strathdearn border, and is wrongly named on the map
as "Carn Dubh aig an Doire." It means—The
Black Cairn of the Dewar's (Pilgrim) Son.

An Sguabach.—There is another Sguabach
south of Loch Cuaich, a few miles from Dalwhinnie, and a Meall an Sguabaich west of Loch
Ericht. It means the "sweeping" one, from
sguab, a besom. The people of Insh—the
village and its vicinity—used to speak of the
north wind as Gaoth na Sguabaich, for it blew
over that hill.

Cnoc Fraing, not *Cnoc an Fhrangaich* as on
the Ordnance map—a conspicuous dome-shaped

hill above Dulnan river.   There is a Cnoc
Frangach a few miles south of Inverness, near
Scaniport.   *Fraoch frangach* means the cross-
leaved heather, of which people made their
scouring brushes.   The brush was called in
some parts *fraings'* in Gaelic.   Compare M. Ir.
frangcán, tansy.

Easga 'n Lochain, with its *caochan* or
streamlet, contains the interesting old word for
" swamp " known as *easg, easga*, or *easgaidh*,
with which we may compare the river name Esk.

A' Bhuidheanaich, in the Ordnance maps
etymologised into *Am Buidh' aonach*, " the
yellow hill or steep," occurs three times in
Badenoch—here behind Kincraig and Dunachton, on the north side of Loch Laggan, and on
the confines of Badenoch a few miles south of
Dalwhinnie.   The idea of " yellowness " under-
lies the word as it is characteristic of the places
meant.   The root is *buidhe* (yellow); the rest is
mere termination and has nothing to do with
aonach, which elsewhere is applied to a hill or
slope.

Coire Bog, &c.—Here we may introduce a
mnemonic rhyme detailing some features of the
ground behind and beside Buidheanaich.

Allt Duinne 'Choire Bhuig,
Tuilnean agus Feithlinn,
Coire Bog is Ruigh na h-Eag,
Steallag is Bad-Earbag.

" The Burn of Dun-ness in Soft Corry, Dulnan and Broad Bog-stream, the Reach of the
Notch, the Spoutie and Hinds' Clump "—that
is the translation of the names.

An Suidhe means the " Seat "; it designates
the solid, massive hill behind Kincraig.

Craig Righ Harailt means King Harold's
Hill, on the side of which his grave is still
pointed out.   As already said, it is unknown
who he was or when he lived.

Coire Neachdradh: Glac an t-Sneachdaidh,
&c.   This corrie is at the end of Dunachton burn
after its final bend among the hills. *Sneachd-
radh* means snows, or much snow—being an
abstract noun formed from *sneachd.*

Ruigh an Ròig: the Reach of the Roig (?) is
eastward of Craig Mhor by the side of the peat
road.   The map places it further along as Ruigh
na Ruaige—the Stretch of the Retreat.

Bad Each is above Glen Guinack : it is mis-
read on the Ordnance map into Pait-an-Eich—
a meaningless expression.   It means Horses'
Clump, and a famous local song[1] begins—

Mollachd gu bràth aig bràigh Bad Each;   ·

curses ever more on upper Bad-each, where the
horses stuck and they could not extricate them.

---

[1] By John Cameron, Kingussie; migrated to America,
where he died about 1891.

Rhymes about the various place-names are common, and here is an enumeration of the heights in the Monadh Liath between Kingussie and Craig Dhubh :—

Creag Bheag Chinn-a'-ghiubhsaich
Creag Mhór Bhail' a' chrothain,
Beinne Bhuidhe na Sròine,
Creag an Lòin aig na croitean,
Sithean Mór Dhail a' Chaoruinn,
Creag an Abhaig a' Bhail'-shios,
Creag Liath a' Bhail'-shuas,
Is Creag Dhubh Bhiallaid,
Cadha an Fhéidh Lochain Ubhaidh,
Cadha is mollaicht' tha ann,
Cha'n fhàs fiar no fodar ann,
Ach sochagan is dearcagan-allt,
Gabhar air aodainn,
Is laosboc air a cheann.

Glen Balloch; in Gaelic *Gleann Baloch.* This name is stymologised on the Ordnance map into Gleann a' Bhealaich—the Glen of the Pass; but the word is *baloch* or *balloch,* which means either speckled or high-walled. To the left the Allt Mhadagain discharges into the Calder : this name is explained on the map as Mada coin, which certainly is not the pronunciation which our *Madagain* reproduces. Madagan is a diminutive of *madadh, a dog, wolf.* There are two corries in Gaick similarly named (Cory Mattakan, 1773).

Sneachdach Slinnean, or Snow Shoulder, is .away on the Moy border.

Meall na h-Uinneig, behind Gask-beg considerably, means the Mass or Hill of the Window.   There are other places so named— Uinneag Coire an Eich (Glen-balloch), Uinneag Coire Ardar, Uinneag Coire an Lochain, Uinneag na Creig Móire, Uinneag Coire Chaoruinn and Uinneag Mhìn Choire, the latter ones being all near one another on the north side of Loch Laggan.   The meaning of the name is an opening or pass, or a notch in the sky-line.   A huge cleft in a rock in the north end of Colonsay is called *Uinneag Iorcaill,* "Hercules' Window"—Prof. Mackinnon.

Iarlraig is the rising ground above Garva Bridge, and is mis-written for Iolairig, place of the eagles.[1]   There is here a rock where the eagle nests or nested.   Compare Auld Cory na Helrick of 1773 with the Allt Coire na h-Iolair of the Ordnance map, both referring to a stream on Loch Ericht side.   There is an Elrick opposite Killyhuntly.   The name is common in North Scotland.

Coire Yairack; Allt Yairack; in Gaelic *Earrag,* as if a feminine of *Errach* (spring).   It is spelt *Yarig* on the 1773 estate map.   Perhaps

1 See Introduction.

it is a corruption of *Gearrag*, the short one, applied to a stream.

Shesgnan is the name of a considerable extent of ground near the source of the Spey, and it means morass land, being from *seasgann*, fenny country, a word which gives several place-names both in Scotland and Ireland. The most notable in Scotland is Shisken in Arran, a large, low-lying district, flat and now fertile.

We now cross Spey, and work our way down the south side.

Dearc Beinne Bige, the Dearc of the Little Hill. The pronunciation is *dirc;* in the 1773 map it is spelt *Dirichk*. It is an oblique case of *dearc*, a hole, cave, cleft; it is found in early Irish *derc* (a cave), and several places in Ireland are called Derk and Dirk therefrom. It occurs at least three times in Laggan—as above; and in *Dirc Craig Chathalain*, the 1773 Dirichk Craig Caulan, or cleft of the Noisy Rock, from *Callan*, noise; and in Dearc an Fhearna.

Coire 'Bhein, the 1773 Cory Vein, is a puzzling name. It looks like the genitive case of *bian*, skin.

Coire Phitridh, at the south corner of Lochan na h-Earba, is given in the map as Corie na Peathraich. The word is probably an abstract or collective noun from *pit*, hollow.

Beinn Eibhinn, the 1773 Bineven, the " pleasant hill," is a prominent peak of 3611 feet high, on the borders of Badenoch and Loch-aber, from which a good view of Skye can be got.

Ben Alder, Blaeu's Bin Aildir, in modern Gaelic Beinn Eallar (Yallar). The word is obscure.

Beinn Udlaman, the Uduman of the 1773 map, on the confines of Badenoch and Perth-shire, east of Loch Ericht, seems to take its name from the ball and socket action, for *udalan* signifies a swivel or joint. Some suggest *ùdlaidh*, gloomy, retired.

The *Boar, An Torc*, of Badenoch is to the left of the railway as one enters the district from the south. The "Sow of Athole" is quite close to the "Boar of Badenoch." We are now at the ridge of

Drumochter, in Gaelic *Drum-uachdar*, or ridge of the upper ground.

Coire Bhoite, or rather Bhoitidh, the *Vottie* of 1773, is two or three miles away, and finds a parallel in the name *Sron Bhoitidh* at the top of Glenfishie, where the river bends on itself. The word *boitidh* means "pig," or rather the call made to a pig when its attention is desired.

Coire Sùileagach, behind Craig Ruadh and Drumgask, means the Corrie full of Eyes, so named from its springs doubtless. The term *sùileach* (full of eyes) is usually applied to streams and corries with whirlpools therein.

Creag Chròcan, not *nan Cròcean* as on the map, is near the above corrie, and is named from the deer's antlers which *cròc* means. Similarly we often meet with *cabar* (an antler or caber) in place-names.

The hill of *Bad na Deimheis*, the *Bad na Feish* of 1773, overlooks Dalwhinnie to the east. The name means the "Clump of the Shears," a curious designation. We now pass over into the forest and district of

　Gaick, in Gaelic *Gàig*, which is the dative or locative of *gàg*, a cleft or pass. It is considered the wildest portion of Badenoch, and the repute of the district is far from good. Supernaturally, it has an uncanny reputation. From the days of the ill-starred and ill-disposed Lord Walter Comyn, who, in crossing at Leum na Féinne— the Fenian Men's Leap—to carry out his dread project of making the Ruthven women go to the harvest fields to work unclothed and naked, was torn to pieces by eagles,[1] to that last Christmas of last century, when Captain John Macpherson of Ballachroan and four others were choked to death by an avalanche of snow as they slept in that far-away bothie, Gaick has an unbroken record of dread supernatural doings.　Duncan

---

1 Hence the expression—Diol Bhaltair an Gàig ort— Walter's fate in Gaick on you—to signify an ill wish or curse on any one.

Gow, in his poem on the Loss of Gaick in 1799,
says :—

> Gàig dhubh nam feadan fiar,
> Nach robh ach na striopaich riamh,
> Na bana-bhuidsich 'gan toirt 'san lìon,
> Gach fear leis 'm bu mhiannach laighe leath'.

Which means that Gaick, the dark, of wind-
whistling crooked glens, has ever been a
strumpet and a witch, enticing to their destruction those that loved her charms. How near
this conception is to that mythological one of
the beauteous maiden that entices the wayfarer
into her castle, and turns into a savage dragon
that devours him! The following verses showing the respective merits of various places have
no love for Gaick :—

> Bha mi 'm Bran, an Cuilc 's an Gàig,
>   'N Eidird agus Leum na Làrach,
> Am Feisidh mhóir bho bun gu bràighe
>   'S b'annsa leam bhi 'n Allt a' Bhàthaich.
> 'S mór a b'fhearr leam bhi 'n Drum-Uachdar
>   Na bhi 'n Gàig nan creagan gruamach,
> Far am faicinn ann na h-uailsean
>   'S iùbhaidh dhearg air bharr an gualain.

The poet prefers Drumochter to Glen-Feshie and
Gaick of the grim crags. The Loss of Gaick is
a local epoch from which to date : an old person

17

always said that he or she was so many years old at Call Ghaig. So in other parts, the Olympiads or Archons or Temple-burnings which made the landmarks of chronology were such as the "Year of the White Peas," "the Hot Summer" (1826?), the year of the "Great Snow," and so forth.

"*Vinegar Hill*," as the maps have it, is to the west of the *Dùn* of Loch an Dùin; the Gaelic is *A' Mhìn-choiseachd*, the easy walking. The English is a fancy name founded on the Gaelic.

A' Chaoirnich, the *Caorunnach* of the Ordnance map, but the *Chournich* of 1773, stands beside Loch an Dùin to the left. The latter form means the "cairny" or "rocky" hill; the other, the "rowan-ny" hill, which is the meaning doubtless. The steep ascent of it from the hither end of the lake is called on the map *Bruthach nan Spàidan*, a meaningless expression for *Bruthach nan Spardan*, the Hen-roost Brae.

Meall Aillig, in the Gargaig Cory (1773), or Garbh-Ghaig (Rough Gaick as opposed to "Smooth" Gaick or Minigaig as in Blaeu's map), appears to contain *aill* (a cliff) as its root form. Some refer it to *aileag*, the hiccup, which the stiffness of the climb might cause.

Coire Bhran, the *Coryvren* of Blaeu, takes its name from the river Bran, a tributary of the Tromie, and this last word is a well-known river

name, applied to turbulent streams, and signifies
" raven."

Caochan a' Chaplich, a streamlet which falls
into Tromie a little below the confluence of the
Bran, contains the word *caplach,* which seems
to be a derivative of *capull* (a horse). There
is a Caiplich in the Aird—a large plateau, the
Monadh Caiplich in Loch Alsh, and a stream of
the name in Abernethy.

Croyla is the prominent mountain on the left
as one enters Glentromie—a massive, striking
hill. It is sung of in the Ossianic poetry of
John Clark, James Macpherson's fellow
Badenoch man, contemporary, friend, and
sincere imitator in poetry and literary honesty.
Clark's (prose) poem is entitled the " Cave of
Creyla," and in his notes he gives some
topographical derivations. Tromie appears
poetically as Trombia, and is explained as *Trom-
bidh,* heavy water, while Badenoch itself is
etymologised as *Bha-dianach,* secure valley.
The Ordnance map renders Croyla as Cruaidh-
leac, a form which etymologises the word out of
all ken of the local pronunciation. Blaeu's
map has Cromlaid, which is evidently meant for
Croyla. The Gaelic pronunciation is *Croidh-la,*
the *la* being pronounced as in English. It is
possibly a form of *cruadhlach* or *cruaidhlach*
(rocky declivity), a locative from which might
have been *cruaidhlaigh.*

Meall an Dubh-catha is at the sources of the Comhraig river. It should be spelt *Dubh-chadha*, the black pass, the word *cadha* being common for pass.

Ciste Mhairearaid or rather *Ciste Mhearad*, Margaret's kist or chest or coffin, is part of Coire Fhearnagan, above the farm of Achlean. Here snow may remain all the year round. It is said that Margaret, who was jilted by Mackintosh of Moy Hall, and who cursed his family to sterility, died here in her mad wanderings.

Meall Dubhag[1] and not *Meall Dubh-achaidh* (Ordnance map) is the name of the hill to the south of Ciste Mairead, while equally *Creag Leathain(n)*, broad craig, is the name of the hill in front of Ciste Mairead, not *Creag na Leacainn*. Further north is

Creag Ghiubhsachan, the craig of the fir forest.

Creag Mhigeachaidh stands prominently behind Feshie Bridge and Laggan-lia. There is a Dal-mhigeachaidh or Dalmigavie in Strathdearn, a Migvie (Gaelic, Migibhidh) in Stratherrick, and the parish of Migvie and Tarland in Aberdeenshire. The root part is *mig* or *meig*, which means in modern Gaelic the bleating of a goat.

---

1 *Meall Dubh-agaidh*, immediately behind Achlum—D. MeD. [Apparently a correction of *Meall Dubhag;* cf. Aviemore.]

Creag Follais, not Creag Phulach (sic) as on the maps, means the conspicuous crag. Similarly

Creag Fhiaclach, not Creag Pheacach (!), on the borders of Rothiemurchus, which means the serrated or toothed crag, a most accurately descriptive epithet.

Clach Mhic Cailein, on the top of Creag Follais. The MacCailein meant is Argyle, supposed to be Montrose's opponent, though it must be remembered that Argyle had also much to do with Huntly at Glenlivet and otherwise.

Sgòr Gaoithe (wind skerry) is behind Creag Mhigeachaidh.

We have now exhausted the natural features of the country so far as the explanation of their names is necessary, and we now turn to the farm and field names—the *bailes* and townships and other concomitants of civilisation. Commencing again at Craig Ellachie, we meet first after crossing the crìoch or boundary the farm of *Kinchyle*, *Cinn-Choille*, wood's-end. Then

Lynwilg, the Lambulge of 1603, *Lynbuilg* (Blaeu), signifies the land of the bag or bulge.

Ballinluig, the town (we use this term for *baile*, which means "farm" or "township") of the hollow.

Kinrara, north and south, on each side of the Spey. This name appears about 1338 as *Kynroreach*; 1440, as *Kynrorayth*; and *Kynrára*

(1603).　The *kin* is easy; it is "head" or
"end" as usual.　The *rara* or *rorath* is difficult.　*Rorath*, like *ro-dhuine* (great man),
might mean the great or noble (*ro*) rath or dwelling-place (the Latin *villa*).

　Dalraddy, Dalreadye (1603), and *Dalrodie*
(Blaeu).　The Gaelic is *Dail-radaidh*, the
radaidh dale.　The adjective *radaidh* is in the
older form *rodaidh*, which is still known in
Gaelic in the force of "dark, sallow."　A
sallow-complexioned **man** might be described
as "Duine rodaidh dorcha."　The root-word is
rod, iron scum or rusty-looking mud; it is a
shorter form of *ruadh* (red).　In Ireland, it is
pretty common, and is applied to ferruginous
land.　The adjective *rodaidh* (dark or ruddy)
might describe the Dalraddy land.　It is in connection with Dalraddy that the great Badenoch
conundrum is given :—

　　Bha cailleach ann Dail-radaidh
　　'S dh' ith i adag 's i marbh.

(There was a carlin in Dalraddy who ate a had-
dock, being dead).　With Dalraddy estate are
mentioned in 1691 the lands of Keanintachair
(now or lately *Cinn-tàchair*, causeway-end),
Knockningalliach (the knowe of the carlins),
Loyninriach, Balivuilin (mill-town), and the
pasturages Feavorar (the lord's moss-stream),
Riochnabegg or Biachnabegg, and Batabog (now

Bata-bog, above Ballinluig, the soft swampy place). Another old name is *Gortincreif* (1603), the *gort* or field (farm) of trees. *Croft-gowan* means the Smith's Croft.

Delfour, *Dalphour* in 1603, and older forms are *Dallefowr* (1569). The *del* or *dal* is for dale, but what is *four?* The Gaelic sound is *fùr*. The word is very common in names in Pictland, such as Dochfour, Pitfour, Balfour, Letterfour, Tillyfour, Tillipourie and Trinafour. These forms point to a nominative *pùr*, the *p* of which declares it of non-Gaelic origin. The term is clearly Pictish. The only Welsh word that can be compared is *pawr* (pasture), *pori* (to graze), the Breton *peur*. *Fùr* has nothing to do with Gaelic *fuar*, for then Dalfour would in Gaelic be Dail-fhuar, that is *Dal-uar*.

Pitchurn, in 1603 *Pettechaerne*, in Gaelic *Bail-chaorruinn*, the town of the rowan. The Pictish *pet* or *pit* (town, farm), which is etymologically represented by the Gaelic *cuid*, has been changed in modern Gaelic to *baile*, the true native word.

Pitourie, in 1495 Pitwery, in 1603 Pettourye, in 1620 Pettevre, &c.; now *Bail'odharaidh*. The adjective *odhar* means "dun," and *odharach*, with an old genitive *odharaigh*, or rather *odharach-mhullach*, is the plant devil's bit. The plant may have given the name to the farm.

Baldow means the black town.

Kincraig, Kyncragye (1603), means the end of the crag or hill, which exactly describes it.

Leault, Gaelic *Leth-allt* or half-burn, a name which also appears in Skye as Lealt, may have reference rather to the old force of *allt*, which was a glen or shore. The stream and partly one-sided glen are characteristic of the present Leault.

Dunachton; Gaelic *Dùn-Neachdain(n)*, the hill-fort of Nechtan. Who he was, we do not know. The name appears first in history in connection with the Wolf of Badenoch. St Drostan's chapel, below Dunachton House, is the *capella de Nachtan* of 1380. We have Dwnachtan in 1381, and Dunachtane in 1603. The barony of Dunachton of old belonged to a family called MacNiven, which ended in the 15th century in two heiresses, one of whom, Isobel, married William Mackintosh, cousin of the chief, and afterwards himself chief of the Clan Mackintosh. Isobel died shortly after marriage childless. Tradition says she was drowned in Loch Insh three weeks after her marriage by wicked kinsfolk.[1] Mr Fraser-Mackintosh has written a most interesting monograph on Dunachton, entitled "Dunachton, Past and Present."

[1] 1475, Baron Macknenan deceased; Lachlan of Gellovy gets the marriage of his daughters [no reference.]

Achnabeachin; Gaelic *Ach' nam Beath-aichean,* the field of the beasts. Last century this land held eight tenants.

Keppochmuir; Gaelic *An Sliabh Ceapanach;* Ceapach means a tillage plot.

Coilintuie or *Meadowside.* The Gaelic is *Coill an t-Suidhe,* the Wood of the Suidh, or sitting or resting. Some hold the name is really Cùil an t-Shuidh, the Recess of the Suidh.

Croftcarnoch; Gaelic *Croit-charnach,* the Cairny Croft.

Belleville is, in its English form, of French origin, and means "beautiful town." The old name in documents and in maps was Raitts, and in the 1776 Roads' Map this name is placed exactly where Belleville would now be written. Gaelic people call it Bail' a' Bhile, "the town of the brae-top," an exact description of the situation. Mrs Grant of Laggan (in 1796) says that Bellavill "is the true Highland name of the place," not Belleville; and it has been maintained by old people that the place was called Bail' a' Bhile before "Ossian" Macpherson ever bought it or lived there. Whether the name is adopted from Gaelic to suit a French idea, or *vice versa,* is a matter of some doubt, though we are inclined to believe that James Macpherson was the first to call old Raitts by such a name. James Macpherson is the most famous—or rather the most notorious—of Badenoch's sons; but though his "Ossian" is a forgery from a historical standpoint, and a purely original work from a literary point of view, yet it is to him that Celtic literature owes its two greatest benefits—its being brought prominently before the European world, and, especially, the preservation of the old literature of the Gael as presented in traditional ballads and poems, and in the obscure Gaelic manuscripts which were fast disappearing through ignorance and carelessness.

Lachandhu, the little loch below Belleville, gives the name to Sir Thomas Dick Lauder's novel.

Raitts—the English plural being used to denote that there were three Raitts—Easter, Middle, and Wester. In 1603 the place is called *Reatt,* and Blaeu has *Rait.* The Gaelic is *Ràt,* and this, which is the usual form in Highland place-names, is a strengthened form of the older *rath* or *ráith* of Old Irish, which meant a residence surrounded by an earthern rampart. It, in fact, meant the old farm house as it had to be built for protective purposes. For the form *ràt* (from ràth-d), compare *Bialaid,* further on, and the Irish names *Kealid* from *caol* and *Croaghat* from *cruach,* which Dr Joyce gives in his second volume of Irish Place-Names to exemplify this termination in *d.*

Chapel-park; Gaelic *Pairc an t-Seipeil. This* is a modern name, derived from the chapel and kirk-yard that once were there, which was known as the chapel of Ma Luac, the Irish Saint. The older name was the *Tillie* or *Tillie-sow,* where an inn existed, whose " Guidwife " was called Bean an Tillie.   Some explain *Tillie-sow* as the Gaelic motto that used, it is said, to be over the olden inn doors, viz., " Tadhailibh so "— " Visit here."

Lynchat is now *Bail' a' Chait;* " Sheep-cot " town, not Cat's-town, is the explanation given by the inhabitants.   [So also *Aodann Chat,* Edincat, in Strathdearn.]

An Uaimh Mhóir, the Great Cave, is a quar- ter of a mile away from the highway as we pass Lynchat.   It is an " Erd-house," the only one of this class of antiquarian remains that exists in Badenoch.   It is in the form of a horse-shoe, which has one limb truncated, about 70 feet long, 8 feet broad, and 7 high.   The walls gradually contract as they rise; and the roofing is formed by large slabs thrown over the ap- proaching walls.   Tradition says it was made in one night by a rather gigantic race : the women carried the excavated stuff in their aprons and threw it in the Spey, while the men brought the stones, large and small, on their shoulders from the neighbouring hills.   All was finished by morning, and the inhabitants knew not what had taken place. From this mythic ground we come down to the romantic period, when, according to the legend, MacNiven or Mac Gille-naoimh and his nine sons were compelled to take refuge here—some say they made the cave, and long they eluded their Macpherson foes. There was a hut built over the mouth of the cave, and at last it was suspected that something was wrong with this hut. So one of the Macphersons donned beggar's raiment, called at the hut, pretended to be taken suddenly ill, and was, with much demur, allowed to stay all night. There was only one woman in the hut, and she was continually baking; and he could not understand how the bread disappeared in the apparent press into which she put it, and which was really the entry into the cave. He at last suspected the truth, returned with a company of men next night, and slew the MacNivens. It is said that this man's descendants suffered from the ailment which he pretended to have on that fateful night.

Laggan, the hollow, now in ruins. Here dwelt the famous Badenoch witch, Bean an Lagain.

Kerrow; in Gaelic *An Ceathramh*, the fourth part—of the davoch doubtless—the davoch of " Kingussie Beige " (1603), with its " four pleuches."

Kingussie. Already discussed under the heading of Kingussie parish.

Ardvroilach; Gaelic *Ard-bhroighleach;* in 1603, *Ardbrelache.* The form *broighleach* seems a genitive plural from the same root form as *broighleag,* the whortleberry. The word *broighlich* (brawling) scarcely suits with *ard,* a height.

Pitmain. The Gaelic is only a rendering of the English sounds : *Piodmé'an.* In 1603 it is *Petmeane.* The reason for their being no Gaelic form of this word is simply this. The great inn and stables of the Inverness road were here. and the name Pit-meadhan, "middle town," was adopted into the English tongue. The Gaelic people, meantime, had been abolishing all the *pet* or *pit* names, and changing them to *Bals,* but this one was stereotyped in the other tongue, and the local Gael had to accept the English name or perpetuate an offending form. He chose to adopt the English pronunciation.

Balachroan; Bellochroan (1603); Gaelic *Baile-'Chrothain,* the town of the sheepfold. Above it was *Coulinlinn,* the nook of the lint, where an old branch of Macphersons lived.

Aldlarie; Gaelic *Allt-Làirigh,* the stream of the *làrach* or gorge.

Strone means "nose."

Newtonmore is the new town of the Moor— An Sliabh.

Clune and *Craggan of Clune.* The Gaelic *cluain* signifies meadow land, whether high or low, in dale or on hill.

Benchar, Bannachar (1603), *Beandocher* (1614), and now *Beannachar,* Irish *beannchar* (horns, gables, peaks), Welsh *Bangor.* It is a very common place-name. The root is *beann* or *beinn* (a peak).

Beallid, in 1603 *Ballet,* in 1637 *Ballid,* now *Bialaid,* so named from being at the mouth of Glen-banchor—*bial* (mouth), with a termination which is explained under *Raitts.* A "pendicle" of it, called *Corranach,* is often mentioned, which probably means _ the "knowey" place.

Cladh Bhrì'd and *Cladh Eadail,* Bridget's and Peter's (?) Kirk-yards, are the one at Benchar and the other along from Beallid, the latter being generally called *Cladh Bhiallaid.* Chapels existed there also at one time.

Ovie, in 1603 *Owey* (and Corealdye, now Coraldie, corrie of streams or cliffs), Blaeu's *Owie,* now *Ubhaidh,* appears to be a derivative of *ubh,* egg: it is a genitive or locative of *ubhach,* spelt and pronounced of old as *ubhaigh.* Mrs Grant describes Lochan Ovie as beauty in the lap of terror, thus suggesting the derivation usually given of the name, viz., *uamhaidh,* dreadful. Some lonesome lakes of dread near

Ballintian are called *Na h-uath Lochan*, the dread lakes.

Cluny, Clovnye (1603), now *Cluainidh*. The root is *cluain* (meadow), and the termination is doubtless that in *A' Chluanach*, a cultivated plateau behind Dunachton, and the dative singular of this abstract form would give the modern Cluny from the older *cluanaigh*.

Balgowan, Pettegovan (1603) now *Bail' a' Ghobhainn*, the town of the smith.

Gask-beg, Gask-more, Gargask, Drumgask —all with *Gask*, and all near one another about Laggan Bridge. There is an older *Gasklone*, Mud-Gask, the *Gascoloyne* of 1603, Gasklyne (1644), and Gaskloan (1691). The form *Gask* appears in the Huntly rental of 1603. The name Gask is common; there is Gask parish in Strathearn, Perthshire, and there is a Gask in Strathnairn, a Gask Hill in Fife, and Gask House near Turriff. The name Gaskan appears more than once, and in one instance applies to a rushy hollow (Gairloch). We have Fingask in four counties—Aberdeen, Fife, Inverness (in the Aird, but the Gaelic is now *Fionn-uisg'*), and Perth. Colonel Robertson, in his "Topography of Scotland," refers Gask to *gasag*, diminutive of *gas*, branch; but this hardly suits either phonetically or otherwise. The word *gasg* seems to have slipped out of use: it belongs only to Scotch Gaelic, and may be a Pictish

word. The dictionaries render it by " tail,"
following Shaw, and mis-improving the matter
by the additional synonym " appendage,"
which is not the meaning; for the idea is rather
the posterior of an animal, such as that of the
hind, which Duncan Ban refers to in this case
as " white "—" gasganan geala," and which
makes an excellent mark for the deer-stalker.
The dictionaries give *gasgan*, a puppy;
gasganach, petulant; and *gasgara (gasgana?)*,
posteriors; all which Shaw first gives. There
is also the living word *gasgag*, a stride, which no
dictionary gives. These derivations throw very
little light on the root word *gasg*, which seems
to signify a nook, gusset, or hollow. The
Laggan gasgs are now " rich meadows, bay
shaped," as a native well describes them. It
was at Gaskbeg that the gifted Mrs Grant of
Laggan lived, and here she sang of the beauties
of the Bronnach stream—the Gaelic Bronach,
the " pebbly " (?)—which flows through the
farm.

Blargie, in 1603 *Blairovey*, in Blaeu *Blariki*,
and in present Gaelic *Blàragaidh*. The termination *agaidh* appears also in Gallovie, which,
in 1497, is *Galowye*, and now *Geal-agaidh*, the
white *agaidh*. The word appears as a prefix in
Aviemore and Avielochan, both being *agaidh* in
Gaelic. The old spelling of these words with a
v, as against the present pronunciation with *g*,

is very extraordinary. The meaning and etymology of *agaidh* are doubtful. Shaw gives *aga* as the " bottom of any depth," and there is a Welsh word *ag*, a " cleft or opening." The word may be Pictish.

Coull, in Gaelic *Cùil*, means the " nook, corner," which the place is.

Ballmishag means the town of the kid, *miseag* or *minnseag*.

Crathie, in 1603 *Crathe*, in Blaeu *Crachy*, now in Gaelic *Craichidh*. The name appears in the Aberdeenshire parish of Crathie, pronounced by Gaelic natives as Creychie; Creychin in 1366. Crathienaird is in 1451, Crachenardy. [Cray at foot of Glenshee is in Gaelic *Crathaigh;* Loch Achray is in Gaelic *Loch Ath-chrathaigh;* ? Ach-ch.] The form *Crathie* possibly points to an older Gaelic *Crathigh*.

Garvabeg and *Garvamore*, the *Garvey Beige* and *Garvey Moir* of 1603. The word at present sounds as *Garbhath,* which is usually explained as *garbh-àth*, rough ford, a very suitable meaning and a possibly correct derivation.

Shirramore and *Shirrabeg*, the *Waster Schyroche* and *Ester Schiroche* of 1603. *Sheiro-more*, in 1773, is in Gaelic *Siorrath Mòr*. With these names we must connect the adjoining glen name, *Glenshirra*, Gaelic *Glenn Sioro*, a name which appears also in Argyleshire, near

18

Inveraray, as Glenshira, Glenshyro (1572), traversed by the *Shira* stream. The root word appears to be *sìr* or *sìor*, long. Some suggest *siaradh*, squinting, obliqueness.

Aberarder, Blaeu's *Abirairdour*, Gaelic *Obair-ardur*. There is an Aberarder (Aberardor in 1456, and Abirardour in 1602) in Strathnairn, and another in Deeside, and an Auchterarder in Strathearn. The *Aber* is the Pictish and Welsh prefix for "confluence," Gaelic *inver*. The *ardour* is etymologised in the Ordnance map as Ard-dhoire, high grove. The word may be from *ard dhobhar*, high water, for the latter form generally appears in place-names as *dour*.

Ardverikie has been explained correctly in the "Province of Moray," published in 1798, as "Ard Merigie, the height for rearing the standard." The Gaelic is *Ard Mheirgidh*, from *meirge*, a standard.

Gallovie.—See under Blargie.

Muccoul is from *Muc-cùil*, Pigs' nook.

Ach-duchil means the field of the black wood.

Dalchully, Gaelic *Dail-chuilidh*. The word *cuilidh* signifies a press or hollow. It means the "dale of the hollow or recess."

Tynrich is for Tigh an Fhraoich, house of the heath.

Catlodge, in 1603 *Catteleitt*, and in 1776 *Catleak*, is in present Gaelic *Caitleag*, the Cat's Hollow; some suggest *cat*, sheepcote. The form *cait* is unusual; we should, by analogy with Muc-cùil and other names where an animal's name comes first in a possessive way, expect *Catlaig* rather than *Caitleag*.

Breakachy, *Brackachye* (1603), is usually explained as *Breacachaidh*, speckled field, which is correct. "Brecacath" (Monymusk) is explained in the 16th century as "campus distinctus coloribus." [Compare Ardochy, Highfield, in Stratherrick, Strathdearn and Lorne.] We shall now cross the hills into Glentruim and up Loch Ericht side. There at Loch Ericht Lodge we have

Dail an Longairt, in 1773 *Rea Delenlongart*, and on the other side of the ridge is *Coire an Longairt* (Cory Longart 1773), while there is an *Eilean Longart* above Garvamore bridge and "Sheals of Badenlongart" in Gaick above the confluence of Bran, according to the 1773 map. *Longart* itself means a shealing, the older form being *longphort*, a harbour or encampment.

Dalwhinnie, in Gaelic *Dail-chuinnidh*, is usually explained as *Dail-choinnimh*, Meeting's Dell; but the phonetics forbid the derivation. Professor Mackinnon has suggested the alternative of the "narrow *dail*." Dalwhinnie was a famous station in the old coaching days, and the

following **verse shows how progress** northwar⸱ ⸱
might be made :—

> Bracbhaist am Baile-chloichridh
> Lunch an Dail na Ceardaich
> Dinneir an Dhail-chuinnidh
> 'S a' bhanais ann an Ràt.

Presmackerach, not the Ordnance *Presmocachie*, is in 1603 *Presmukra*, that is *Preasmucraigh*, bush of piggery or pigs.

Dalannach, which the Ordnance map etymologises into *Dail-gleannach* or Glen-dale, was in 1603 *Dallandache*, and is now Dail-annach. The old form points to the word *lann* or *land*, an enclosure or glade. The Irish *Annagh*, for *Eanach*, a marsh, will scarcely do, as the name appears in Loch Ennich in its proper Gaelic phonetics.

Crubinmore, *Crobine* (1603), now *Crùbinn*. The names *Crubeen*, *Cruboge*, *Slievecroob*, &c., appear in Ireland, and are referred by Dr Joyce to *crùb*, (a paw, hoof), *crúibin* (a trotter, little hoof). The Gaelic *crùbach* (lame), and *crùban* (a crouching), are further forms of the root word, a locative case from the the latter form being possibly our Crubin, referring to the two "much back-bent hills there."

Invernahavon, *Invernavine* (1603), means the confluence of the river, that is, of the Truim with Spey.

Ralia, Gaelic *Rath-liath*, means the grey *rath* or dwelling-place.

Nuide, Nuid (1603), *Noid* (1699), now *Noid*. The derivation suggested for the name is *nuadh-id*, a topographic noun from the adjective *nuadh* or *nodha*, new; of old, "Noid of Ralia."

Knappach, in Gaelic *A' Chnapaich*, the hilly or knobby land. It is a common place-name, especially in Ireland, appearing there as Knappagh and Nappagh.

Ruthven, which is also the first form the name appears in in 1370, when the "Wolf" took possession of the lordship of Badenoch. It was here he had his castle. In 1380 the name is *Rothven* and *Ruthan*. The name is common all over Pictland, mostly in the form Ruthven, but also at various times and places spelt Ruthfen, Ruwen, Ruven, Riv(v) en, &c. The modern Gaelic is *Ruadhainn*, which simply means the "red place," from *ruadhan*, anything red. The *v* of the English form lacks historic explanation. *Brae-ruthven* gives the phonetically interesting Gaelic *Bré-ruadhnach*.

Gordon Hall (so in 1773 also) is in Gaelic *Lag an Nòtair*, the Notary's Hollow, for it is a hollow. The name and its proximity to Ruthven Castle mutually explain one another: Gordon Hall was doubtless the seat of the Gordon lords of Badenoch, when the castle of Ruthven was changed to barrack purposes. Here the rents used to be "lifted" for the Gordon estates.

Killiehuntly, Keillehuntlye (1603), Blaeu's *Kyllehunteme,* in present Gaelic *Coille-Chun-tainn,* the wood of Contin. Huntly is in Gaelic *Hundaidh,* and M'Firbis, in the 16th century, has Hundon; hence arises the English form. The popular mind still connects it with the Huntlies. Contin is a parish in Ross-shire, and there was a Contuinn in Ireland, on the borders of Meath and Cavan, which is mentioned in connection with Fionn's youthful exploits. It has been explained as the meeting of the waters, *con-* (with) and *tuinn* (waves), but the matter is doubtful.

Inveruglas, Inneruglas (1603), in Gaelic *Inbhir-ùlais,* the *inver* of *Ulas,* although no such stream exists now, receives its explanation from the old Retours, for in 1691 we have mention of Inveruglash and its mill-town on the water of Duglass, which means the stream passing the present Milton. Hence it means the *inver* of Duglass or dark stream, *dubh* (black), and *glais* (stream).

Soillierie, in Gaelic *Soileiridh,* means the "bright conspicuous place," on the rising beyond the Insh village.

Lynchlaggan stands for the Gaelic *Loinn-Chlaiginn,* the Glade of the Skull, possibly referring to the knoll above it rather than to an actual skull there found; the name is applied in Ireland to such skull-like hills.

Am Beithigh (not *Am Beithe*), means the Birch-pool; a locative form.

Farletter is the old name for Balnacraig and Lynchlaggan, and it appears in 1603 as *Ferlatt* and *Falatrie* (1691). It took its name from the hill above, now called *Craig Farleitir*. The word *Farleitir* contains *lëitir*, a slope or hillside, and possibly the preposition *for* (over), though we must remember the Fodderletter of Strathavon with its Pictish *Fotter*, or *Fetter*, or *Fother* (?).

Forr is situated on a knolly ridge overlooking Loch Insh, and evidently contains the preposition *for* (over), as in *orra* for *forra*, on them. The last *r* or *ra* is more doubtful. Farr; in Strathnairn and Sutherland, is to be compared with it.

Dalnavert, in 1338 and 1440 *Dalnafert*, in 1603 *Dallavertt*, now in Gaelic *Dail-a'-bheirt*, which is for *Dail na bhfeart*, the dale of the graves or trenches, from *feart*, a grave, which gives many place-names in Ireland, such as Clonfert, Moyarty, &c.

Cromaran is possibly for *Crom-raon*, the crooked field.

Balnain is for *Beal an àthain*, the ford mouth.

Ballintian, the town of the fairy knoll, was called of old *Countelawe* (1603) and *Cuntelait* (1691), remembered still vaguely as the name of the stretch up the river from Ballintian, and caplained as *Cunntadh-làid,* the counting (place) of the loads! Perhaps, like Contin, it is for *Con-tuil-aid,* the meeting of the waters, that is, of Feshie and Fernsdale, which takes place here.

Balanscrittan, the town of the *sgriodan* or running gravel.

Bulroy, for *Bhuaile-ruaidh,* the red fold.

Tolvah, the hole of drowning.

Achlean, for *Achadh-leathainn,* is broad field. Beside it is Achlum, for *Achadh-leum,* the field of the leap.

Ruigh-aiteachain may possibly be a corruption for Ruigh Aitneachain, the Stretch of the Junipers.

Ruigh-fionntaig, the Reach of the Fair-stream.

In the Dulnan valley is *Caggan,* the Gaelic of which is *An Caiginn,* and there is "a stony hill face" in Glen-Feshie of like name.

ANNAT

ANNAT

Much mystery is made to attach to this name, though, as a matter of fact, the word is simple enough as to meaning. It is obsolete both in Scotch and Irish Gaelic, and it is usually glossed by *eaglais* (church) simply. There was, however, a difference between the general term *eaglais* and the restricted word *annóid*. The *annóid* church was that in which the patron saint (of the monastery or monastic district) was educated or in which his relics were kept (*i mbi taisi in erloma*). The first time we meet with it in literature is in the Book of Armagh (circa 800 A.D.), and there Iserninus, or Iarnan, is left at a certain spot by St Patric to found his monastery (*manche*) and his patron saint's church (*andoóit*). The Old Irish form is *andóit*, with the last vowel long; and its derivation is disputed. Dr Whitley Stokes suggests *antitas*, antiquity ("ancient church"), as its origin, a late Latin term, the

phonetics being the same very much as in
Trianaid, O.I. Tríndóit. Unfortunately *antitas*
is a figment of the philological brain to explain
antas (G. *antatis*), which is glossed by
" senatus " or senate, its meaning being practically that of *ecclesia*, which became the Gaelic
eaglais. The phonetics here are exactly those
of Trianaid. We may take it that mediæval
Latin *antas*, from *ante*, before, and really meaning " council of ancients," is the ancestor of
annaid.

The relation of the *annóid* to other churches
in the district was one of superiority and
antiquity. It is especially contrasted with the
dalta church (cf. Kildalton), founded by a member of the same community as the founder of
the original church and monastery, and the word
may be translated as " sister " or " fosterling "
church. A further church, another step below
it, was the *conpairche* (co-parishioner) church
under the tutelage of the original founder. Two
words are general, *eaglais* and *ceall* or *cell*, now
known only by its locative *cill* (Kil-), the latter
meaning a smaller church than the other usually,
being from Lat. *cella*, a cell. Other church
names meet us having slightly different meanings :—*teampull*, church, originally " temple ";
clachan, church, Irish *clochán*, a stone bee-hive
monastic hut; *seipeal*, Middle Irish *sépell*, a late
word from *chapel*; *neimheadh*, glebe, Old Irish

nemed, chapel, Gaulish *nemeton*. This last is the original Celtic name for a temple, and comes from the same root as *nèamh*. It appears rarely —Rosneath (old Neveth), Navity once or twice, and especially in Roskeen, where Mr Watson in his "Ross-shire Place-Names" has shown the word to exist in Nonakil (neimh' na cill'), Dalnavie, Knocknavie, Inshnavie, and Newmore (neimh' mhór). *Annóin* or *Andóin* (church) is another name that only appears in the glosses.

Annaid is therefore not a native word. Its chance resemblance to the eastern goddess Anaitis has been responsible for much "Druidism," and bad speculation on Celtic religion generally. In this connection we may mention two other interesting ecclesiastical words. The first is Manachainn or Monastery, the Gaelic name of Beauly. The other is the early Irish *apdaine* or *abthaine*, abbacy, or "abbey land" also, whence our two or three Appins, about which also much nonsense is usually written. As *abthane*, a supposed title, the word puzzled the historians for many centuries, until Skene, himself first a victim, discovered the mistake. In proof of the above facts in regard to *annaid*, the many glossaries of early Irish published with Irish texts must be consulted, but a fair account of the matter can be got from the third volume of the published *Senchus Mór*.

GAELIC "AIRIGH," SHEILING,

IN

NORSE PLACE-NAMES

GAELIC "AIRIGH," SHEILING, 'IN NORSE PLACE-NAMES

THE new Saga book of the Viking Club discusses the origin of *ark* and *erg* in the place-names of northern England, and tries to overturn the theory that they are from Norse *hörgr* (*Horg*), and Anglo-Saxon *hearg*, a sacrificial " grove " of heathen times. The new theory regards them as being from Norse or Danish *erg* or *œrg*, a shieling or dairy farm, a word undoubtedly borrowed by the Norse as the Orkney Saga fully proves, and as several place-names in the Highlands and Isles still prove. Dr Colley-March was the originator of the new theory in a paper printed in 1890 in a Liverpool antiquarian society's transactions—and I have not seen it; but as Dr Isaac Taylor in his excellent work on " Names and their Histories " (1896), holds by

19

the *horg* theory, Dr March's view is either unknown to or rejected by the English experts on
place-names.   The difficulties in both theories
are great : *horg* can hardly be used with other
than a god's name outside epithets; of course it
is used alone in Harrow.   It is difficult to equate
Grims-argh in Preston with a deity.   Again the
borrowed *arg* of the Norse cannot without great
difficulty be connected historically with northern
England.   In the Highlands the termination *ary*
in place names is common, less so is *sary;* the
latter nearly always comes from the possessive *s*
before *ary,* and in the Norse *ärg;* the former
may belong to other endings, especially *-garry*
(N. *gerdi,* G. *gearraidh,* outland beyond township ploughed land).   The only literary reference in Norse to *arg* or *erg* is in the Orkney Saga,
where we have the place called by them Asgrims-
ærgin practically glossed by the expression
" *erg,* which we call *setr* (sheiling)."   Asgrims-
ærg is now called Askary or Assary, at the north
end of Loch Calder in Caithness.   When one
compares the original form Asgrims-ærg with
the present Askary or Assary, one is compelled
to tremble (metaphorically) for the etymologist
of Western Isles names of Norse origin.   Dr
Anderson points out that many places in Caithness present this termination—Halsary, (Hall,
or, perhaps, Hallvard!), Dorrery, Shurrery,

Blingery, &c. Sutherland presents at least three—Gearnsary, Modsary, and Gradsary, but with Asgrims-ærg before our eyes, we refuse at present to consider them, though Mr Mackay of Hereford has made a decent attempt to etymologise them in Vols. XVII. and XVIII. of Inverness Gaelic Society Transactions. To regain confidence, we must go to the happy sheiling grounds of -sary and -ary in the Uists. In North Uist we have two distinct districts given over to Aulasary, which, of course, is Olafs-arge (*arge* must have been the oldest form, as we shall see), and which means "Olave's Sheiling." In the same island is Obisary, which stands for Hopsarge, "Sheiling in the Bay." There, too, we have Langary from *lang,* long; Risary, from *Hris,* copse; Horisary (hörgs, "grove"?), Dusary, Vanisary, and Honary. In South Uist are Vaccasary and Trasary, in Barra is Ersary (Eric's-arge?). Ardnamurchan seems to contain some : Brunery (*brunnr,* spring), Smirisarary ("smear or butter"?), Alisary and Assary, in Glenelg Skiary. But these last five I do not know the pronunciation of, and may not be rightly included. Perhaps some native may oblige on this point. The Gaelic *airigh,* misspelt *airidh,* is in early Irish *airge,* dairy or a place where cows are, which in old Irish would be *arge,* at which stage the Norse borrowed it

from the Scots.   Personally I believe that it was
adopted only in the Highlands by them.   B
the bye, its initial use has been suggested for
Arkle in Sutherland, that is Arg-fell, "Sheiling's Fell"; if so, the difficult *ar* or *ark* of Arbol,
in Easter Ross, might so be explained.   The
English forms from *arg* generally show *ark*, if
the root is initial in the word.   In future it is
hoped that any Gaelic *writer* who reads the above
will write *airigh,* not *airidh,* for "sheiling."

GLENSHIEL

GLENSHIEL

THE glen is, as usual in such cases, named after the river Shiel. There is another river Shiel and Loch Shiel forming the southern boundary of Moidart. It is mentioned by the Dean of Lismore, who gives the bounds of the Clanranald as—

Eddir selli is sowyrrni.
" Between Shiel and Loch-hourn (Sorn)."

Fortunately, we can go back eight hundred years further than the Dean's time, and we find the southern Shiel in Adamnan twice under the form of Sale. The phonetics here are all right, for Old Irish *saile*, saliva, is in modern Gaelic *sile*. The old Celtic form of the river's name would be Salia, the root being *sal*, sea, salt, saliva. The root *s-val*, swell, is also possible. The name likely is Pictish, and therefore we are forced to fall back on original Celtic roots for an explanation.

TOMNAHURICH

TOMNAHURICH

Your correspondent, "Clach," has forgotten the late "Clach's" (Alex. Mackenzie) derivation of Tomnahuirich; this was Tom-na-Fiodhraich, "Hill of the Wood." In favour of this he quoted Thomas Mackenzie, headmaster of Raining's School, and after 1843 connected with the High School. Old Thomas declared the "f" was dropped within the memory of people living in his time, and the old *cailleachs* of the town used to go out to get firewood there, speaking of it as "dol an fhiodhrach." But this is fanciful. The word *fiodhrach* does not mean "wood" in the sense of *trees*, but of *logs* for shipbuilding; even so it is rare. Again, we have the Gaelic pronunciation of Tomnahurich recorded in the Fernaig MS. (1690) in the "Prophesie about Inverness." "There will be battle—

        i dig McPehaig i mach
        Lea layn agus lea luhrich
        Tuitti ni Ghayle ma saigh
        Ma voirlumb toim ni hurich

—in which Macbeth will come forth with sword and armour, and the Gael will fall over other on the Bordland of Tom-na-hurich.'' Mr Thomas Mackenzie's derivation is simply impossible, and it is grammatically bad. Ballifeary no doubt means '' Town of the Watch,'' but I know no Gaelic words that could make Tomnahurich into ''Watchman's Hill.'' A very usual derivation has been the ''Boat Hill,'' from its turned up boat shape, and with this fancy the cemetery at the top seems to have been made into a sort of ship's shape. The name *iubhrach* for boat is poetical, and derived from the name of the fatal mythic vessel that conveyed Clan Uisneach back to Ireland. The name simply means the '' Yew Ship.'' For, after all wanderings, we must fall back on the manifest meaning. Tom-na-h-Iubhraich means simply '' Hill of the Yew Wood ''; *iubhrach* means a yew wood, from *iubhar*, yew, just as *giuthsach* means '' Pine-wood '' (Kin-gussie is Cinn-ghiuthsaich, older *ghiúsaigh*); *beitheach*, birch-wood, and so on. The old Irish for *iubhar* was *ibar* and the Gaulish stem is *eburo*, common in place names and even tribal names. York was called Eburacum, which is much the same form as *iubhrach*, which stands for Celtic *Eburākon*.

PLACE-NAMES

OF

ROSS AND CROMARTY

PLACE-NAMES OF ROSS AND CROMARTY. By W. J. Watson, M.A. (Aberd.), B.A. (Oxon). Inverness : Northern Counties Printing and Publishing Co. 1904. 10s 6d.

MR WATSON's book on the place-names of Ross and Cromarty holds a unique position : it is the first attempt by a Gaelic-speaking Celt, trained in modern philologic ways, to give in book-form the results of a thorough investigation into the names of a large county, and, incidentally, to give a practical epitome of Scottish place-names. Many years ago—in 1887—Professor Mackinnon published in the *Scotsman* a series of articles on "Place and Personal Names in Argyle," marked by that modern scholarship which native Gaelic speakers so abundantly lack in dealing with such matters, but, unfortunately for the public, he has never gathered them into book-form. There have also been several other competent, and, at the same time, Gaelic-speaking philologists who dealt with the place-names of different localities in papers and articles more or less fugitive. Mr Watson, however, is really the first Gael in the field with a work which can be honestly called scientific, which systematises its results in a way helpful for investigators in this difficult subject. It has only been too painfully evident of late years that only a learned native Gael—or a German!—can really deal with the Celtic names of Scotland. Hitherto the authors of works on Scottish place-names have not taken the trouble to learn the Gaelic language—and that, too, a language which possesses a double set of inflections, initial, and, as usual, final, not to mention the fact of its difficult Continental pronunciation. It is no wonder that one Sassenach writer on the subject, on getting from a Highlander the correct Gaelic form of a certain combination which he meant for the explanation (*by appearance*) of a certain place-name, rejected this correct form of spoiling his derivation, and kept his own original wrong combination! Such a scientist as the late James Macdonald of Huntly, who honestly tried to acquire the language, never attained complete correctness in reproducing Gaelic names pronounced to him by the natives. What with the Gaelic article causing aspiration and eclipsis, bewildering to a non-Celt, and the other phonetic and syntactic *finesse* of a language which has undergone more than ordinary philologic change, Gaelic is a language which only a very well trained outsider can have anything to do with. This training our place-name philogists as yet refuse to undergo. And there are also the history of the lan-

guage—its changes through hundreds of years
—and the history of the country during the
same time, all to be taken into account.   It may
truly be said that the writer who undertakes to
deal with the Celtic place-names of Scotland
must undergo no ordinary linguistic and historic
training.

Mr Watson fulfils all the requirements of the
philologist we need to elucidate our Celtic place-
names.   His Introduction of some hundred
pages is a mine of practical information, thoroughly systematised.   In dealing with Gaelic
names, the student will be first struck with the
large place which he gives to suffixes   To the
ordinary philologist every ending in -ach is for
achadh, " field "; Mr Watson shows this suffix
to be old Celtic -ācum, denoting " place of,"
such as Carn-ach, " place of cairns," or Dornoch, " place of hand-stones."   He shows with
clearness how suffixes combine : Muc-ar-n-aich,
" place of pigs," where we have three suffixes
(ar, an, ach).   One important point which he
brings out is the undoubted existence of a
diminutive -aidh or-idh, at least in old Pictland.
He adduces lochaidh, badaidh, and lagaidh as
outstanding examples.   These suffixes seem to
be the old Celtic ending in -io-s, or fem. -ia, the
latter very common in river names.   The difficulty here, however, is the modern Gaelic pro-

20

nunciation in final -*idh*, not -*e* as in usual Gaelic. The Welsh, however, pronounce, or rather spell, this ending (-*io-s*) in its modern form as -*ydd*. It would seem that in this diminutive ending -*aidh* we have distinctive traces of Pictish or Brittonic pronunciation of these place-names. We have such diminutives in old Gaelic in certain personal names, such as Barre (St Barr) for Barrio-s, and this again for Barro-vindos or Barrfhind, which we know to be the full name of the Saint. Those acquainted with the old charter forms of place-names know that -*ie*, the Scottish form of G. -*aidh*, is continually interchanged with -*in*. This last, which does not usually exist in a Gaelic form, must be the old Pictish stem-ending (from -*iô*, gen. -*inos*) in *n*, known well in Scottish Gaelic, and giving rise to the modern Gaelic plural, just like the weak stems in the Teutonic languages. Material for pursuing this and kindred points will be found in abundance in Mr Watson's volume. We may also note his excellent tabulation of Norse vowels and consonants in Gaelic; it should be very useful to students of Northern names. But does not Homer nod in explaining Saraig as Saur-Vík (Mud-bay), the phonetics of which by the table result in Sòraig? Compare Soroba, Sorby, and English Sowerby.

The main body of the work deals *seriatim* with the twenty-nine mainland parishes of Ross and with Lewis in general. Each parish forms, as it were, a chapter by itself; the place-names are dealt with in separate articles, vocabulary-wise, but not in alphabetical order. The "English" or map-name is given first; then the old forms from charters, documents, or histories; then the Gaelic form, where such is existent; and, lastly, the meaning or derivation. Mr Watson has heard all the pronunciations personally, and he has visited practically every corner of the county. On this head the work is most thoroughly done, and the derivation offered suits the characteristics of the place, if it be named after any characteristics. The county name Ross he is inclined to derive from Brittonic or Pictish sources, corresponding to Welsh *rhos*, "a wold," rather than from Gaelic *ros*, "a promontory," but the words are no doubt ultimately the same. Cromarty contains the adjective *crom*, "bent," but the old forms are puzzling, and the modern Gaelic Cromba` points only to *crom-bath*, "curved sea." Mr Watson restores the old name as Crom-b-ach-dan, the *b* being a development (of Pictish times?) and the rest mere suffixes, the total meaning "Bay Place." Pictish, Norse, and Gaelic names jog one another all over the county, but, as the author well shows, there is a marked difference between Easter Ross names and those of Wester Ross, the latter being more

Gaelic and more modern really.   The Norse element stops at the Beauly and Tarradale and Eskadale (Ash-dale, lately explained as Uisge-dail!).   Pictish names are common in East Ross.   One of these we have in Bal-keith, doubtless for older Pit-keith; Gaelic, Baile-na-Coille, a translation which, as Mr Watson points out, seems to prove that Keith means "wood," from a word allied to Welsh *coed*, "wood"; Gaulish *ceto-*, allied to English *heath*.   Dal-keith is therefore Brittonic in both elements, "Plateau of the wood" (Welsh *dol*, Pictish *dul*, *dal*).   Space does not allow us to follow Mr Watson further in quoting his interesting deriva-tions, but we must mention some old or peculiar words which he has been enabled to recognise or rescue.   Strikingly happy is his derivation of the place-names Nonakil ("church-land"), Newmore, Dalnavie, and Navity, from the old Gaelic *nemed* (*neimhidh* now), "a sacred place," which we have also in Rosneath. *Eirbhe* or *airbhe*, "a wall," is found in Altna-harrie, etc.; *rabhan*, a kind of bulrush; *saothair*, a neck that joins a "dry-island" to the shore, a promontory covered at high tide; *faithir*, the steep face of an old raised beach; *feodhail*, a side form of *faodhail*, "a ford," from Norse *vadhill*, "shallow water"; *sleaghach*, a rifted or gullied slope or hill, from the same root as *slighe*, "path," literally "a cutting" (root *sleg*, "hit," "cut "). On the west coast *cathair* means a "fairy knoll," while *sithean* means a considerable hill with no notions of fairies attached thereto. Mr Watson rightly queries *druineach* as Druid; the meaning is artist, artificer, sculptor (Mr Carmichael's *draoineach*). Irish *druine* means " art," even " needlework." We demur to Mr Watson's derivation of Killearnan. True the Gaelic is Cill-Iurnain, which might point to a St Iturnan, only the name Iturnan is a misreading for Itarnan, a true Pictish name and a saint's name also. Ernin or Ferreolus was a favourite saint and a favourite saint's name, and to a root-inflected form of Ernin or Iarnan we must refer Iurnan.

Mr Watson has added a valuable index to his work, containing over three thousand words, and showing by a device with the full stop where the main accent rests. Many of these words naturally belong to districts outside Ross. Indeed the volume, as already said, is a microcosm of Scottish place-names, the Anglic Lothians and the Merse being left out of account. It lays a sound basis for the further study of Scottish place-names on modern philologic lines.

PLACE NAMES

OF

ELGINSHIRE

THE PLACE NAMES OF ELGINSHIRE. By D.
Matheson, F.E.I.S.   Stirling : Eneas Mackay.   1905.

MR D. MATHESON, lately head of an educational
institution in Elgin, and now editor of the
Northern Times, is the latest recruit to the slowly
increasing authors on place names.   His work
on the '' Place Names of Elginshire '' is a handsome volume of over two hundred pages, published by Eneas Mackay, Stirling, and dedicated
to Mr Carnegie.   Works on place names have
steadily been getting more scientific as their
authors have studied the science of language and
the possibilities which the history, the physical
features, and the languages of the localities dealt
with afford.   The authors have also profited by
reading what has recently been done by others
in the same line.   Mr Matheson, however,
stands by himself, and is a law to himself on
language and history.   He has consulted Skeat's
Etymological Dictionary, but not with profit; he
does not know that there is a corresponding
Gaelic Etymological Dictionary, considered of

equal authority according to leading Celtic scholars.   The latter

> " Wad from many a blunder free him
> And foolish notion."

No doubt Mr Watson's book on the "Place Names of Ross-shire" came out too late to be of use to him; this is a pity, if Mr Matheson would have utilised the methods and results attained there—which is doubtful.   Mr Johnston, of Falkirk, he does quote; it is a pity that he did not use even this indifferent work to better purpose.   In short, Mr Matheson belongs to the old school of etymologists.   He has no compunction to refer a Moray name to a German, Dutch, or Scandinavian origin straight away, without considering the question of how the Germans, for example, could ever have planted a name in Moray.   Thus, for Knockgranish, near Aviemore, he gives: "from the Gaelic 'Cnoc,' a hill, and the Teutonic 'Gran' or 'Grense,' a boundary," the latter being a German word.   How could he get his Germans up to the heights of Craigellachie several centuries ago?   Besides, Granish is famous in works on Druid lore, as our author should have known.   Again, Balvatton, in Cromdale, is taken from Gaelic 'baile' and Norse 'vatn,' water.   Were the Vikings anytime about Grantown?   Of course, the name means 'Town of the clump (badan).'   In his Scandinavian eagerness, he antedates them by 600 years. Lossie, Ptolemy's Loxa, dates to 120 A.D. at least; the Vikings came in 800 A.D.; yet our author calmly asserts that Loxa is Laxa of Norse, ' salmon river ' ! It means ' winding river ' (Old Gaelic *losc*).   In matters Gaelic, Mr Matheson belongs to the school of the late Colonel Robertson, famed for his '' Topography of Scotland.''   We thought that Mr Matheson knew Gaelic; we are now doubtful.

In history Mr Matheson's work is '' second hand of second hand,'' and his introduction is an extraordinary jumble.   Lollius Urbicus, about whom only a few words exist recording the fact of his building the thirty-two mile wall, is represented as conquering to the Beauly Firth, calling the district southward Vespasiana !   Where in the world did Mr Matheson get this utterly absurd statement?   His confusion in regard to Ptolemy is quite inexcusable, as excellent editions of that author's Geography of Scotland can be easily got at (Gaelic Society's Trans. XVIII.; Proc. Society of Antiquaries, XI., by Captain Thomas).   There he could see that Burghead was in Ptolemy's original ' Greek ' (not Latin) Pteroton Stratopedon, or ' winged camp,' and that such ' fool ' work as Tor-an-duin, founded on Ptolemy's word Pteroton, was beneath notice. Mr Matheson has the Scandinavians on the brain.

One third of his Moray names, speaking roughly, he refers to Scandinavian sources; now it is safe to say that not one name in Moray is due directly to the Scandinavians. They never colonised there, and the only recorded battle fought by them in Moray was that of Torfnes, in which they defeated King Duncan (probably). The assertions of the Saga, when examined judicially, show that the Norse made a " blood-red " foray through Moray to Fife. Undoubtedly they held part of the old province of Moray—the Ross portion—and this is the foundation for the Saga statements. From place names we know they stopped at Beauly river, the old limit of the province of Ross. All Mr Matheson's Norse derivations may be unmercifully excised, but with what a result to the book ! That there are Norse and Dutch names in Moray we do not doubt; but these were brought in by the English and Norman-French planted in the district in the 12th century to replace the transported natives. This is historical, and if Mr Matheson had studied the Teutonic names in Moray with these facts of the 12th century in his mind, he would certainly have added to our knowledge both of place names and history. A few of the names brought in by these colonists from Lothian, Danish Cumberland, and, even, Flanders, may be pointed out. Hatton is in Moray three times—' heathton ' (Taylor); common in England; Overton,

Harestanes, Middleton, Whiterigs, Unthank (useless land), Oakenhead or Aikenhead (Blaeu), Orton, Ogston, Coleburn (compare Cold-beck of Cumberland), Ormiston, Mundale (Mundwell or 'Inlet-field' over the borders, whence the Border surname Mundel—Norse in origin), and several others. This would have been a fertile field of research; but Mr Matheson's Scandinavian wet blanket is over it all.

Mr Matheson wastes much space by giving the derivation not only of the place name, but the derivation also of the constituent words. Thus, if a place is called 'Hill-head,' surely for ordinary purposes it is sufficient to say "from Eng. 'hill' and 'head.'" No! Mr Matheson must etymologise both 'hill' and 'head'—thus :—

"*Hillhead.*—Middle English *hil, hul*, Anglo-Saxon *hyll*, Dutch *hil*, Latin *collis*, Lituanian [*sic!*] Kalnas, a hill, and head from the Middle English *hed*, heed, heued, Anglo-Saxon heafod, Dutch hoofd, Icelandic hofud, Latin caput, Greek Kephale [*sic!* really allied to Eng. *gable*], Sanskrit Kapala, literally a skull, and by usage a head, or end."

Such is the passage, with all its imperfections of typing (not due to the printer) and derivation. If Mr Matheson had dropped these useless additions to simple *hill* and *head*, he would have reduced his book by about one half.   But the

worst of it is that he iterates these lists every
time the respective words turn up, and if the
derivations are all awry, as they are usually in
Gaelic, the constant repetition is doubly irritating. The Gaelic word *lag*, with its derivatives
lagan and *logie*, occur very often, but nearly
every time we have this piece of atrocity
attached :—

. " Gaelic *lag*, *lug*, German *lucke*, and cognate
with the Latin *Lacus*, and Greek *Lakkos*, a
hollow or lake."

Now it is just possible that ' lag ' may be allied
to German ' lucke,' gap (Kluge is doubtful about
its derivation), but certainly it is not allied to
either of the Latin or Greek words, which agree
with Gaelic ' loch.' Mr Matheson has been very
unwise to touch Gaelic derivation, considering
his knowledge of the subject, and the further
fact that his particular derivation work is already
competently done and placed before the public
in dictionary form.

Some other leading errors must be pointed
out. The termination ' -as,' ' -us,' ' -ais ' is
common in Moray, as it is in all Pictland. Mr
Matheson, in an evil moment following old Shaw,
made this to be ' eas,' waterfall, though Shaw
adds the idea of ' water ' generally. The number of waterfalls in Moray would have been
counted by scores were this derivation true.
The suffix denotes ' place,' ' station,' and is no

doubt derived from the root 'ves,' 'vos,' dwell, be, allied to Greek 'astu,' a city, Sanskrit 'vastu,' a place, and perhaps to Gaelic 'fois.' Dallas means 'plane place,' from old 'dul,' now 'dail'; Rothes, 'place of *raths* or granges'; Duffus, 'dark place'; Forres, 'lower place,' Pictish 'voter,' 'fother,' 'for,' 'far'; Forres, Mr Matheson says, appears in Ptolemy as Varris —which is not the case; Granish, 'rough place' (gràn), not 'grense' of German (Mr M.), nor 'grian' of the Druidists; and here add 'gourish,' of Ach-gourish, etc., 'place of goats.' Similarly Pityoulish is for Pit-geldais, the root 'geld' (Geldie, etc.) denoting 'water,' as in old Eng. 'child' (Chillam), a spring, Norse 'kelda,' spring, whence St Kilda. The prefix 'lyne' appears very often in the Strathspey portion of Moray. Mr Matheson derives this from 'linne,' pool. It is safe to say, but with one exception, not one of the many names so prefixed comes from 'linne.' The word is 'loinn,' locative of 'lann,' a land, a glade, Welsh 'llan,' of which our author speaks so often. Here Mr Matheson has failed in his duty towards Gaelic and local pronunciation: 'loinn' is very different in pronunciation from 'linne,' and the mistake is inexcusable. Besides, there are no pools near most of the places so named; here Mr Matheson fails in his facts. As a matter of fact, he does not know the County from a linguistic standpoint.

His Gaelic derivations are naturally best tested by the Highland border parishes—Abernehy, Duthil, Cromdale, and Edinkillie. The ' aber ' of Abernethy is from ' od-' or ' ad-ber,' Lat. ' af-fer,' root ' fer,' ' ber,' bear; "there never has been any doubt " about this among modern philologists till Mr Matheson has cast it. Abernethy is derived by Mr Matheson from Aber n-aitionn, ' confluence of the broom '; we cannot characterise this piece of ineptitude. The rivers Lochy and Lochty come from Loch-dae, ' Black ' (loch) and ' dae ' (goddess), not from Lochdubh, as Mr Matheson says; for Adamnan distinctly speaks of ' Nigra dea ' as the translation of the Lochaber Lochy. ' Tobar,' well, is not the same as ' dobhar,' water, nor as ' tiobar,' well, though the first and last are both from the root ' bhru,' spring. Auchtercheper, in Duthil, is for Achadh-da-tiobar, ' field of the two wells,' not Mr M.'s ' uachdar-ceap-tir,' which is impossible in view of the Gaelic sounds. Ry-voan, in Abernethy, is ' Bothie-reach,' not ' peat-reach.' Mr Matheson spells this common word Ry very badly as ' reidh '; it is ' ruigh,' a stretch or piece of land at the base of a hill, also ' a fore arm.' Causor, in Abernethy, is Cabhsair (causeway), not ' Casair.' The Desher of Duthil is not from Lat. ' disertum,' but from Gaelic ' deisear,' south side, Loch-tay Disher, where also is old Toyer, still ' tuathair.' Seemingly Duthil is an

assimilation of Tuathail (north side), to Desher
on the south side of the same hill. Carr-Bridge,
Drochaid Charra, is from ' cartha,' a pillar stone,
old Irish ' coirthe.' The pillar stone or stones
are there. Slochd surely is from Gaelic ' sloc,'
a pit, gully. Gallovie, as in Laggan, is a derivative of ' geal,' ' White-land.' Lochnellan,
Loch-an-ellan, is ' Loch with Isle.' It is curious what a *penchant* the amateur philologist has
for ' àilean,' green spot, which is really rare in
place names. So is ' àite,' place; it scarcely
occurs, yet according to the amateur it is every-
where. Inverallan is from Allan river; this
river-name is common in Pictland and Welsh-
land, and is possibly from the root ' pal,' Lat.
' palus,' marsh. Anyway, it is not from ' àilean,'
a green. The derivation given for Knockando
—' Cnocan-dubh '—shows that Mr Matheson
never heard the Gaelic of the name, which is
Cnoc-cheannachd, ' Market knoll.' Even the
Sassenach etymologists know this, and use it as
a warning name! Dalchapple is derived by Mr
M. from ' caibeal,' a chapel, which in Scotch
Gaelic is ' seipeal.' Of course the name means
here and elsewhere ' Dell of the horses (capull).'
Fionnlarig is ' White pass,' from ' làraig,' a
pass, ' learg,' hill-side.

Mr Matheson, of course, gives himself un-
bridled license in regard to hybrids; Gaelic,

21

English, and other Teutonic roots are welded together indifferently. The worst case is that of Ptolemy's Tvesis, now known to be Spey (Scotch 'spate' allied). This Mr Matheson writes Teussis, and derives from the Greek Teukrion; on what principles, we wot not. Where a word begins as Gaelic, Mr Matheson should remember, it will end in Gaelic. A funny hybrid is recorded in Pit-airlie; this is Pictish 'pet' and Eng. 'early'! He shows a preference for the out-of-the-way rather than the evident etymology. Cummingston is from St Cummein, not from the Cummings. Is this likely? Blinkbonny appears thrice, each time with a new derivation; first, French 'blanc,' white, Gaelic 'ban,' hill [sic]; second, Fr. 'blanc,' G. 'bàn,' white ('White-white'!); third, as 'blink' of Eng. and 'bonny' of Sc., which, of course, it really is. Rev. Mr Johnston gives several other places so named, and translates it 'Belle-vue.' The Pictish 'pett' or 'pit' is not allied to English 'pit' (p. 150), as the modern discussions on the Pictish question should have taught Mr Matheson. The places called Bauds seem to be from the plural of G. 'bad,' a clump—'place of clumps.' Very many other mistakes could be pointed out in the names of the Laigh of Moray, apart from the Highland parishes. Elgin, as a name, cannot be separated from Glen-elg; the word 'elg' in ancient Gaelic means ' noble.' As for Moray, its oldest forms are Mureb, Norse Mærhæfi, now Morro or Mortho. The whole points to a Pictish Moriti, dative pl. Moritobis, whence Murref of early documents and Norse Mærhæfi. It would aspirate into Morthaibh, acc. Morthu (Pictish Moritos), admirably suiting the modern phonetics. The root is ' mor ' of ' muir,' sea, and the Gaulish tribal name Morini is its exact parellel. The meaning is ' Sea-side folk.' The exact value of Mr Matheson's book we care not to assess. Of course, every one interested in place names should have it. If he had given the old forms of the names with dates, this in itself would be of great value; if he had indicated the pronunciation with accented syllable, this also would be, *pace* Mr Matheson, of great importance. But his references to old forms are vague and sometimes misleading, as when he means by old or primary form-what he conceives to have been the old form. As a working list of names, with some historic facts, the book will do.

PLACE-NAMES

OF

SCOTLAND

A Review of " Place-Names of Scotland "
by the Rev. James B. Johnston, B.D.,
Falkirk. Published by Mr David Douglas,
Edinburgh, 1884.

" Place-Names of Scotland " is the name of
a book by the Rev. James B. Johnston, B.D.,
Falkirk, published by Mr David Douglas, Edinburgh. The proper title of the book should
have been something like that of Colonel
Robertson's work on the Gaelic Topography of
Scotland. Both books deal mainly with the
Gaelic names of Scotland, real or supposed, and
both are equal in philologic value. Indeed, Mr
Johnston's work is distinctly worse than his predecessor's on many points, despite his having
the advantage of several works that have
appeared since Colonel Robertson's pioneer
book of over twenty years ago. Mr Johnston
has at least a nodding acquaintance with Professors Mackinnon and Rhys, and, really, from
the state of philologic knowledge in Scotland at
present, we should have expected much better
results. He confesses to only an amateur's

knowledge of Gaelic, but he might have saved himself the trouble of the confession. His work too plainly reveals the fact. And we need not wonder at his saying in regard to Gaelic spelling, " that there is probably no language in the world in which the eye can give less help to the tongue." This is simply nonsense. Few languages are written more strictly according to rule, and, if Mr Johnston had only taken the trouble to master these rules, he would have saved himself from any amount of bad etymologising.

Gaelic is only one portion—though the largest—of the equipment necessary for one that is to tackle the place-names of Scotland. A knowledge of the principles and practice of philology is absolutely necessary; and, though Mr Johnston knows some philologists like Professors Rhys and Mackinnon, and quotes them, yet personally he knows nothing of philology. When he has to trust to his own unaided resources, the result is philologically lamentable. Again, a clear conception of the history of Scotland is necessary for the place-name etymologist. Were the Gaels really the first inhabitants of Scotland? and is one justified in looking for Gaelic place-names in South-Eastern Scotland? Is it not the case that Gaelic did not penetrate south of the Forth until the Macalpine dynasty (844-1033)? We omit Galloway, and the western coast as far as the Clyde. The Gaelic place-names that occur in the Edinburgh district clearly belong to Gaelic that had already borrowed deeply of the Norse. The prefix *dal*, a dale, is a Gaelic word borrowed from the Norse; and the Dalkeiths and Dalrys south of the Forth prove that they were so named much later than the year 800, when the Norsemen came first. Another point is the Pictish question. Were the Picts also Gaels? Skene, of course, says they were : they spoke a low Gaelic dialect, he says—whatever that may mean. But Mr Johnston, who accepts Skene's views, does him a real injustice by supposing that he ever maintained the absurd idea that the Cornish was a Gaelic language. That language is Brythonic of the Brythonic. Could Mr Johnston not decide that point himself by testing the language philologically, instead of pitting Skene against Rhys?

Further, Mr Johnston has not made himself acquainted with all the literature of his subject. Professor Mackinnon's articles on Argyllshire Place-Names he knows, and also Sir Herbert Maxwell's Topography of Galloway. It is doubtful if he has consulted Captain Thomas's two contributions on the Place-Names of the Hebrides and of Islay, in the Society of Antiquaries' Transactions. They are, outside Pro-

fessor Mackinnon's articles—and he owes much
to Captain Thomas—the best thing done in
Scottish topography.   Mr Johnston has overlooked many of Captain Thomas's derivations,
which are correct, while his own are not.
Further, many papers have appeared in the
Transactions of the Inverness Gaelic Society on
this subject, all of them being good, some being
excellent.   Dr Cameron's paper on Arran
Place-Names appeared in Volume XV. It would
have saved Mr Johnston from etymologising
Lamlash as Lan-Maol-Iosa, for it was the island
that was called Lamlash, that is, Eilean-Molais,
the Isle of Molas, a well-known Irish saint. We
may mention Mr Mackay's excellent series of
papers on Sutherland Place-Names in the same
Transactions, Mr Macbain's Badenoch Place-
Names, and Mr Maclean's papers on Alness and
Kiltearn.   Besides, Dr Whitley Stokes passed
in review the old Pictish names in the Philological Society's Transactions last year.   He
clearly showed that *aber* and *pet* or *pit*, as prefixes, are Pictish, and that Pictish belongs to
the Welsh group. Besides, Pictland extended
from the Forth to the Orkneys, and Pets and
Abers can be traced as far north as Sutherland
and as far west as Drumalban.

Mr Johnston opens with some chapters on
general principles, where he passes in review
the characteristic of Celtic, Gaelic, Norse, and

other place designations. We need not speak of his philology. Suffice it to say that he equates the Welsh *pen* with Gaelic *ben*, and concludes, like Skene, that Welsh p may appear as Gaelic b. Now, Gaelic *beann* has a very good Welsh equivalent in Welsh *ban*, of like meaning and use; while *pen* is the corresponding form to Gaelic *ceann* or *Kin-*. Gaelic final r is never lost like the Norse r; so Geldie cannot be Gelder, nor Orchy be *urchar*, a cast. *Aber* is not strengthened either to *ar* or *ab*, but a syllable is left out, if it repeats the same sound as the previous one, or there is a metathesis of the r as in Arbroath. Hence the Aberbreachy of 1334 loses one of its *bers* and now appears as *Abriachan*, which Mr Johnston absurdly etymologises into *Abhriabhach*, grey water. And here we say something of Mr Johnston's *abh* and *an* for water. *They are mere figments of his own and other etymologists' imagination.* No such words exist or have existed in the Gaelic language, and yet several scores of Mr Johnston's derivations depend upon these words! The *an* which terminates several river names is a mere adjective termination seen to advantage in the Gaulish river-names Sequana or Matrona. The word *aoi*, isthmus, is a Norse word, and cannot form the root of Iona, nor can *i*, island, which again is the *ey* of Norse borrowed. Mr Johnston's lack of knowledge of Gaelic makes him use the absurdest of Gaelic words, so long as the sound suits. Some of the words he offers are obsolete, some rare, and some are, as already said, mere figments of the dictionary-maker. The Gaelic *uisg*, water, has nothing to do with the Pictish Esk, Ptolemy's Iska. Mr Johnston's theory about Hybrids is ridiculous, and both his examples are demonstrably wrong. Newtonmore, where he regards *more* as Gaelic *mòr*, big, is really Newton-muir, the Muir's Newton—Baile-ùr-an-t-sléibh in Gaelic! His Garrabost is explained by Captain Thomas as Geirabost or Geirr's Bost or Farm, and not Garbh Bost, the rough farm. If Mr Johnston wants a proper hybrid he must look for forms where the sense of the older word has been forgotten. Such a case occurs in a name like Strath-halladale, where the idea of *dale* is repeated twice, the Gaels not recognising that the terminal *dal* meant a dale.

We may now take a few specimens of Mr Johnston's derivations, beginning at Inverness. He suggests that Ness may be from *nios*, from below; but *nios* has the long *i* sound and the *i* of the Gaelic for Ness is short. We need not speak here or elsewhere of how inapplicable the sense of the Gaelic words offered is to the river or place-name. Clachnacuddin is etymologised as Clachcudachan or St Cuthbert's stone, not Clach nan cìdainn, the tubs' stone. Clachnaharry fares equally badly : the root is given as *carraid*, strife, instead or *aire*, watching. Nairn is for *an arn*, the flank, where the word *arn* is a figment of the lexicographer. Ross means really a wood or moor, not a promontory. Moray is of course *Mor abh*, big water! Yet it is clear that the root is *mor*, sea, for the vowel is short. Aberdeen may represent the confluence of either Dee or Don, it seems. The Dee he takes from the Gaelic *Deabhadh*, draining, though Ptolemy's *Deva* makes it clear that it and his Devana or Divona, now Don, both mean "goddess," and indicate the existence of river worship, of which we hear from Gildas.

"Philology founded on sound is not sound philology," and when Mr Johnston etymologises Knockando as Cnocan-dubh, black hillock, he commits two blunders : he should attend to the place of the accent on words; that shows where the main root of the word lies, the accent being in this case on the *and*; and he should know that the real Gaelic name of the place is Cnoc-cheannachd or Market hill, as old Shaw carefully explained over six score years ago. The Gaelic accent is of course on the first part of *Ceannachd*. Aviemore is abh mor, big water; but the Gaelic pronunciation is *Agaidh mhór*, the big *agie*, whatever that may be. Balintore is given as Baile an Deoraidh, the Dewar's town, but the name really means the town of the Bleaching.

Balfour, and the other words in *four*, is a glaring example of bad etymologising.   In these words, the accent is on the *four*, which clearly shows that this is the main root.   But Mr Johnston explains *four* as for *fuar*, cold.   Yet Dalfour, if for cold dale, would undoubtedly in Gaelic be Dailfhuar, that is Dal-uar, with the accent on the Dal and the *f* entirely gone.   The *four* of these words must stand for *pour*, a Pictish word denoting pasture land—if we may guess from the Breton *peur*, Welsh *pawr*.   This etymology, suggested in "Badenoch Place-Names," has been accepted by Dr Whitley Stokes in his revised edition of his Pictish vocabulary.   Curiously the prefix *both*, habitation, which is so common in Gaelic Place-Names, finds scarcely a place in our author's work.   Yet Boleskine, Balquidder, and several others show this prefix.

Mr Johnston is not satisfied with one or two root words, in explaining a name of any length, and he generally manages to stick on an extra *abh*, *an*, or *ach* (for *achadh*, field).   Cabrach is for cabar-achadh, deer field, whereas the *ach* here and elsewhere is the adjective termination. Conan is for con-ân, or caoin abhuinn, gentle river, which, as a matter of fact, it is not. Glencoe is variously derived from *cu*, *coin*, dog, or from *coill*, wood, or from *comair*, confluence. Yet the Gaelic name is Gleann-comhann, or narrow glen. Mr Johnston's alternative derivations are always irritating, and the fact of his giving them shows how utterly unreliable and unscientific his work is. Culloden is given as *Cul-lodan*, back of the pool; but the Gaelic is Cuilodair. Culross is anciently Culenross, or Holly-wood. Dalarossie is not the field of the *ros* or promontory, but Dail-fhearghuis, or Fergus' dale. Dalnavert is not Dal-na-bhaird, Bard's dale, but Dail-nan-feart, dale of the graves. The word *dabhach*, four ploughgates, is not from *damh-ach* (sic!), ox field, but from *dabhach*, a tub or corn measure. Dulnan is not Dail an án, river dale, but *Tuilnean*, from *tuil*, flood. The Earn is not Ear án, east flowing, for the Gaelic is Eire, with long e, and its genitive is Eireann, the same name as Ireland. Auldearn is in Gaelic Allt-Eire or Earn Stream. Feshie cannot be from *fásach*, desert; it is a river name, and the root vowel is short e, not long a. Garry cannot be from *garbh*, rough; the Gaelic is Garadh. The Gaelic *gàrradh* is merely the English *garden* borrowed. Gask is not for *crosg*, a crossing. Urquhart is absurdly explained by Ard-a'-cheàird, smith's height. Now, Adamnan, about 700, gives this name as Airchartdan, where the *air* is clearly the preposition, and the root word is *cartd* or *card*. With this name we must connect Kincardine, which seems a half Pictish word for " end of the rowan wood"; not *cinn gairdein*, head of the arm, as Mr Johnston has it. We might deal thus with over a third of Mr Johnston's some three thousand words. The work is a mass of guess-work, slavishly following the spelling, and forgetting too often the history of the word or its present sound. Indeed, without indicating the modern sound of the word and the place of the accent, such books as this are worthless. Mr Johnston gives from the *Origines Parochiales*, the oldest forms of many names, and we must say that this is the most valuable contribution he has made to the elucidation of the Place-Names of Scotland.

THE PLACE-NAMES

OF

ARGYLL

THE PLACE-NAMES OF ARGYLL. By H. C. Gillies, M.D. London: D. Nutt. 1906.

DR GILLIES' work has been received with a universal chorus of praise by the press, from the London "Tribune" to the *Oban Times*. The reviews were commendably short, for they showed no marks of familiarity with Gaelic place-names. There has been, therefore, no expert opinion offered as yet to our knowledge; and as Ian Maclaren has just said, "the present day is a day of experts; the day of amateurs is past," adding that in any subject we seek expert advice when we wish to know. There are very few experts in Celtic scholarship or in Gaelic scholarship to-day in Scotland, but their number is increasing with fair rapidity, thanks to our Celtic Chair. In this work on Argyll Place-Names, Dr Gillies comes forward on his own credentials as an expert in Gaelic philology in its most difficult aspect, that of elucidating place-names. He says :—" I am quite aware that the work is far from perfect. No person could make it perfect; and certainly no one in my position, with my poor scraps of available time, could do it better. I believe it is as nearly correct as any one could make it." Now here Dr Gillies gets a little mixed in his climax. First, he can do it as well as any man in his position as regards time; second, the work is as good as any man can do, time or not! Really the Doctor protests too much. The book, however, takes the same Sir Oracle tone throughout. The work of previous writers he ignores or overlooks, except in one or two cases. For instance, a careful study of Mr Watson's work on the Place-Names of Ross-shire, which, by its excellent introduction is at once a text book and an example book for the study of Scoto-Celtic place-names, would have saved Dr Gillies many absurdities in his Norse etymologies; for Dr Gillies has quite a craze for explaining names as of Norse origin. A feature of the work is its perversity; long established etymologies are thrust aside for something new or bizarre (as in the case of the county name), or the obvious derivation is overlooked, generally for a Norse one. Again, the format of the book is bad. What is wanted is to give first the map or post-official name; then the modern Gaelic pronunciation; thirdly (if the word is difficult) its oldest forms and changes; lastly, its derivation, with proof adduced, such as the suitability of the explanation to the character of the place. Then the etymologist should, if possible, see the place and hear the name pronounced, or at least he should get a description of the place and hear the pronunciation. As regards the ancient forms, Dr Gillies takes up the monstrous position that they are not necessary, and that, too, when he is professedly dealing with Norse words and difficult Gaelic words. He certainly saves himself much research, but at what risk? Who would for a moment think that modern Askary stands for Norse Asgrims-erg, the "àirigh" of Asgrim? Or Scrabster for Skára-bólstadhr? Then again Dr Gillies has clearly trusted for his form of the name to the ordnance map in too many cases; this is evident, and he admits it in some cases. The motto with the expert in place-names is to accept no ordnance map name unless it is verified. Dr Gillies has had some predecessors in the field of Argyll Place-names. Professor Mackinnon wrote a series of eighteen articles in the. *Scotsman* on the "Place and Personal Names of Argyle" in 1887-8, when he showed the sound, sane scholarship and literary expositive power that ever since has marked his work. And in place-names, sanity and scholarship must conjoin; running after the bizarre or fanciful is fatal. Rev. Mr MacNeil's "Guide to Islay" contains mostly expert-produced derivations, the late Hector Maclean, Captain Thomas, and Dr Macbain having helped. Drs Reeves and Skene went over the names of Iona and Tiree, making valuable lists and exhuming old church names.

So much for preface. The name Argyll is in G., Earraghàidheal; early Gaelic, Airer-gáidhel (Annals of Ulster), i n-airiur Gaoidheol (Three Fragments), etc. The word here is "oirear," district, coastland; Irish, oirear, early Irish, airer. M'Vurich speaks of Argyll as being divided into two districts—"Oirer a deas," Argyll proper; "oirer a tuath," North Argyll to Lochbroom. The name means the "Coastland of the Gael," or, as the 12th century writer puts it in Latin, "Margo Scottorum." The Gael in Ireland and in Scotland bore one or two names, Scot and Gàidheal being the favourites among the people themselves. The present view of Celtic scholars accords with the old annals, not with Skene and later writers. Professor Kuno Meyer writes "that no Gael ever set foot on British soil save from a vessel that first put out from Ireland." The annals put the first invasion of the Scots about 160 A.D., the leader being Cairbre Riada, son of Conaire II., King of Ireland. Other invasions followed, and the Scots and Picts joined to attack Roman Britain. Indeed, about 360 A.D., King Crimthann ruled both Britain or Alba and Ireland. The most important colony came in 501 with the sons of Erc. The Scots latterly extended their conquests south and north, so that when the Norse came in 794 they called the Minch the Scotland Fjord and the Pentland Firth the Pictland Fjord.

Soon· thereafter the Scots took supreme rule.
The above are not Dr Gillies' views. Firstly, as
to Argyll.   He has created a new Irish word for
the occasion; this is " oir-thir," East-land, from
" air" or " oir," before, on, and tìr, land.
Now there is an old and a modern Irish word
like this—" airther," the east, front part; it
comes, as Dr Whitley Stokes points out, from
the comparative of air—comparative in ter,
Greek tero-s.   He gives the old Celtic as
(p)areitero-s, allied to Latin per, pro.   Like
English prepositional comparatives, it is used as
a noun.   It will be seen that Dr Gillies creates
a new word in oir-thìr, for tìr has nothing to do
with the Irish word.   Besides the tìr would pre-
serve its long sound in the compound oir-thír.
This argument topples one of the Doctor's card
houses.   Then as to his history.   In Argyll, he
says, Gaelic " has been there from the beginning."   Getting more poetical, after the Biblical
manner—but somewhat after, he adds :—" It is
written in the rock."   Now this same patriotic
Gael allows that Eachairn, and especially Echdach
(nominative Echaid), are the Gaelic descendants
of Ptolemy's Epidii, the inhabitants of Kintyre,
the *p* of which proves it Pictish or Brittonic!
Gaelic " each " is Welsh " ep," " eb."   As a
matter of fact the Gael did not visit the Epidii for
at least forty years later.   Argyll was then in
the hands of the Picts, who spoke a Brittonic

tongue. It is scarcely worth while noticing that he deduces Fergus Mac Erc's pedigree from Conn Ceudchathach, and not from his son-in-law, Conaire II., descended from Conaire Mór; but such are the unfailing facts according to the annals. He *will* antedate the coming of the Norse by two hundred years; why, one cannot see. Some harum-scarum youth lately announced that a German professor held this belief; but when proof was asked in face of the overwhelming evidence on the other side, it was discovered that the "Norsemen" were the hired men that slew St Donnan and his 52 followers in Eigg or in Sutherland; the annals call them "pirates," using the Latin term *piraiti*. The "Saint's Life" is responsible for a queer story of a queen taking vengeance on Donnan through hired pirates. The evidence that the Norse first came in 793 to the East Coast and burnt the great Monastery of Lindisfarne is firstly contemporary, and, secondly, Dr Gillies ought to know that what affects the Church for good or bad is sacredly recorded. "The Norsemen made a bee-line for the monasteries," once they discovered their wealth. The Norse appeared in Scotland Fjord in 794, and visited Iona, according to one account; in 795 they appeared on the Irish coasts; in 802 they sacked Iona; in 806 they slew the whole *familia*, 68 souls. Dr Gillies, of course, calls the pirates who killed Donnan " Norsemen "—no mistake about it.

Other little foibles are there. The Scots are felt in modern Argyll as Easterlings, or Alban-aich even. He is unaware that Alba meant Great Britain till the 10th century (see for instance Cormac's Gloss, " Mug-eíme"). The Druids, too, appear. Innis Drynich—he hesitates between " droighneach," thorn-wood, and " Druidhnich," Druids. The meaning of this last word, for it is genuine, " druineach," is artist or artificer, ornamentator. The name appears in Cladh nan Druineach (Iona). Cnoc Druidean he corrects to Cnoc Druidhean, but Bishop Reeves, who was there, makes it " Knock of Starlings "! The Church part of the book is fairly done. St Finlagan he has missed; his chapel was in Island Finlagan, where the Lord of the Isles afterwards held high festival. This is all the more remarkable as Mr MacNeill's " Guide " tells all about " Sanctt Finlagane at p. 74. The name was used in a patronymic; Archibald M'Linlagan was at Stremnish in 1686; this is M'Gill Fhinnlagan. The name is a double diminutive of Findlug, which the Scottish Gael corrupted into Findlaoch, whence Finlay. The funniest mistake is about isle Davaar. It is called the Island of " Sanct Barre," 1449-1508; the form Davaar is for older Do-Bharre, " thy St Barre," on the same principle as Mo-Barre,

or Mo-luoc, etc. Dr Gillies devotes a paragraph
to Davaar, and seems to accept the popular derivation "Double-pointed" isle. At anyrate, his
history is at fault. Another saint with "do"
has put him wrong; this is in Kildavie, which he
renders as St David's. It is really dedicated to
Do-Bhì, whom he knows as Mo-Bhì. There is
another such in Skye, which the present writer
also rescued from other saints. Mundu, as from
Mo-fhindu, is good enough phonetics for Dr
Whitley Stokes, and Dr Gillies need not boggle
at it. Brannan is not from "bran," raven; the
saint's name is really Brénaind, the Brīanult of
Martin. Maoldoraidh is a good name in itself,
it is not Maoldeóradh. Maolrubha means
" slave, or king of the promontory." Dr Reeves ·
hesitates between "rubha," patience, or promontory. For examples of such names as Maol,
with abstract, material or place-names, see
Gaelic Society Trans. XX. There is a St Finan
apart from the Findans; he is in Ardnamurchan,
Glengarry, and Abriachan. The root is "fín,"
shining, which appears in Glen Fìnain, or Glenfinnan; not fionn, as Dr Gillies has it. Where
is Kilmodan explained?

Looking at the district and island names we
first find Dr Gillies shaking his head over the too
easy derivations of Cowal and Lorn, from the
names of the grandson and son of Erc. For the
former he suggests, after much thought, the

" feckless " idea of " comhdhail," a meeting!
Had he looked at Irish names like Fer-managh,
Kinel-ea, or Iv-erk, he would see that these were
personal names originally. Men of Monach, Kin
of Aodh, and O'Ercs, used now as land names.
The " Chronicles of the Picts and Scots " makes
it clear that these two names were originally
Cinel Loairnd and Cinel Comgaill. The " Cinel"
simply was dropped in course of time. The
tract on the Scots of Dalriada shows other such
" Cinel " names, and it is worth while examining it to see if more district names might not be
unravelled. Gigha isle, M'Vurich's Giodhaigh,
he derives from Norse " gjá," a chasm, bay,
borrowed into Gaelic as " geòdh," creek, and
" ey," island, the whole being equal to Gjá-ey,
" rift island." The Norse called it Gudhey,
God's isle. Dr Gillies knows better than the
Norse themselves. Kilmaillie he renders into
Gaelic as Cill A' Mhailuibh; there is deep reason
for the Gaelic article. Dr Gillies has evolved
from his inner consciousness a set of " black
friars" before " friar" times, and calls them
" mael," tonsured one, " dubh," black. The
worst of it is that " mael," devotee, is never
qualified by an adjective. When it is, the word
is a confusion for " mál," prince, as Mael-
mordha for Mál-mordha, " great prince," the
name of some thirty kings and lords recorded in
the " Four Masters." Maeldub is " Dark lord,"

and is the name of four saints. But Maeldub could never produce the phonetics of "Màili" of Kilmallie. If Dr Gillies could assure us that Màldubh preserved its *á*, though changed to *ao* elsewhere, then we should allow his derivation from Maeldub, meaning "Black Prince." The Kylmalduff cited by Dr Gillies as the first form of Kilmaillie belongs really to Inveraray; the mistake is quite inexcusable. Dalmaillie and Invermaillie contain river names. It is a common word possibly from a Celtic "Madlios," root *mad*, wet, as practically the Doctor says, without, however, giving the root forms.

Our author (Dr Gillies) thinks he has made a distinct hit in his derivation of Ardnamurchan. The word appears in Adamnan (704) in the nom. pl. and dat. pl., thus :—Artda-muirchol and Artdaib-muirchol. The first part means "heights," not height (Dr G.); Reeves made murchol into "sea-hazels," and Bodley's librarian lately made it into "heights of the sea of Coll," which is not so bad. Our author at any-rate accounts for the modern *n*; he makes it to be Ard na mur(dh)ucan, "height of the sea nymphs"; the word murdúchand means syren in early Irish, from muir, and dúchand, singing (K. Meyer). The length of the *u*, we fear, spoils Dr Gillies' beautiful derivation; it won't leave the word in its most modern form. In Gaelic it gives three syllables. Besides, it does not a bit suit Adamnan's phonetics; he was most accurate, and the MS. was written only a few years after his death. He cannot be trifled with even over the *l* at the end. Rum seems to appear in connection with St Began, called "of Rumm" (676), Norse "rymr" won't do (Dr G.). Eigg is also in Adamnan, but the Doctor has no hesitation in taking it from Norse "egg," edge, which is absurd, as Euclid has it. Adamnan calls it Egea, possibly from "eag," cleft. It is so. Canna isle he deduces from "kunnu," know—a very poor "look-out" indeed, especially as to vowels. The word "cana" means porpoise in older Gaelic. Mull appears as Malaeus in Ptolemy, and so the Norse Múli, a point, is out of the question; Adamnan has Malea. The modern phonetics are correct—liquid *a* short becoming *u* (ball, buill). This really should be a lesson in rash etymologising, for even otherwise Muile, with its short vowel, could not come from Múli with long *u*. But Dr Gillies calls it the "manifest derivation"! Truly with him "vowels count for nothing." Of course Coll (G. Colla) comes incontinently from the Norse —here from "Kolla," a hind. The minister of the island, who has made a most capable survey of the place-names, and who gave the results to the Inverness Gaelic Society, says he has found plenty hazel in the north of the isle, at the nearest landing point to the mainland. The

name comes, as does Colonsay, from "Coll,"
hazel. Colonsay appears in Adamnan as Colosus
—no *n*—and is pre-Norse. Our author takes it
from Norse "kollr," hilltop, another "feckless"
derivation. Iona and Islay possibly belong to
the same root; here we deal with "funda-
mentals." The root seems to be Celtic
"(p)í," Aryan pi, pí, water, drink. We know
it in the Esk rivers, Ptolemy's Iska. Iona might
be Aryan Pì-va, Pi-vi (locative); Islay, Pí-lia.
Islay appears in Adamnan as Ilea, yet Dr Gillies
thinks the termination is Norse "ey," island,
and yet the Norse called it nothing but Il, not
Il-ey! Such is the philology of imagination.
Dr Gillies does not etymologise the roots of Iona
or Islay. We may add the Awe river, Adamnan's Aba, which of course contains the root of
"abhainn," nearly "naked"; the same root,
with double stem, is in Avich. Dr Gillies was
to explain it by a note to p. 58, but in this, as in
other cases, there is no note.

Some words our author has strangely missed
the form and force of are these :—"Aoirinn,"
mass, the offerendum, whence Inchaffray, in
1190 Inchaffren. It occurs in Rhu na h-aoirinn,
Eilean na h-aoirinn, and Erin, Iring (Ardnamurchan). They are places where mass was
held outside. The Doctor here suggests that
very much over-worked Norse word "eyrr," a
beach. The *n* he does not explain, for the word

was never adopted into Gaelic, and the *n* cannot
be the Norse article, which the Doctor does not
seem to know about. "Longart," shieling,
encampment, comes from longphort, originally
meaning "harbourage"—"ship"—port. Taylor, the water poet, speaks of the hunting booths
in the Grampians as Lonquhards (1618). Dr
Gillies cannot explain it, since "the supreme
scholar of our time, not·only of Gaelic, but of
all languages, has failed with the word." The
scholar meant we do not know; perhaps the
Doctor speaks "sarcastic," but the word was
explained in Inverness Gaelic Society Trans.
fifteen years ago. "Lochay" is an unfortunate
miss; Professor Mackinnon in 1887 explained
the word as the translation of Adamnan's
"Nigra dea," his Loch-dae in the index of
chapters. The ending is the gen. of the old
Gaelic word for "goddess." There are several
rivers of this name all over Pictland. River
worship was rife among the Celts as Gildas so
tragically tells us. "Feòirlinn" is another word
over which he hesitates, and at last he lands
wrongly regarding "linn" as pool, and "feoir"
as fjara, ebb, of Norse. The word means
"forthing" or farthing—farthing land; it is
common all over the West Coast; its phonetics
(N. fjordhungr) are represented by "birlinn,"
Norse "byrdhingr." "Doirlinn" is surely
native. Elerig, Iolairig, etc., of which some

two hundred or more occur, usually as Elrig or
even Eldrig, is for " eileirig," an obsolete word
meaning the place where the deer were driven
into, a cul-de-sac, generally beside a hillock or
hill, where the deer-slayers took their place.
The word is in the " Book of Deer " (ind-elerc),
now Elrig. This explanation has been public
property for ten years. Glen Amaind should
be compared to the famous Glen Almond; the
river name Almond is good Celtic "Ambona,"
root amb, ab. " Leth-allt " is a burn with one
high bank, for the word originally meant " cliff,
height " (Lat. *altus*), and its Scotch use is 'due
doubtless to Pictish. " Laimbrig," a landing
place, has been explained as Norse " Hladh-
hamarr," pier or landing rock, plus the word
" vík," a bay (Gaelic Society Trans., XXI.,
317). " Corpach " is rightly explained first,
but why fly to Norse " Korpr," raven? Are
there really Norse words in Lochaber at all?
We think not—at least not east of the Linnhe.
"Corran" means a point, the fem. is " corrag,"
finger; it is common in the Isles; what has
corran, a sickle, to do with it? The root of
corran, sickle, is " kerp, korp," to cut (Stokes).
Dr Gillies follows good company in etymologising
Nant (better Neannt). It is an Englified form
of the native rapid pronunciation 'n-ann-da for
'n abhainn dubh, " Black river." With Coille

or Drochaid prefixed the word is wonderfully
" crashed." together.

Dr Gillies has not done well in trusting to the
ordnance maps. The gem of the book is p. 59;
here on the Awe near its junction with the loch
the map has "Conflicts," and below "1300-
1308," referring, of course, to the feud between
MacDougall and Bruce. The Doctor thinks the
place is called "Conflicts," and gives a Gaelic
"Coingheal"! The map has Clenamachrie,
Dr Gillies corrects to Gleann na machrach, but
the true name is Cladh na Macraidh (Churchyard
of the Young Men). The name Cormac on the
same page is mismanaged; while another Cladh
on page 58 is given as Cleugh and derived from
Scots. Cluniter (51) is rendered Claon-leitir,
whereas it is a sand-bank—Claon-oitir; Drum-
synie, on page 52, is Drum-sineidh, not from
sian. To take a place or two in Coll, for example—Airivirig is locally and by fact Airigh-
mhaoraich, not from N. borg; Airinabost has no
"har" in the name (shieling-ton); Ascaoineach
is for Asknish (ash or ship ness); Clabhach stands
for A' Chlabaich, and comes from clab—it has
nothing to do with the words for "kite"; Foill
is not "treachery," but N. Fjall, hill; Gallan-
ach is so named from a water plant of yellow
colour growing there, and called by the natives
gallan. The most extraordinary miss of all is

23

in the case of Pharspig, Skerray—'' I can make
nothing of it '' (Dr G.), but the local people know
it to be from a very usual name for the sea-gull
—'' farspag.'' Loch Ghille-Caluim is really L.
Cille-Chainnigh, from Kil-Kenneth, St Kenneth,
where the church is. Glen Brander is from
'' Brandradh,'' ravens (abstract pl.). Tiretig-
ean (p. 36) cannot be from Aodhagain or Egan.
That he has trusted to these maps is also proved
by such remarks as at p. 72—'' I do not know
the local history.''

As regards the Norse names, Dr Gillies gets
more in love with Norse derivations as the book
progresses.

Proaig he will not have as Norse Broadbay,
but it is pronounced like the Gaelic of Brodick
save for the initial p, which is not likely to be
Norse anyway. Gaelic often interchanges b and
p in borrowed words; the dictionary amply
proves that. Crosprig and Librig show final
'' brekka,'' bank, or possibly '' berg,'' hill, in
the form '' brg.'' Melfort is surely N. mela-fjord,
'' bent firth,'' from the common word '' melr,''
bent grass. Seil Isle is no doubt Norse; the
Gaelic Saoil is phonetically the ideal form of
Norse '' seil.'' Soroba is the common Norse
place-name '' Saur-bær,'' mud or swamp or
sour-ton. It appears as Sowerby in Yorkshire,
Sorbie in Galloway, and two or three times in
the Highlands. Gleann Fhreasdail and Loch

Restill are surely from "Risdal," copse-dale,
and not from "providence." Raoiceadal might
be from "reykr," reek; Geodha an t-sìl rather
refers to N. sìl, herring; Leòdamus is Leod's
moss (compare Skye, Strolamus, Skulamus, from
Sturli and Skuli). Mi-mheall is possibly "mjo-
fjall," narrow hill. Ernach is certainly not from
"eyrr"; the termination is Gaelic. Beinn
Thuncairidh is likely Tunga-gerdhi, not sunna.
There are many words, however, where Dr
Gillies goes against the phonetic laws which
govern the passing of words from Norse into
Gaelic. Thus final or intervocalic kk, pp, tt,
become simply k, t, p; k, t, p become g, d, b; g,
d, b get aspirated and disappear practically.
Trodigal cannot be from trodhi; bodhi (sunken
rock) is bodha; Lagal garve cannot come from
lagr; this would be "lagh," as it is. Final rdh
at the end of a second word becomes rd, rt, as in
Suain-eart; "nd" also similarly becomes d, as
in "miosad," narrow sound. Troternish is no
exception, for the n of Thróndar-nes is still heard
and is preserved in old documents (M'Vurich,
Tróntarnis); we do not know if Trudernish is
allied. Suaineart is given correctly derived
from Sveinn-fjord, but at p. 11 Norse "jördh,"
our "earth," is introduced very unnecessarily.
The word is not allied to Gaelic aird, point, which
is allied to Greek "ardis," of like meaning. A
bad blunder is taking Saddel from sand-dale; the

old form of the word would here save such non-sense—Sagadull (15th cent.), M'Vurich's Sagh-adal. "Faodhail," a ford, is missed; it is from Norse "vadhill," a ford, a shallow between isles where horses pass (Miss Freer, "Outer Isles").

Terminal -aidh in river names is Pictish; it is for -ia, from -ios, -ia. Welsh represents this by -ydd; Pictish by -aidh or -idh, and Gaelic by -e. Terminal -an in river names has nothing to do with "abhainn"; it stands for Gaulish -ona (Matrona, Divona—our Don), -ana. "Ard" is the Irish for "height," but Scotch Gaelic allows a locative according to locality. "Aoineadh" is a good Gaelic word, and cannot be from N. "enni." "Leac" is also a good word for "cheek," its locative being "leacainn," so commonly used for hill-sides. The Doctor says —"Leac, a check, a word with which I am not familiar"—just like his "leac" in making him-self arbiter of what is Gaelic, old or new (for its use in a school book see "Higher Gaelic Read-ings," p. 78). Gleann-a-Comhann: the Doctor regards this *a* as the article; it is simply a glide vowel following *n*, and doing duty for the Irish eclipsis. Loch Sween and the old name Syffin is from old Suibhne, a well-known name in Ire-land. Sweyn Mac Sweyn is also found in char-ters and documents (Coll register in Dr Johnson's time; he spoke to Mrs M'Sweyn). There are three or four confusing surnames of this kind—

MacShui'ne (Argyll, M'Queen), M'Suain (Skye,
M'Sveinn), M'Swan, M'Aoidhean (M'Quien,
Skye); possibly MacCuinn from Conn; but this
last name is not found in Highland documents.
It belongs to early history.   Tormoid is from
Thormund (final nd to d); Ivarr, Iomhar, is for
Ingvarr.   Clan Ean Murguenich is surely the
famous or infamous MacIans of Ardnamurchan.
Dermot, son of Fergus Cerrbél, was the good
King whom Ruadan cursed.   Gometra stands for
Godmundar-ey, " Godmund's Isle "; Hermitra
for Hermund's.   The name Oighrig or Effric is
not from òigh; the Abbess of Kildare had this
name in 738, and it was spelled Aithbhric, later
Africa.   These are some of the errors which we
find in Dr Gillies' Place-Names of Argyll.   They
are not all that we, or better still, one more
acquainted with the county, could point out, but,
as Mercutio says, " 'Tis enough."

INDEX

Index

Note: - The stress accent is indicated by a full stop placed before the stressed syllable - e.g. Aber.arder is stressed on the third syllable; .Aberscaig is stressed on the first.

A

Bute, xx, 78

C.

E.

F.

G.

I.

N.

O.

P.

S.

V.

W.

Y.

.

Printed in the United States
23531LVS00002B/106

9 780902 664098